PRINCETON UNIVERSITY STUDIES
IN PAPYROLOGY

No. 1

Edited by ALLAN CHESTER JOHNSON

PAPYRI IN THE PRINCETON
UNIVERSITY COLLECTIONS

PAPYRI IN THE PRINCETON UNIVERSITY COLLECTIONS

VOL. II

EDITED WITH NOTES

BY

EDMUND HARRIS KASE, JR.
Instructor in New Testament Greek
Princeton Theological Seminary

PRINCETON
PRINCETON UNIVERSITY PRESS
1936

Copyright, 1936, by
Princeton University Press

Printed in the United States of America
by J. H. Furst Company, Baltimore, Maryland

PREFACE

Five years have elapsed since the publication of *Papyri in the Princeton University Collections* by Professors Allan C. Johnson and Henry B. Van Hoesen. During this period work upon the unedited texts still remaining in the collection,[1] of which there are at least four hundred,[2] has continued without interruption. Individual students, working under the direction of Professor Johnson, have published from time to time single texts that appeared to be of more than average interest.[3] And in addition many other texts have been transcribed and studied with a view to ultimate publication.

The time has at last arrived when it seems both expedient and practicable to systematize the method of publication. To this end the preparation of a volume of representative texts was projected by Professor Johnson and entrusted to the writer in the spring of 1933, and it has been decided that this volume shall be considered the second in a series initiated by the earlier work of Professors Johnson and Van Hoesen, to which reference has been made above. The present volume is thus Vol. II of a series entitled *Papyri in the Princeton University Collections*.[4] Texts published in this series, as in other similar collections, will be numbered consecutively from volume to volume, thus facilitating reference to individual texts. In accordance with this plan the ninety-three texts presented in the pages which follow have been assigned the numbers **15-107**, the texts in Vol. I being numbered **1-14**.

As the writer looks back over the last three years he realizes that those who have contributed directly or indirectly to the preparation of this work are many. To all who have thus assisted him, both individuals and in-

---

[1] Really two collections, consisting in part of papyri owned by Princeton University and in part of texts loaned to the University by Mr. Robert Garrett. The former are designated by the symbol AM; the latter are referred to as the Garrett Deposit.

[2] Recently augmented (September, 1935) by the acquisition of about forty non-literary and two literary texts, the gift of Mr. John H. Scheide.

[3] Cf. Kenneth S. Gapp, "A Lease of a Pigeon House with Brood" (*T. A. P. A.*, LXIV [1933], 89-97); Oscar W. Reinmuth, "Two Prefectural Edicts Concerning the *Publicani*" (*C. P.*, XXXI [1936], 146-162); and Edmund H. Kase, Jr., "A Papyrus Roll in the Princeton Collection" (Baltimore, 1933).

[4] It will be observed that Vol. II differs from its predecessor in format. Uniformity in this respect, it is admitted, would have been desirable, but the smaller pages of the older volume are not altogether satisfactory for the publication of papyri, requiring as they do the frequent division of lines and making difficult the inclusion of plates. It was therefore decided to sacrifice outward uniformity in the interest of practical considerations.

stitutions, he desires now to express his deep appreciation. Of this large number there are several toward whom he feels an especial sense of obligation. Among these should be mentioned the Rockefeller Foundation, whose generous financial assistance, extended through the Council of the Humanities of Princeton University, made possible the preparation and publication of this volume, and the Board of Trustees of Grove City College, which, acting through the president of the College, Dr. Weir C. Ketler, granted to the writer an extended leave of absence, that he might return to Princeton to undertake the work of transcribing and editing the texts which are now being published.

Others whom the writer has consulted in connection with special problems and to whom he desires to express his gratitude include the late Professor A. S. Hunt, Mr. H. I. Bell, Dr. Sherman L. Wallace, Dr. Oscar W. Reinmuth, Dr. Ellwood M. Schofield, Mr. William Frederick Shaffer, Mr. Sidney P. Goodrich, and Mr. William M. Spackman.

But it is to Professor Allan Chester Johnson that the writer acknowledges his heaviest obligation. To him he owes both the suggestion and opportunity of undertaking the work which he has just completed; with him was shared some of the work of transcribing the texts; and from him has come many a fruitful suggestion bearing upon the interpretation of individual documents. His constructive advice and constant encouragement have been of great assistance to the writer at every stage of his work.

Complete responsibility for the transcriptions and commentaries is assumed, of course, by the writer.

EDMUND H. KASE, JR.

Princeton, N. J.
9 October 1936.

CONTENTS

	PAGE
Preface	v
List of Plates	viii
Table of Papyri	ix

TEXTS

		PAGE
I.	The Epistle of St. James (**15**)	1
II.	Documents of the Ptolemaic Period (**16-19**)	3
III.	Documents of the Roman Period:	
	a. Official (**20-22**)	9
	b. Declarations and Petitions (**23-30**)	12
	c. Contracts (**31-39**)	23
	d. Taxation (**40-53**)	38
	e. Accounts and Lists (**54-64**)	55
	f. Private Letters (**65-74**)	63
	g. Magic and Astrology (**75-76**)	72
IV.	Documents of the Byzantine Period:	
	a. Petitions (**77-78**)	74
	b. Contracts and Orders (**79-87**)	76
	c. Taxation (**88-94**)	84
	d. Accounts and Lists (**95-96**)	87
	e. Private Letters (**97-106**)	93
	f. Magic (**107**)	102

INDEXES

		PAGE
I.	Kings and Emperors	105
II.	Consuls	106
III.	Indictions	107
IV.	Months and Days	107
V.	Personal Names	107
VI.	Geographical	114
VII.	Religion	115
VIII.	Magic and Astrology	116
IX.	Official and Military Terms	116
X.	Professions, Trades and Occupations	117
XI.	Weights, Measures and Coins	117
XII.	Taxes	118
XIII.	General Index	119

LIST OF PLATES

I.	**20, 40**	⎫
II.	**26, 66**	⎪
III.	**29**	⎪
IV.	**37, 38**	⎪
V.	**42**, recto	⎬ at the end
VI.	**42**, verso	⎪
VII.	**39, 50**	⎪
VIII.	**96**, recto	⎪
IX.	**97**	⎪
X.	**102**	⎭

TABLE OF PAPYRI

		Date (A.D. except **16-19**)	PAGE
15.	The Epistle of St. James	5th cent.	1
16.	Report of Legal Proceedings	158 B.C. (?)	3
17.	Receipt for the Payment of Rent (?)	2nd cent. B.C. (?)	6
18.	Grain Accounts	Late 3rd cent. B.C.	6
19.	Letter	2nd cent. B.C.	8
20.	Edicts of Prefect	2nd cent.	9
21.	Financial Report	236/237	10
22.	Official Letter	246-249	11
23.	Petition to the Chief of Police	13	12
24.	Registration of Live Stock	21	12
25.	Petition to Strategus (?)	1st-2nd cent.	14
26.	Pilot's Receipt	About 154	14
27.	Declarations Concerning the Delivery of Garments	191/192	18
28.	Registration of Live Stock	219	19
29.	Petition to Strategus	258	21
30.	Petition to Strategus	About 264	23
31.	Deed of Divorce	79 or 80	23
32.	Loan of Money and Wheat	99	25
33.	Loan of Wheat	126	26
34.	Repayment of Loans	144	27
35.	Receipt for Payment of Debt	About 161	29
36.	Partnership Contract	195-197	29
37.	Receipts for Payment of Rent on Leased Land	255 and 256	30
38.	Roman Will	About 264	34
39.	Lease of a Melon Garden	3rd cent.	37
40.	Embankment Certificate	49	38
41.	Receipt for the Trades' Tax	50	40
42.	Grain Accounts	93	41
43.	Receipts for Poll-Tax (λαογραφία)	141	44
44.	Receipt for Poll-Tax (συντάξιμον)	141	45
45.	Receipt for Poll-Tax (λαογραφία)	174	46
46.	Account Recording Payments of Dike-Tax	2nd cent.	46
47.	Receipt for Poll-Tax (λαογραφία)	2nd cent.	47
48.	Receipt for τέλος μόσχου θυομένου	206	48
49.	Tax Receipt	217 (?)	49

TABLE OF PAPYRI

		A.D.	PAGE
50.	Receipt for ἀννῶνα στρατιωτῶν	255	49
51.	Custom-House Receipt	3rd cent.	50
52.	Tax Accounts	3rd cent.	51
53.	Tax Accounts	56 and 57	53
54.	Wage Account	Early 1st cent.	55
55.	Alphabetical List of Names	1st cent. (?)	57
56.	Account	153/154	57
57.	Soldier's Expense Account	2nd cent.	58
58.	List of Names	2nd-3rd cent.	59
59.	List of Names	2nd-3rd cent.	60
60.	Account	2nd-3rd cent.	60
61.	Account	264	61
62.	Account	3rd cent.	62
63.	List of Names (?)	3rd-4th cent.	62
64.	Account	Late 3rd cent.	63
65.	Letter	40 (?)	63
66.	Letter	1st cent.	64
67.	Letter	1st-2nd cent.	65
68.	Letter	2nd cent. (?)	65
69.	Letter	2nd cent.	66
70.	Letter	2nd-3rd cent.	67
71.	Letter	3rd cent.	68
72.	Letter	3rd cent.	69
73.	Letter	3rd cent.	70
74.	Letter	About 300	71
75.	Horoscope	138-161	72
76.	Erotic Incantation	3rd cent.	73
77.	Petition to the Prefect	Early 4th cent.	74
78.	Petition to the *Proximi* of a City	6th cent.	75
79.	Division of an Inheritance	326	76
80.	Order for Payment of Money	About 337	77
81.	Repayment of a Loan	344	77
82.	Dialysis	481	78
83.	Declaration of Payment of Money out of a Deposit	5th cent.	80
84.	Sale of a House	5th cent. (?)	81
85.	Sale of a Slave	5th cent. (?)	82
86.	Order for Delivery of Oil	6th cent. (?)	82
87.	Loan with Surety	612	83
88.	Account of Arrears of Wine	5th cent.	84
89.	Receipt for Poll-Tax (διαγραφή)	6th cent.	84
90.	Receipts for μερισμός	6th-7th cent.	84

		A.D.	PAGE
91.	Receipt for μερισμός	6th-7th cent.	85
92.	Receipt for Poll-Tax (ἀνδρισμός)	6th-7th cent.	85
93.	Receipt for ἐμβολή	7th cent.	86
94.	Receipts for δημόσια	7th cent.	86
95.	Inventory of Stolen Property	4th cent. (?)	87
96.	Wage Account	551/552 or 566/567	88
97.	Letter	326/327	93
98.	Letter	4th cent.	94
99.	Letter	4th cent.	96
100.	Letter	4th cent.	96
101.	Letter	4th cent.	97
102.	Letter	4th cent.	98
103.	Letter	5th cent.	99
104.	Letter	5th cent.	100
105.	Letter	6th cent.	101
106.	Letter	6th cent.	101
107.	Gnostic Fever Amulet	4th-5th cent.	102

15. The Epistle of St. James

Garrett Dep. 7742.   8.7 × 6.5 and 6 × 6.5 cm.   Oxyrhynchus.   5th cent. A.D.

Two small fragments of the Epistle of St. James containing on the recto ii. 16-18 (frag. a) and ii. 21-23 (frag. b), and on the verso ii. 23-25 (frag. a) and iii. 2-4 (frag. b). These fragments are not to be confused with another papyrus (P. Oxy. 1171 = $\mathfrak{P}^{20}$ [Gregory-Dobschütz]), also deposited in the Princeton University Library (AM 4117), which presents the text of James ii. 19–iii. 9.[1]

The two fragments form part of one leaf of the original codex, one (frag. a) containing the first eight lines from pages 29 and 30,[2] the other (frag. b) the last eight lines from the same pages. It would thus appear that in this manuscript (almost certainly of the Catholic Epistles alone) the Epistle of James occupied a unique position, for the fourteen missing leaves (pages 1-28) would have provided just enough space (making allowance for titles) for the three Johannine Epistles and the opening section of James (i. 1–ii. 16), whereas this space would be insufficient to accomodate the two Epistles of Peter in addition to the missing portion of James. Such an arrangement of the Catholic Epistles appears to be wholly without precedent. And yet this should occasion little surprise in view of the striking lack of uniformity shown by manuscripts and canonical lists with respect to the order of these books. The various arrangements of the seven Catholic Epistles are conveniently tabulated by Moffatt, *An Introduction to the Literature of the New Testament*, 17.

The text of these fragments agrees on the whole with the textual group represented chiefly by manuscripts B, ℵ, and C. It agrees with A, however, in reading τὸ στόμα (τὰ στόματα B, ℵ, C) in iii. 3, and it is probable that it had τί τὸ ὄφελος in ii. 16 (τί ὄφελος B, C). Other significant divergences

---

[1] A re-examination of the original of P. Oxy. 1171 convinces me that the printed text requires revision in the case of two words: γεινεσθα[ι in place of γεινεσθε (line 18) and μεγα⟦υ⟧λαυχει instead of μεγαλα αυχει (line 26), υ having been corrected to λ by the original scribe. In addition I would suggest the following minor revisions of the text: αδικιας η[(line 28), δεδαμα]σται (line 34), κατα]ρωμεθα (line 39).

[2] It is no longer possible to read the page numbers with certainty. Both readings were made in the spring of 1936 and verified by Professor A. C. Johnson, Dr. E. M. Schofield, Mr. C. T. Fritsch, and the present writer. Later in the spring an attempt was made to improve the legibility of the text by resorting to the use of chemicals, but unfortunately both numerals were practically obliterated at that time. It is still possible to discern traces of the λ on the verso, but on the recto nothing remains of the κθ which was formerly visible close to a fold in the upper margin. The writer does not question the reading of either numeral, but Dr. Schofield, it should be noted, would prefer to dot both letters in the case of the numeral on the recto.

from the principal manuscripts are the omission of ἔχεις in ii. 18 (a unique reading) and the omission of σου before χωρίς in the same verse (in agreement with 442 and ff). For probable variants in iii. 2 see below.

The manuscript should probably be assigned to the second half of the fifth century.[3]

For the transcription of the text, as well as for most of the introductory material which appears above, I am indebted to Dr. Ellwood M. Schofield. This text has been recently edited by Dr. Schofield in a doctoral dissertation (*The Papyrus Fragments of the Greek New Testament* [1936]) now on deposit in manuscript form in the library of the Southern Baptist Theological Seminary, Louisville, Kentucky. A detailed commentary will be found on pages 206-216 of this work.

On the verso Dr. Schofield reads only a ν in line 17 and a dot in the line above. I have added to his readings in these lines, for I believe that the long vertical stroke extending downward from line 16 may be the tail of a ρ, and in the following line I find traces of a letter before ν, this letter possibly being an ι. I have accordingly inserted these letters in the text and would suggest that the two lines be restored as follows:

[ος ανη]ρ [δυναμενος χαλιν] / [αγωγε]ιν [και ολον το σωμα].

There appears to be no question about the ν in line 17. The position of this letter makes it impossible to read χαλιναγωγῆσαι. On the other hand the space requirements would be satisfied by reading the present infinitive. This reading, if correct, is unique. Space considerations likewise suggest reading δυνάμενος in the lacuna (so ℵ) rather than δυνατός, the reading found in the other uncial manuscripts.

RECTO

Frag. a.

κθ

[τα επιτηδεια] του σωματος	ii. 16
[τι το οφελος] ουτως και η πι	17
[οτις εαν μ]η εχη εργα νεκρα	
[εστιν καθ] εαυτην αλλα ερε[ι	18
5 [τις συ πιστ]ειν καγω εργα εχ[ω	
[δειξον μοι] την πιστιν χω[ρις	
[των εργων και] εγω [σοι δειξω	
[εκ των εργων μο]υ τη[ν πιστιν	

(9 lines lost)

[3] Mr. H. I. Bell, in preparing an inventory of the papyri acquired by Princeton University in 1928, dated this text tentatively in the "sixth (?) century."

15. THE EPISTLE OF ST. JAMES

Frag. b.

[θυσιαστηριον βλεπε]ις ο[τι   ii. 21-22
[η πιστις συνηργει] τοις εργ[ο
20 [ις αυτου και εκ των ε]ργων η πι[σ
[τις ετελειωθη και επλ]ηρωθη η γρ
[αφη η λεγουσα επι]στευσε[ν   23
[δε Αβρααμ τω θω και ε]λογισθη
[αυτω εις δικαιοσ]υνην και

VERSO

Frag. a.

λ

φ[ι]λος θυ εκ[λ]η[θη ορατε οτι εξ   ii. 24
εργων δικαιου[ται ανος και ου
[κ εκ] πιστεω[ς] μο[νον ομοιως   25
[δε και] Ρααβ' η πο[ρνη ουκ εξ ερ
5 [γων ε]δικαιωθη [υποδεξαμε
[ν]η τους αγγελ[ους και ετερα
[οδω εκ]βαλο[υσα ....
π̄]ῡς̄ [

(7 lines lost)

Frag. b.

.....]ρ[iii. 2
.....]ιν[
[...] των ϊ[ππων τους χαλινους   3
[ε]ις το στ[ομα βαλλομεν εις
20 [τ]ο πιθεσθ[αι αυτους ημιν και
ολον το σ[ωμα αυτων μεταγο
μεν ϊδου [και τα πλοια τηλι   4
καυτα [

16. REPORT OF LEGAL PROCEEDINGS

Garrett Dep. 7614.   18.5 × 22 cm.   Fayum.   158 B.C.(?)

A fragmentary column containing a portion of an official record of a trial held in the court of the χρηματισταί, sitting in Crocodilopolis, in the Fayum. Although the details of the case remain obscure, it would appear that someone connected with the case had been instructed on the thirteenth of Mechir, in the twenty-third year of an unnamed ruler, to appear in court on the same day to attend the rehearing of the case. His appearance in court was prevented, however, by the fact that on that same day he was occupied in taking a letter from the πράκτωρ (ξενικῶν ?) in Crocodilopolis (?) to the ἐπιστάτης of the village of Philadelphia.

The lower portion of the record, as it is here preserved, contains the statement of this person as offered to the court in explanation of his failure to appear on the thirteenth as instructed. Not only would it have been impossible, he states, to reach Crocodilopolis on that day, by reason of the distance involved, but the journey, even if possible of accomplishment, would have been of no avail, for the sitting of the court would have been adjourned before his arrival. On the following day, he goes on to explain, he delivered another letter, receiving it from the ἐπιστάτης and taking it to the πράκτωρ. This letter was turned over to the court on the succeeding day, the court messenger (ὑπηρέτης) having received it from the πράκτωρ.

The opening lines (1-8) apparently contain the conclusion of a statement covering the nature of the case, the names of the interested parties, and perhaps an announcement of the decision of the χρηματισταί to hold a rehearing, this decision having been reached on the eleventh of the month. It is further stated that two days later a messenger of the court served notice of the retrial. Beyond the fact that the case was concerned with a small vineyard, nothing is known of its nature or outcome.

For discussions of the legal procedure in the Ptolemaic period see Mitteis, *Grundzüge*, 1-22; Semeka, *Ptolemäisches Prozessrecht*; and the recent dissertation by Berneker, *Zur Prozesseinleitung im Ptolemäischen Recht*.

It would appear that lines 1-8 are the continuation of a previous column, of which the concluding letters of four lines are visible along the left edge between lines 8 and 9 (cf. note to line 8).

A date near the middle of the second century is required by the character of the two hands. The twenty-third year (lines 5 and 8) may, therefore, reasonably be assumed to be that of the joint reign of Philometor and Cleopatra (i. e. 159/158 B.C.). A date near the close of the preceding reign of Epiphanes (183/182) is a less probable alternative.

```
          ] Ἰσοδώρου τοῦ [καὶ ...6-8... Ἀλ]εξανδρέω[ς
     τῶν οὔπω] ἐπηγμένων [εἰς δῆμον Ἡ]φαιστιέα
     ... καταγ]ενομένων ἐν Φ[ιλαδελ]φεί[αι] τῆς Ἡρακλείδου
     μερίδος τ]ῶν ἐκ τῆς αὐτῆ[ς .]οι κώμης [..4-5..]ε τῶν
5    [χ]ρ[ηματι]στῶν, ὧν εἰσαγωγεὺς Θεογένης, τοῦ κγ (ἔτους),
     Μεχεὶρ ιᾱ.     ὑπὲρ ἀμπελῶνος (ἀρουρῶν) δ, ἐξ οὗ
     ἀποφέρεται τὰ καθ' ἔτος γενήματα καὶ [....8-10....]λ̄γ.
     παρ[ηγγ]έλη διὰ Πέλοπος ὑπηρέτ[ο]υ, (ἔτους) κγ, [Μ]εχεὶρ ῑγ.

(Hand 2)   Πῶς οὖν δυνατόν ἐστιν τῆς παραγγελίας
10         γενομένης τῆς ῑγ, ἐν ἧι καὶ παρὰ τοῦ πράκτο-
```

16. REPORT OF LEGAL PROCEEDINGS

ρος εἰλήφην τὴν ἐπιστολὴν πρὸς τὸν ἐν Φιλαδελφείαι ἐπιστάτην,
εὐθέως καὶ ἀναδικῆσαι ἐ[ν] τῆι αὐτῆι ἡμέραι
ἐν Κροκοδίλων πόλει, τ[οσοῦ]το τὸ μῆκος
15 ἡμέρ[α]ν ἀπέχον εἰς τὴν πόλιν. εἰ δέ τις καὶ
λάβοι ἀναιβηκέναι εἰς τὴν πόλιν, οὔτε καὶ
τοὺς χρηματιστὰς καταλάβοι ἔτι καθημένους,
τ[ό]δε πάντων δεινότατ[ο]ν.
ἐπιστολὴν εἴληφα παρὰ τοῦ ἐπιστάτου [π]ρὸς
20 τὸν πράκτορα τῆς ιδ̄, καὶ παρὰ τοῦ πράκτορ[ο]ς
π[ρο]σενήνεκται ιε̄ τοῖς χρηματ[ι]σ[τ]αῖς
δι'] ὑπηρ[έ]του Δημητρίου.

16. Read ἀναβεβηκέναι.

1. Ἰσοδώρου. For the unusual spelling cf. SB. 419 (Ἰσοδώρα).
2. [εἰς δῆμον Ἡ]φαιστιέα. No deme of this name is otherwise attested.
5. For the duties of the εἰσαγωγεύς see Mitteis, *Grundzüge*, 4-5.
6. Traces of an additional letter are visible following the numeral (δ). A fraction is required, perhaps one-eighth (assuming a relationship with the numeral in the following line).
7. Perhaps [τὰ ἐπιγεν(ήματα)], although the numeral which follows is difficult to explain. For λ̄γ one might read alternatively κ̄γ (= 3 talents). Cf. O. Strassb. 26.
8. παρ[ηγγ]έλη. For the form see Mayser, *Grammatik*, I, 381. The technical meaning of this verb is discussed by Meyer, P. Hamb. 25, introd., according to whom it represents an official, rather than a private, summons. Just below this line, at the left, are to be found the ends of four lines from a preceding column. Only a few letters remain from each line:]τον;] . . . ;]τε;]ιαντι.
11. ἐπιστολήν. It is quite possible that it was the purpose of this letter to inform the ἐπιστάτης of the decision of the court to rehear the case. He may have been previously instructed by the πράκτωρ to carry out the provisions of the verdict as pronounced by the court at the conclusion of the original trial. In view of the prospective retrial it was but natural for the πράκτωρ to rescind his previous orders. Reference is made in lines 19-22 to the reply written by the ἐπιστάτης.
13. ἀναδικῆσαι. This verb is found in P. Lille 29. 4, where it must be understood in the sense of *make an appeal for the rehearing of a case*. But here the actual renewal of the action, rather than the appeal for a renewal of the same, would appear to be intended. That ἀναδικῆσαι is equivalent to the Attic ἀναδικάσασθαι is pointed out by Meyer, *Jur. Pap.*, 71. I. 4, note.
15. ἀπέχον εἰς τὴν πόλιν. Cf. P. Teb. 92. 4. Philadelphia was situated about eighteen miles from Crocodilopolis.
16. λάβοι ἀναβεβηκέναι. The use of λαμβάνω c. inf. in the sense of *undertake* appears to be new. For the closest parallels cf. Liddell-Scott-Jones, s. v., I. 11 and II. 4.

17. Receipt for the Payment of Rent (?)

Garrett Dep. 7693. 6 × 6.5 cm. Philadelphia. 2nd (?) cent. B.C.

It does not seem possible to say with certainty whether the accompanying fragment offers a small portion of a receipt for the payment of rent or the opening lines of a somewhat briefly worded lease. Receipts in the form of a *homologia* (cf. P. Amh. 55) are relatively rare, although this form is commonly found in leases. On the other hand, one misses the elaborate and detailed phrasing so characteristic of documents of the latter class (cf. P. Teb. 105. See, however, P. Teb. 107).

```
   Παποντῶς Νεκφερ[ῶτος
   Σωκράτῃ Ἀπολλωνίου [                   Φιλαδελ-
   φείας. ὁμολογῶι ἐφ' ὃν [                ἐν τῶι
   πέμπτωι γύῃ περὶ Φ[ιλαδέλφειαν          ἄρουραι
5  τέσσαρες μετρήσει [                     τῆς μισ-
   θώσεως ἐκφο[ρίου ?                      καθ'-
   ἔτος  ισαι[                             κριθ-
   ῆς ἀρτάβ[ας ?
   πα[ρ]ασιμε[
10 πα[
         .    .    .    .    .    .    .    .
```

3. ὁμολογῶι ἐφ' ὃν [. κλῆρον is almost certainly to be supplied in the lacuna. The reading ἐφ' ὃν (for ὅσον) βούλει would be most unusual in a lease from the Ptolemaic period. Cf. Waszynski, *Bodenpacht*, 91. For the spelling cf. P. Teb. 111. 4.

4. πέμπτωι γύῃ. For numbered γύαι (*plots*) see P. Ryl. 142. 14, note.

18. Grain Accounts

AM 8908. 9 × 17 cm. Provenance unknown. Late 3rd cent. B.C.

A portion of a column from a grain account. Several names appear, opposite each of which a quantity of wheat (of barley, however, in one instance) has been entered. The exact quantity in each case cannot be determined, owing to the loss of the column of figures at the ends of the lines. In a few instances the occupation of those whose names appear has been indicated, one being designated as a ὑδροφόρος, another as a μάχιμος, and a third as an ἀρτοκόπος. The entry in line 14 (εἰς τὸν βοτανισμόν) suggests the possibility that many of these payments were made to individual workmen as wages for agricultural services.

On the verso there are portions of two columns of a summarized grain account arranged by months, the extant sections referring to Phamenoth (?) and Pharmouthi. Separate entries are found for each day in the month, these being classified and totalled at the end of each month. A similar arrangement of accounts is seen in P. Lond. 131. The daily entries are usually not large, seldom exceeding three or four artabae. Totals from only one month (Phamenoth ?) are preserved. These show 75½ artabae of wheat, 1 artaba of wheat ἐξ ἀχύρου (evidently wheat secured by winnowing chaff), an unascertainable quantity of wheat mixed with barley, and 20 and odd artabae of barley.

The accounts on the recto and verso may be related, that on the verso furnishing a summarized statement of the total daily outlays to various individuals. It should be noted, however, that with one exception (line 8) all of the entries on the recto cover payments of wheat, whereas in the account on the verso more prominence is given to payments of barley, though the wheat entries still predominate.

```
       κ . . . . . αρ[
      Θεοφίλωι δικαίωι ζ[
                σιτονετοισ[
       Δημητρίωι          πυρ(οῦ) [
    5  Δωρίωνι            πυρ(οῦ) [
       Φιλοκράτει         πυρ(οῦ) [
       ὑδροφόρωι Φιλήμον[ος
       δόντος             κρι(θῆς) [
       Δείωι Συριακῶι τ[
   10  Διονυσίωι μαχίμωι       π[υρ(οῦ)
       Τιμαίωι            πυρ(οῦ) [
       Πετεμίνει          πυρ(οῦ) [
       Νικασίππωι         πυρ(οῦ) [
       εἰς τὸν βοτανισμὸν τοῦ [
   15  Κασέπωι            πυρ(οῦ) [
       Πετεσούχωι καταρχ . . [
       ἀρτοκόπωι [
```

VERSO

```
       Col. I                              Col. II
    ς̄    πυ[ρ(οῦ)]      δ          38    . . [
         κρι(θῆς)        αL              /  πυρ(οῦ)      οεL
 20  ζ̄   πυ[ρ(οῦ)]      αγ́         40   καὶ ἐξ ἀχύρου ⁊ α
     η̄   πυ[ρ(οῦ)]      ηLγ́              κρι(θο-) ⁊ ἐξ ἀχύρου [
    [θ̄]  κρι(θῆς)       βL               κριθῆς           κ . .
    [ῑ]  πυρ(οῦ)         ζ
    [ῑα] πυρ(οῦ)        βLγ́              Φαρμοῦθι
 25  ῑβ   πυρ(οῦ)        βLγ́         ᾱ     πυρ(οῦ)       δL
```

	ῑγ	πυρ(οῦ)	ε	45	θ̄	πυρ(οῦ)	δ[
	ιδ	ἐξ ἀχύρου			ῑ	⊬	ε
		πυρ(οῦ)	ιθβ́		ῑα	πυρ(οῦ)	θL
		τῆι αὐτῆι			ῑβ	πυρ(οῦ)	αL
30		⊬ / ε			ῑγ	πυρ(οῦ)	δ
	[ι]ς̄	ἐξ ἀχύρου		50		κρι(θῆς)	L
	[ ]	⊬ ιδβ́			ῑδ	⊬	ι[
	[ ]	⊬ α			ῑε	⊬	β
		κρι(θῆς) γ			[ῑς]	⊬	δ
35	ῑη	κρι(θῆς) ε			[ι]ζ̄	κρι(θῆς)	β
	ιθ	κρι(θῆς) β					
	[	]′					

15. Κασέπωι. The same name should evidently be restored in SB. 3795.

19. Letter

Garrett Dep. 7692.   22.5 × 13.5 cm.   Fayum.   2nd cent. b.c.

A fragmentary letter from Pamnous to Euphron, in which the writer mentions that he has given instructions to send a boat to him at Alabanthis. His sister will accompany him on the proposed journey. Next the writer appears to instruct his correspondent to provide a three-couched cloth tent (σκηνὴν σακκίνην τρίκλινον) for their use during the visit. The rest is obscure.

In the form of a postscript there is appended the statement that Apollodorus has received payment for some pitch. The rather illegible notations which appear in the left-hand margin seem to refer to the sending of the boat on the nineteenth of the month.

      Παμνοῦς Εὔφρονι χαίρειν. καθότ[ι κ]αὶ πα[ροῦσιν ὑμῖν
      μετέδωκα ὑπὲρ τοῦ πέμψαι μοι πλοιάριον εἰς Ἀλαβ[ανθίδα
                                            καιτηναι[
      ἀνακομισ[θ]ήσομαι ἐγώ τε καὶ ἡ ἀδελφὴ   χαρην[
      σιδοσι[.]δεμο καὶ σκηνὴν σακκίνην τρίκλινον [
      μημενη
  5 τὴν δὲ τιμὴν διασάφησον ὅπως ἐξαποστείλωσι α[
                                         σιτ [

  7 ἀπέχει δὲ καὶ Ἀπολλόδωρος τὴν τιμὴν τῆς πίσσης εκ [

In the margin at left:
(Hand 2)   ....[.]..ῑη
         ...ευρον
10 πέμψουσι

τὸ πλ[οιάρ]ι(ον)
τῆι ιθ̄ [.]...
ἐμ ἡμέραι.

On the verso:
14 (Hand 1) Εὔφρονι.

4. τρίκλινον. For the couch as a unit of measurement see McCartney, *C. P.*, XXIX (1934), 30-35. Cf. P. S. I. 533. 2, 5.

20. Edicts of Prefect

AM 8931.   12 × 8 cm.   Provenance unknown.   2nd cent. A.D.   Plate I.

Fragments of two edicts of a prefect whose name has been lost. The first of these (a) deals with the malpractices of the τελῶναι, who were reported to be seeking unjustly to exact money from transient visitors. Those of their victims whose time was short were seized, with the result that many offered to purchase their freedom in order to secure a speedier release. The edict orders an immediate cessation of such practices. To this there has been joined what appears to be a fragment of a second edict (b), written, however, by a different hand. Both documents have been recently edited by O. W. Reinmuth (*C. P.*, XXXI [1936], 146 ff.), whose detailed commentary presents a penetrating analysis of these texts.

(a)

[ἔπαρχος]
Αἰγύπτου λέγει·
Κατηχοῦμαι τοὺς τελώνας
δι[ν]ῶς σοφίσασθαι τοῖς διερ-
5 χομένοις καὶ ἀπαιτεῖν τὰ
μὴ ὀφιλόμενα αὐτοῖς ἐπὶ πλεῖ-
ον] καὶ κρατεῖν τοὺς ἐπιγομέν[ο]υς
ἵνα] καὶ τὸ τάχιον ἀποχωρῖν τι-
νὲς ἐξωνήσωνται. παραγγέλ-
10 λω [δὲ] οὖν αὐτοῖς παύσασθαι τῆς
τοιαύ]της πλ[ε]ονεξίας παρ[α-
χρῆμα ? .] ατε[

. . . .

(b)

. . . .
(Hand 2)   ...[.......]...[
βαίη τοῖς ἐπάρ[χοις ?
15 ρω ζήτησιν εγ[

ἀναγκαῖον ἡγη[σάμην ?   δια- ?]
τάγματι παρὰ ἡγ[εμόνος ?
τὴν τῆς εἰρήνη[s
αν πρὸ παντὸς [
20 σιας χρήζοντ[αι ?
σι χωρὶς πάσης τ[ἐ-]
πὶ τὰς κρίσεις παρ[
ται ἐντεῦθεν κ[στρα-]
τηγοῖς κίνδυν[ον ?   παραγ- ?]
25 γέλλω ανοχνι[
            . . . .

8. ἀποχωρὶν. I had previously read ἀποχωρίσ[ι]s, but the reading of the infinitive, as proposed by Reinmuth (op. cit., 149), is abundantly confirmed by the original, as I now discover upon renewed examination.

11. τοιαύ]της. This reading I owe to Reinmuth.

21. FINANCIAL REPORT

Garrett Dep. 7639.   11 × 11 cm.   Alexandrian χώρα.   236/237 A.D.

The following fragment furnishes the name (Αὐρήλιος Εὐδαίμων) and date (236/237) of a στρατηγὸς τῆς Ἀλεξανδρέων χώρας. It was not previously known that the administration of the Alexandrian χώρα remained in the hands of a strategus subsequent to the introduction of an Alexandrian βουλή in 202 A.D. Cf. Bilabel, P.-W., art. *Strategos*, 219. The only other text in which this official is attested is the undated P. S. I. 870, which the editor assigns either to the second or third century A.D.

The document appears to have contained a report of receipts and expenditures submitted by the strategus to some other official, perhaps to the epistrategus of the Delta region. Only the opening lines have been preserved. On the verso there is found a short account which seems to be unrelated to the text on the recto. This account was written by a different hand and, though partially obliterated, would appear to be otherwise complete. It is thus likely that a portion of the original papyrus was torn off to receive the shorter account on the verso. The publication of the latter is hardly justified by reason of the unsatisfactory condition of the text. It would be of interest to know the manner in which this document found its way to Oxyrhynchus or the Fayum, where it was probably discovered.

Παρὰ Αὐ]ρηλίου Εὐδαίμονος στρατηγο[ῦ
τῆς Ἀλ]εξανδρέων χώρας,
λόγος ἀρ]γυρικὸς τῶν εἰσπεπραγμένων
...5-7...]πων δεδαπανημένων ε [..]
5 ..3-5..ῳκ]ονομημένων ἀριθμήσεων

21. FINANCIAL REPORT

> month] τοῦ ἐνεστῶτος γ (ἔτους) τῶν κυρ[ίων
> ἡμῶν Α]ὐτοκράτορος Γαΐου Ἰουλίου Οὐήρου
> Μαξιμί]νου Εὐσεβοῦς Εὐτυχοῦς Σεβαστοῦ
> [καὶ Γαΐου Ἰουλίου Οὐήρου Μαξίμου τοῦ]
> 10 [ἱερωτάτου Καίσαρος κ.τ.λ.]

2. τῆς Ἀλεξανδρέων χώρας. That this was a nome and not public land belonging to the city of Alexandria (οἶκος πόλεως Ἀλεξανδρέων) is the view of Wilcken, *Grundzüge*, 286, 308. It is also possible that the Alexandrian χώρα consisted of land situated in various nomes in which the Alexandrians enjoyed certain rights. This land may have been under the administrative supervision of a special strategus rather than subject to the administration of the regular nome officials. It would thus be proper to speak of the Alexandrian χώρα as a nome only in the administrative sense.

22. OFFICIAL LETTER

AM 8939.   10 × 21 cm.   Oxyrhynchus.   246-249 A.D.

An official letter addressed to Aurelius Philoxenus, strategus of the Oxyrhynchite nome, concerning arrears of wheat owed on ὑπάρχοντα γενηματογραφούμενα (cf. Wilcken, *Grundzüge*, 297-298). About fifteen letters have been lost from the beginning of each line. Hardly enough remains to provide a basis for a satisfactory reconstruction of the text.

A date late in the reign of the Philippi seems assured by the name of the strategus to whom the letter is addressed. Cf. Bilabel, P.-W., art. *Strategos*, 211. Aurelius Philoxenus is known to have held this office in the year 247/248 (P. Oxy. 2123), whereas Aurelius Dios is attested for the years 244-245/246 (P. Oxy. 81, 1119, 1662).

> Ὁ δεῖνα   Φιλό]ξενος στρατηγῷ Ὀξυρυγχίτου χαίρειν.
>   ]ας περὶ πυροῦ ὀφειλομένου
>   τῶν ὑ]παρχόντων γενηματογρα-
> φουμένων   ὑπὸ τῆς] τοῦ ἰδίου λόγου ἐπιτροπῆς
> 5   ]ευσα. φρόντισον οὖν κατὰ τὰ πολ-
> ιτευόμενα   ]ς τὴν μερισμένην
>   ] καθ' ἑκάστην ἀρτάβην δρα-
> χμὰς   τέ]σσαρας ἄνευ τινὸς ὑπερθέσεως
>   καταβε]βλημένων πράξας τὸ ἀργύριον
> 10   ] Πλουτάρχῳ δεκαδάρχῳ συνόν-
> τος ?   ]νος ὑπηρέτου τῆς ἐπιτροπῆς
>   ]μενον εἰς τὴν λαμπροτάτην
>   τῶν Ὀξυρυγχιτῶν πό]λιν καὶ λημματισθησόμενον
>   τοῖς τῆς ἐπιτρο]πῆς λόγοις. ἐρρῶσθαί σε εὔχομαι.
> 15 L ? Ἰουλίων Φιλίππ]ων τῶν κυρίων, Θὼθ ι.

1. Read Φιλοξένῳ.

7–8. Space considerations suggest reading δρα|[χμὰς τριάκοντα τέ]σσαρας, although the prevailing price of wheat was much lower at this period. Cf. P. Lond. 1226. 10 (12 dr.) and B. G. U. 14. II. 14 (14 dr.). A twofold penalty may possibly be involved in the present instance, or the higher price may reflect a temporary shortage of grain. Neither δέκα nor εἴκοσι would satisfy the space requirements.

23. Petition to the Chief of Police

AM 8909.   9 × 18.5 cm.   Theadelphia.   13 A.D.

A complaint addressed to Quintus Pacillius Euxinus, ἐπιστάτης φυλακιτῶν, by Harthotes, son of Marreis, in which the writer reports the nocturnal intrusion of shepherds into his fields, resulting in the loss of half an aroura of hay, and enters a petition for redress. Similar petitions are found in P. Ryl. 124 ff. For the office of ἐπιστάτης φυλακιτῶν see P. Ryl., pp. 117 f.

The text of this petition has been published with a brief commentary by Professor S. H. Weber (*T. A. P. A.*, LVI [1925], xlii).

Κοΐντωι Πακιλλίωι Εὐξείνωι
ἐπιστάτηι φυλακιτῶν
παρὰ Ἁρθώτου τοῦ Μαρρείους
τῶν ἀπὸ Θεαδελφείας δημο-
5   σίων γεωργῶν. τῆι νυκτὶ τῆι
φερούσηι εἰς τὴν ιη τοῦ Φαρμοῦ(θι)
τοῦ μβ (ἔτους) Καίσαρος ἐπιβαλόν-
τες οἱ τῆς κώμης ποιμένες
εἰς τὰς ὑπ' ἐμοῦ γεωργου-
10   μένας βασιλικῆς γῆς
κατενέμησάν μου χόρ-
του ἡμιαρούριον. διὸ ἀξιῶι
ἐὰν φαίνηιται κατα-
σταθῆναι τοὺς ἐγκαλου-
15   μένους ἐπὶ σὲ πρὸς τὴν
ἐσομένην ἐπέξοδον.
        εὐτύχ(ει).

24. Registration of Live Stock

Garrett Dep. 7640.   6.5 × 33 cm.   Oxyrhynchus.   21 A.D.

A declaration addressed to the strategus of the Oxyrhynchite nome in which the declarant states the number of sheep and goats which she is

24. REGISTRATION OF LIVE STOCK

registering for the current year (20/21 A.D.). Analogous texts are listed by Westermann-Kraemer (P. Cornell 15, introd.), who present an exhaustive analysis of this material. To this list should now be added P. Ross. Georg. II, 13. See also **28**.

This would appear to be the earliest extant declaration of this type. It was presented to the same toparch, Sarapion, who functions in a similar capacity in P. Oxy. 245 (26 A.D.) and P. Oxy. 351 (28 A.D.). He may thus have held this office continuously for eight years or longer. That another toparch may also have held office for more than six years at this period is pointed out by Oertel, *Liturgie*, 163. The date of our text (Τῦβι λ) indicates that the declarant is presenting a πρώτη ἀπογραφή (cf. P. Oxy. 246. 20). See also Meyer, *Sav. Zeit.*, LII (1932), 386-387.

The name of the strategus (line 3) has been almost obliterated, but the remaining traces favor the reading Χαιρέαι. Chaereas thus served continuously from 21 to 28 A.D. (cf. Bilabel, P.-W., art. *Strategos*, 210), perhaps remaining in office for three three-year terms (*ibid.*, 226).

For the text on the verso see **55**.

```
        Πρό(βατα) ρθ,
        α[ἰ(γας) γ].
        Χαιρέαι στρατηγῶι
        παρὰ Τααρχωρσίας
 5      .....[.]...[..]. ἀπ[ο]γ[ρ]άφο[μαι
        εἰς τὸ ἐνεστὸς ζL
        Τιβερίου Καίσαρος
        Σεβαστοῦ τὰ ὑ[π]άρ(χοντά) μοι
        πρόβατα ἑκατὸν ἐν-
10      νέα, αἶγας τρεῖς,
        / πρ(όβατα) ρθ, αἰγ(ες) γ, καὶ τοὺς
        [ἐπακολου]θ(οῦντας) ἄ[ρ]ν(ας) καὶ ἐ[ρί-
        φους, ἃ νεμήσετα[ι
        περὶ Πέλα τῆς πρὸ(ς) λί-
15      β(α) τοπ(αρχίας) καὶ δι' ὅλου τοῦ νο(μοῦ)
        δι(ὰ) νο(μέως) Πετσείριος υἱοῦ
        Πετσείριος λαογρ(αφουμένου)
        περὶ Σέσφθα τῆς
        κάτω τοπαρχ(ίας), ὧν
20      καὶ τάξομαι τὸ κ-
        αθῆ[κ]ον τέλος.
  ∠             ε[ὐτ]ύχ[(ει)].
        Σαραπίω(ν) τοπ(άρχης) ἀναγέγρ(αφα)
        πρόβατα ἑκατὸν ἐν-
```

25 νέα, αἶγας τρεῖς, / πρ(όβατα) ρθ,
    αἰγ(ες) γ. Lζ Τιβερίου Καίσαρο[ς
        Σεβαστοῦ, Τῦβ(ι) λ.

1–2. Similar dockets are found at the head of P. Oxy. 74 and P. Cornell 15.
20–21. τὸ καθῆκον τέλος. Sc. τέλος προβάτων. The longer expression is found, however, only in an ostracon receipt from Upper Egypt (O. Tait, p. 20, 114). Wallace (*Taxes in Roman Egypt from Augustus to Diocletian*, s. vv.) identifies this tax with the ἐννόμιον.

25. Petition to Strategus (?)

AM 8927.   7 × 6.5 cm.   Oxyrhynchus.   1st-2nd cent. A.D.

A fragmentary portion of the opening lines of a petition addressed to Tiberius Claudius Sara[pion], who was perhaps a strategus. No strategus of this name is attested, however. The same name occurs in P. Oxy. 364 (94 A.D.), where its possessor is described as being an ex-agoranomus of Alexandria. An identification of this strategus with any one of the three Oxyrhynchite strategi who bore the name Sarapion (cf. **27**, introd.), and who held office between 191 and 221 A.D., is excluded by chronological considerations, for both the name Tiberius Claudius and the character of the writing point to a much earlier date.

```
    Τιβερίωι Κλαυδίωι Σαρα[πίωνι στρατηγῷ ?
    παρὰ Εὐπόρου Ἀπετε[
    ωνος τῶν ἀπ' Ὀξυρύγχω[ν πόλεως
    τῇ]ς θυγατρός μου [
5   ..]εισης ἀπὸ το[ῦ
       ]...κοπτο[
       ]..τ..[
.   .   .   .   .   .   .   .
```

26. Pilot's Receipt

AM 8930.   8 × 13 cm.   Philadelphia.   About 154 A.D.   Plate II.

In the following statement the skipper (κυβερνήτης), in command of three boats engaged in the transportation of grain down the Nile to Alexandria, acknowledges to the σιτολόγοι of Arsinoïte Philadelphia the lading of 8627¼ artabae of wheat. Such statements were commonly issued in triplicate, two copies being despatched to the strategus of the nome or division from which the grain was being exported, while a third copy was delivered to the sitologi from whom the cargo had been received. Among analogous documents of the Roman period may be cited P. Oxy. 1259, 1260, 2125, Stud. Pal. XX. 32, and P. Lond. 256a (= W. Chrest. 443).

It is apparent that the present text is closely related to P. Warren 5 (*Aegyptus*, XIII, 240 ff.), although the shipments recorded in the two documents vary in quantity and hence would appear to have been made in different years. The late Professor A. S. Hunt, to whom I am also indebted for the rehabilitation of lines 21-23, very kindly made a comparison of the hands. Although Professor Hunt described the hand of the Princeton text as more upright and more careful than the first hand of the Warren papyrus, yet he concluded, by reason of the closely similar formation of the letters, that the identity of the two hands might be reasonably assumed.

Reference is made in lines 20-25 to an ἐπίσταλμα issued jointly by two officials, the first of whom is described as being both royal scribe (βασιλικὸς γραμματεύς) of the Themistes division and acting-strategus (διαδεχόμενος καὶ τὰ κατὰ τὴν στρατηγίαν) of the Heracleides division. Although the papyrus is badly mutilated at this point, it would appear that the second official was the royal scribe of the latter division. During the first part of the third century A.D. such authorizations seem regularly to have required the coöperative action of the strategus and royal scribe of the nome or division from which the shipment of grain was being made (cf. P. Oxy. 1259. 8-9, 2125. 8-11, and Stud. Pal. XX. 32. 1-2, 10-11). Earlier in the Roman period, on the other hand, the strategus appears to have acted independently in this regard (cf. P. Oxy. 276. 13-15). The present text furnishes the earliest evidence for the joint action of the two officials (cf., however, Biedermann, *Studien zur ägyptischen Verwaltungsgeschichte in ptolemäisch-römischer Zeit. Der* Βασιλικὸς Γραμματεύς, 81 ff.).

Temporary vacancies in the office of strategus were usually filled by the appointment of the royal scribe of the same nome or division to serve as acting-strategus (cf. Biedermann, *op. cit.*, 100 ff., Oertel, *Liturgie*, 297 f., and Wenger, *Die Stellvertretung im Rechte der Papyri*, 57 ff.). Our Princeton text furnishes a unique instance of the appointment to this office of a royal scribe from another division. Close parallels to this procedure are supplied, however, by B. G. U. 199. 1-4 and 1023. 1-2. In the former instance a strategus of the combined Themistes and Polemon divisions is shown to serve also as acting-strategus of the remaining Heracleides division. In the latter the office of royal scribe of the Themistes division is associated with that of acting-royal scribe of the Polemon division. It is thus apparent that the prefect in making such appointments was at liberty to exercise his judgment (cf. Wenger, *op. cit.*, 64).

It is impossible, in the absence of explicit internal indications of date, to assign this text to a definite year. Its close relationship to P. Warren 5 suggests, however, a date in or around A.D. 154 (cf. Wilcken, *Archiv*, XI, 131). The concluding portion of the document has been lost.

The transportation system has been discussed in its various phases by numerous writers. References to the older literature will be found in the more recent works by Frisk (*Bankakten aus dem Faijūm*, 5 ff.) and Westermann-Keyes (*Tax Lists and Transportation Receipts from Theadelphia*, 98 ff.). See also Kunkel, *Archiv*, VIII, 183 ff., who discusses the transportation of grain in the late Ptolemaic period.

    Σιτολ[όγ]οις Φιλαδελφίας
    Ἀρσινοείτου Ἡρακλείδου μερίδος
    Ἀχαιὸς Φαθρήους τοῦ Πετεφνούθιος
    τῶν ἀπὸ κώμης Ἄθρας ὅρων
5 τοῦ Προσωπείτου νομοῦ πίστι Διδύμου
    τοῦ καὶ Ἑρμείου διὰ Σερήνου Διδύμου
    Ἀλθαιέως γραμματέω[ς] κυβερνή-
    της πλοίων γ̄, ἀγωγῆς — Ἠψ,
    ρ ᾱ — πζ⟦s⟧, Lσ μγs,
10 γ(ίνονται) — Ἠωλς, μεθ' ἃς ἑκουσίως
    ἀπεγόμησε — σ, ρ ᾱ — β, Lσ — α,
    γ(ίνονται) (πυροῦ) (ἀρτάβαι) σγ, τὰς λοιπὰς τῆς ἐν-
    βολῆς — Ἠφ, ρ ᾱ — πε, Lσ μβs,
    (γίνονται) (πυροῦ) (ἀρτάβαι) Ἠωκζs, ἐξ ἀπ[οσ]τόλου
15 Δομιττ[ίο]υ Ῥούφου ἐπιτρόπου Νέας
    πόλεω[ς] ὁμολογῶ μεμετρῆσθαι
    καὶ ἐνβε[βλ]ῆσθαι παρ' ὑμῶν ἀφ' ὅρ-
    μου Κ[ερκῆς] ὥστε εἰς Ἀλεξάν{ξαν}δ(ρειαν)
    κατα[χθῆ]ναι εἰς τὸν ἐν τῇ Νέᾳ
20 πόλ[ει χειρ]ισμὸν ἐξ ἐπιστάλμα-
    τος [Πτολεμ]αίου βασιλ[ι]κ[οῦ] γρα(μματέως)
    Θεμί[στου μερ]ίδος διαδ[εχ]ομένου
    κα[ὶ] τ[ὰ κατὰ τὴ]ν στρατη[γίαν] Ἡρακλεί-
    [δου μερίδος καὶ ..⁶⁻⁸.. βασι]λικοῦ
25 [γραμματέως Ἡρακλείδου μερίδος   ]
      . . . .

11. απεγομησα has been altered to απεγομησε.   12–13. αγω|γης has been altered to εν|βολης.   14. Read Ἠχκζs.

3. Φαθρήους. Cf. Παθρήους (P. Warren 5. 14), Φατρέους (P. Oxy. 242. 3), Φατρῆτο(ς) (*Archiv*, VI, 427. 32), and Φαθρῆτι (P. Lond. 29. 3). See also O. Oslo, p. 49.

4. κώμης Ἄθρας ὅρων. The reading in SB. 674. 3 (κώμης Ἄθρα ὅρων) is thus confirmed.

5. πίστι Διδύμου. The same expression occurs in P. Warren 5. 15. That Didymus is thus indicated to have acted as surety for Achaius has been pointed out by Hunt (note *ad. loc.*) and Wilcken (*Archiv*, XI, 131).

8–10. ἀγωγῆς κ.τ.λ. It is evident that the term ἀγωγῆς, which usually refers to the carrying capacity of the boats (cf. P. Amh. 138. 5 and P. Mon., pp. 56 f.), is here applied to the actual cargo, for there have been included in the total of 8830½ artabae (line 10) the two fractional extras (1% and ½%), which regularly formed part of the latter. The purpose of these two additional percentages has long remained obscure (cf. the note to P. Oxy. 1259. 16 and Oertel, *Liturgie*, 213). Kalén (P. Berl. Leihgabe, pp. 298 f.) rather plausibly seeks to connect these with the 1% φιλάνθρωπον and ½% ἐνοίκιον θησαυροῦ, two fees collected at the granary on grain received by the sitologi. The inclusion of these extras in shipments destined for Alexandria may reflect, according to Kalén, the responsibility of the sitologi for the purity of the grain. Any deficiency which might result from the presence of sand or other impurities would be sufficiently covered, one might suppose, by these extras. Yet that such was not always the case is shown by P. Oxy. 708 (= W. Chrest. 432), where, on the basis of the sample tested, the detected impurities amounted to 2½%. The fact that in this instance the restitution of the entire amount of the deficiency was required of the sitologi from whom the shipment had been received in no way invalidates Kalén's hypothesis, for the round number (2000 artabae) would appear not to have included the customary extras. It is interesting to note, however, that in addition to the 50 artabae thus required of the sitologi in making good their deficiency provision was made for the delivery of an additional ¾ artaba (διάφορον), amounting to 1½% of this total. For *deductions* of 1½% in shipping cf. P. Iand. 138.

11. ἀπεγόμησε. The purpose of unloading a portion of the cargo is uncertain. Similar reductions of the cargo are not recorded elsewhere. Perhaps the pilot desired to avoid the risk of overloading one of his boats. For the size of the boats engaged in such service see Reil, *Beiträge zur Kenntnis des Gewerbes im hellenistischen Ägypten*, 89. The verb ἀπογομέω (cf. ἀπογομόω) is found only here among published texts. Cf. the listing by Gradenwitz, *Heidelberger Konträrindex der griechischen Papyrusurkunden*, 91.

14. The net total remaining after the deduction of 203 artabae has evidently been given incorrectly. We should expect to find Ἠχκζ̄ς, which would represent the sum of the figures given in the preceding line. After the original cargo had been reduced by 203 artabae, there would remain a total of 8627½ artabae.

15. Domittius Rufus appears to be otherwise unknown. For the ἐπίτροπος Νέας πόλεως see Wilcken, *Grundzüge*, 369 f. and *Hermes*, LXIII (1928), 59 ff. A list of these officials is presented by Calderini, Θησαυροί, 57.

17–18. ἀφ' ὅρμου Κ[ερκῆς]. For the identification of Κερκή with the modern Riqqa see Wilcken, *Archiv*, XI, 131 f. and P. Teb. 823. 6, note. It is not unlikely that grain shipments from Philadelphia were regularly carried overland to this point and thence transported by water to Alexandria.

19–20. τὸν ἐν τῇ Νέᾳ πόλει χειρισμόν. Cf. Oertel, *op. cit.*, 124, note 2.

21. [Πτολεμ]αίου βασιλ[ι]κ[οῦ] γρα(μματέως). The same official appears also in P. Col. 1 recto 4, VIII. 6 (155 A.D.). See Westermann and Keyes, *Tax Lists and Transportation Receipts from Theadelphia*, 133 f. Lists of the royal scribes of the Themistes division are presented by Biedermann, *op. cit.*, 114; Martin, *Archiv*, VI, 171; and Paulus, *Prosopographie der Beamten des Ἀρσινοΐτης Νομός*, 134 f.

24. There is a gap in the list of the royal scribes of the Heracleides division extending from 153 to 159 A. D. Cf. Martin, *Archiv*, VI, 165. Our text probably falls within these dates. Thus it is not possible to restore with

certainty the name which has been lost from this line. Διόφαντος is known, however, to have served in this capacity in 151 and 153, and may have continued in office after the latter date. The exact number of letters to be supplied in the lacuna is necessarily uncertain, but space considerations favor the restoration of not more than eight letters, and the conditions would be most satisfactorily met by the restoration of only six.

27. Declarations Concerning the Delivery of Garments

AM 8947.   11 × 10 cm.   Oxyrhynchus.   191/192 A.D.

A declaration addressed under oath to the strategus of the Oxyrhynchite nome by some official connected with the office of the juridicus. On the assumption that the texts on recto and verso are related, it is probable that the declaration concerned a shipment of garments destined for Alexandria, which the strategus is urged to despatch promptly. It appears from P. Lips. 57 that the office of the juridicus was in some way concerned with the delivery of requisitions of clothing supplied to the gladiatorial school in Alexandria. The text supplies the name of an otherwise unknown juridicus, Suillius Julius (cf. Rosenberg, P.-W., art. *Iuridicus*, 1153).

On the verso there is a second declaration (in a different hand) likewise addressed under oath to the strategus, informing him that the delivery of certain garments of stated value will be made in accordance with instructions received from him. That the articles were destined for shipment to Alexandria would appear from line 15. The name of the strategus (line 8) is new. This Sarapion is not to be identified with the two strategi of the same name who served several years later. Cf. P. Oxy. 1197 (211 A.D.) and 61 (221 A.D.).

Although the part played by the juridicus in connection with the requisition suggests, as indicated above, that the garments were destined for the gladiatorial school in Alexandria, it is also possible that the clothing was required for the use of the army. In the Byzantine period collections of clothing were frequently made for military purposes. Cf. P. Oxy. 1448, introd.

]λισοι ὑπὸ Σουιλλίου Ἰουλίου τοῦ κρατίστου
δικαιοδότου ἧς ἐστιν
Σαραπίωνι ? τῷ σ]τρ(ατηγῷ) Ὀξ(υρυγχίτου) χαίρειν. τὸ [..]
ἐξ ἔθους πεμπόμενον ἀμφὶ ἃς
] αχων φρόντισον πρὸ καιροῦ διαπέμψασθαι
ἐπιμελέστ(ερον)
ἐρ]ρῶσθ(αί) ⟨σε⟩ εὔχο(μαι). (ἔτους) λβ̄ Αὐτοκράτορος Καίσαρος Λουκίου Αἰλίου
5   Αὐρηλίου Κομμόδου Εὐσεβ]οῦς Εὐτυχοῦς Σεβαστοῦ Ἀρμενιακοῦ Μηδικοῦ
Παρθικοῦ

27. DECLARATIONS CONCERNING THE DELIVERY OF GARMENTS

Σαρματικοῦ Γερμανικοῦ μεγίστου Βρετα]ννικοῦ, [month, day, καὶ] ὀμ-
μν(ύω) τὴν Λουκίου Αἰλίου
Αὐρηλίου Κομμόδου Σεβαστοῦ τύχην   ] ως
σεσημ(είωμαι) καὶ τοῖς

. . . .

Verso

(Hand 2) Σαραπίωνι στρα(τηγῷ).
Θῶνις ἀπελε(ύθερος) Ἀπολλωνιανο(ῦ) τοῦ κ(αὶ) Διον[υσίου ?
10 νιου ἀμφο(τέρων) Ἑρμίππου Ἁδριανείω(ν) τῶν καὶ [
Σαραποῦτ(ος) ἀπ' Ὀξ(υρυγχιτῶν) πόλ(εως) ὀμνύομ(εν) τὴν Αὐρη[λίου
κ.τ.λ. τύχην ποιήσειν
παράδ(οσιν) καὶ συντείμ(ησιν) τῶν κατασκευασθέ[ντων
Ὀξ(υρυγχιτῶν) πόλ(εως) παρικλ( ) γ̄ (δηναρίων) τε χω( ) παλλίω(ν)
ζε(υγῶν ?) λ[
πη (δηναρίων ?) β̄ ζε(υγῶν ?) λδ ἀκολ(ούθως) τοῖς γρα(φεῖσιν) ὑπὸ
Σου[ιλλίου Ἰουλίου ?
15 ἔτι δὲ καὶ καταπλε(ύσεσθαι) εἰς Ἀλεξ(άνδρειαν) σὺν τοῖς πλ[οίοις
τῶν κελε(υσθέντων) ἐν τῷδε τῷ νομ(ῷ) απαρ[
καὶ παραμενεῖν ἄχρι ἂν [.]τε ā ἱματι[
τῆς παραδ(όσεως) γράμματα, ἢ ἔνοχ(οι) ε[ἴ]ημεν τ[ῷ ὅρκῳ
Ἀδριανῷ ιβ.

19. Read Ἁδριανοῦ.

13. παρικλ( ). Cf. P. Lips. 57. 28 (περ κλων).

28. Registration of Live Stock

Garrett Dep. 7659.   8.5 × 19.5 cm.   Oxyrhynchus(?).   219 A.D.

A return covering a flock of 15 sheep, 10 lambs, and 3 goats reported for the year 218/219 A.D. It would appear that an identical return had been made in the previous year. The flock subsequently suffered a loss of 10 sheep, a loss which was balanced, however, by the birth of 10 lambs. The lambs of the previous year were numbered, in accordance with the usual practice (cf. P. Cornell, p. 79), among the sheep of the current year. The size of the flock thus remained unchanged.

For similar returns see **24**, introd. A few lines have been lost from the beginning of the text. Numerous erasures, corrections, and repetitions impair the sense of what remains. The corrections were made by the original writer, having been inserted by him between the lines of the text. For the convenience of the reader the lines containing these revisions are designated by the letters a-f, the numbered lines representing the text as originally written. Only those words are enclosed within doubled square brackets which were actually stricken by the writer.

It is not apparent why the original draft of the return was so extensively revised. The declarant seems to have been in a confused state of mind, as is shown both by his revisions and by the absent-minded repetition of the oath formula in line 22. Perhaps the source of his confusion should be sought in the similarity of the two returns.

```
1   [                        ἀπεγρ(αψάμην)]
2   τῷ [διελ(ηλυθότι)] [[α (ἔτει ?)]] ἐπὶ τῆς α(ὐτῆς) κώμης
3   πρόβ(ατα) τ(έλεια) ιε̄, ἄρν(ας) ῑ, αἶγ(ας) γ̄,
a                   διελ(ηλυθότα) α (ἔτος)
4   ἃ γείνεται πρὸς τὸ [[ἐνεστ(ὸς)]]
5   [[ἔτος]] πρόβ(ατα) τέλ(εια) κε̄, αἶγ(ες) γ̄
b                                   μετ' ἀ-
6       ἐξ ὧν διεφθ(άρη) [[πρόβ(ατα)]] ·
c   πογρ(άψασθαι) καὶ ἐξαριθ(μήσασθαι) λείπ(εται) τ[ῷ ἐ]νεσ(τῶτι) (ἔτει)
                                πρόβ(ατα) τέλ(εια)
7   τέλ(εια) ῑ, καταλείπ(εται) πρόβ(ατα) τέλ(εια)
d        [[καὶ πρόβ(ατα)]] καὶ προσ-
8   ιε̄, αἶγ(ες) γ̄, [[ἃ καὶ ἀπογρ(άφομαι)]]
e   επακο(λουθοῦντες) ἀπὸ γο(νῆς) τοῦ α (ἔτους) ἄ[ρ]ν(ες) ι, (γίνεται)
                                [[κε̄]], ἃ γείνεται
9   πρὸς τὸ ἐνεστ(ὸς) β (ἔτος) ἐπὶ τῆς α(ὐτῆς)
f   πρ[ό]β(ατα) κε̄, ἐξ ὧν διεφθ(άρη) τῷ α(ὐτῷ) α (ἔτει)
10  κώ(μης) καὶ τοὺς ἐπακολ(ουθοῦντας) ἀπὸ γο-
    νῆς ἄρν(ας) ῑ, ἃ νεμήσεται
    περὶ τὴν α(ὐτὴν) κώ(μην) καὶ δι' ὅλου
    τοῦ νομοῦ διὰ νομέως
    Ἀμμωνίου καὶ ὀμνύω
15  τὴν Μάρκου Αὐ[ρ]ηλίου
    Ἀντωνίνου Εὐσεβοῦς
    Εὐτυχοῦς Σεβαστοῦ τύχην
    μὴ ἐψεῦσθαι. ἔτους β̄
    Αὐτοκράτορος Καίσαρος
20  Μάρκου Αὐρηλίου Ἀντωνίνου
    Εὐσεβοῦς Εὐτυχοῦς Σεβαστοῦ
    τύχην μὴ ἐψεῦσθαι.
    ἔτους β̄ Αὐτοκράτορος Καίσαρος
    Μάρκου Αὐρηλίου
25  Ἀντωνίνου Εὐσεβοῦς
    Εὐτυχοῦς Σεβαστοῦ,
```

Μεχεὶρ ε⁻. Αὐρήλιος Ἀμμώ-
νιος] Πτολλᾶτος δι' ἐμοῦ
....]απιδου. ἐπιδέδωκα
30 καὶ ὤμ]οσα τ[ὸ]ν ὅρκον ὡς π(ρόκειται).

29. Petition to Strategus

Garrett Dep. 7627.   10 × 20.5 cm.   Philadelphia.   258 A.D.   Plate III.

A petition to the strategus of the Heracleides division of the Arsinoïte nome in which the appellant reports an accident involving severe injury to his brother. Although the details are uncertain, it appears that one of the brothers, Atammon, fell from a roof in the village of Kaminou, the accident having been in some way occasioned by an attack of Libyans. The injured man having received no medical attention, his brother petitions the strategus to take cognizance of the situation in order that his life may be spared. Reference is made to a simliar petition in P. Oxy. 52. 8. Official investigations of accidents involved a physician's report (cf. P. Oxy. 52 and B. G. U. 647).

The reference to an invasion of Libyans is of considerable historical interest. It is well-known that the empire was severely shaken on all sides by barbarian invasions during the later years of the reign of Valerianus and Gallienus. The present text yields important contemporary evidence for similar unrest along the Egyptian border. There appears to be no other reference to a Libyan raid at this time (cf. Bates, *The Eastern Libyans*, 236). Attacks from this source became increasingly common after this date according to Honigmann, P.-W., XXV, 198.

The two brothers, Atammon and Asoeis, appear in two other Princeton texts (**37** and SB. 7474) written by the same, or a very similar, hand.

Single vertical and horizontal folds have caused severe damage to the papyrus, breaking it into four pieces of about equal size, and occasioning the loss of several letters in the center of each line.

Αὐρηλ[ίῳ Ἀπολλω?]νίῳ τῷ καὶ Ἱέρακι
στρα(τηγῷ) Ἀρσι(νοίτου) Ἡ[ρακλείδου] μερίδος
παρ' Αὐ[ρηλίου Ἀσό]ειτος Παυ-
σείρεως [ἀπὸ κώ]μης Φιλαδελ-
5 φίας ἕν[εκα] τοῦ ἀδελφοῦ μου
Ἀτάμμ[ω]ν[ος κ]αταγενομένων
ἐν κώμῃ [Κα]μίνου. διὰ τὴν γενο-
μένην ἡμ[ῖν] ὑπὸ τῶν Λιβύων
ἐπέλευσι[ν τ]οῦ ἀδελφοῦ μου
10 Ἀτάμμωνο[ς πρό]χθες καταπε-
σόντος δι[. . . . .]ων ἀπὸ δώμα-

τος ἠσ[θένησε]ν ἐν τῇ αὐτῇ
κώμῃ ὁ ἀ[θεράπευ]τος καὶ αὐτοῦ
πλήξ| εἰς πολλὰς] ἔχοντος
15 ἀλλὰ καὶ [ἀθεραπε]ύτου γενομένου ἐπι[δίδωμι] τάδε τὰ βιβλ[ί-
δια ἀξι[ῶν ἐν καταχω]ρισμῷ γε-
νέσθαι μὴ [μηδὲν] ἀνθρωπεινὸν αὐτῷ σ[υμβ]ῇ. διευτύχει.
20 Ἀσόει[ς ἐτῶν] μ, ἀντικ(νημίοις) οὐλαί.
Ⅼϛ// Α[ὐτο]κρατόρων Καισάρω[ν
Πουπλίου Λικιν[νίο]υ Οὐαλεριανοῦ
καὶ Πουπλίου Λ[ικι]ννίου Οὐαλεριανοῦ
Γαλλιηνοῦ Γερ[μ]ανικῶν μεγίστων
25 Εὐσεβῶν Εὐτ|υχῶν καὶ Π]ουπλίου Λικιννίου
Κορνηλίου Σαλ[ωνίνο]υ Οὐαλεριανοῦ
τοῦ ἐπιφαν[εστάτου] Καίσαρος Σεβαστῶ(ν),
Θὼ[θ .]α‾.

6, 10. αταμ'μ.

1. Ἀπολλω]ρίῳ. The reading is very uncertain. No strategus is attested for the Arsinoïte nome between the years 245 and 260 (cf. Bilabel, P.-W., art. *Strategos*, 197). An Αὐρήλιος Ἡρακλείδης (cf. B. G. U. 244) is known to have held this office during the reign of Gallienus (260-268), but his name cannot be read here.

7. ἐν κώμῃ [Κα]μίνου. Cf. Stud. Pal. XX. 90. 4. The residence of the brothers in this village was probably transitory. They had leased a plot of land near Tanis in 252 for a period of five years (cf. SB. 7474), but the term of this lease had just expired.

11. δι[.....]ων. Some phrase indicating the manner of the fall seems to be required. The dotted letters are almost certainly correct.

15. καί. The final letter could be as easily read as τ, yet καί must be intended.
16-19. Cf. the similar request in B. G. U. 45. 15-19.
18-19. μὴ [μηδὲν] ἀνθρωπεινὸν αὐτῷ σ[υμβ]ῇ. Paratactic negative purpose clauses are common in the papyri. Cf. Mayser, *Grammatik*, II¹, 237 and II³, 81. For the doubling of the negative see Mayser, *op. cit.*, II², 567.

20. ἀντικ(νημίοις) οὐλαί. The word order is unusual, for οὐλή regularly precedes the designation of the part of the body on which the scar is found. The plural ἀντικ(νημίοις) is suggested both by the plural οὐλαί and the absence of a definite reference to either the right or left shin. Such identification data commonly accompanied petitions for assistance (cf. Hasebroek, *Das Signalement in den Papyrusurkunden*, 85).

25-27. For Saloninus as Caesar cf. P. Giss. 50. 34, note and P. Oxy. 1273. 44, note.

30. Petition to Strategus

Garrett Dep. 7645b.   16.5 × 7.5 cm.   Hermopolis.   About 264 A.D.

Only the opening lines have been preserved, but the fragment is not without interest. The presence of the name Asclatarion, also called Coprilla, furnishes an approximate date for **38** (see page 34), in which the same woman is instituted as an heiress in a Roman will. The date is determined by the text on the verso (**61**), an account of receipts and expenditures from the year 263/264.

The fragment also furnishes the name of Αὐρήλιος Σπαρτιάτης ὁ καὶ Χαιρήμων, a hitherto unknown strategus of the Hermopolite nome (cf. Bilabel, P.-W., art. *Strategos*). In line 7 reference is made to a γενόμενος βουλ(ευτικὸς) ὑπηρ(έτης). Cf. C. P. R. 20. I. 12.

Αὐρηλίῳ Σπαρτιάτῃ τῷ καὶ Χαιρήμονι στρατηγ[ῷ
    Ἑρμοπολ(ίτου)
παρὰ Αὐ(ρηλίας) Ἀσκλαταρίου τῆς καὶ Κοπρίλλης Ἑρμίνου
τοῦ καὶ Ἀσκληπιάδου Χαιρήμονος Ἑρμοπολ(ιτοῦ) ἀναγρ(αφομένης)
5 ἐπ' ἀμφόδ(ου) Φρουρ(ίου) λιβός, συνεστῶτος αὐτῇ Αὐ(ρηλίου) Ἀγαθοῦ
Δαίμονος τοῦ καὶ Ἑρμαίου ...... ον [....]ου τοῦ καὶ
Κ... βουσ... γενομένου βουλ(ευτικοῦ) ὑπηρ(έτου) [τῆς αὐ(τῆς) Ἑρ]μοῦ
    πόλ(εως)

Traces of letters from an additional line.

. . . .

31. Deed of Divorce

Garrett Dep. 7663.   9.5 × 11.5 cm.   Fayum.   79 or 80 A.D.

A deed of divorce drawn up by Haraisis, the divorcée, acting with her guardian, in which she acknowledges to Thouonis, from whom she has separated, the receipt of her dowry. The text in its present fragmentary state supplies only the barest outline of the introductory portion of the agreement, yielding neither the amount of the dowry, the name and relationship of the guardian, nor the exact date of the original contract of marriage.

Divorce contracts are not numerous. A list of those which have been published is furnished by S. G. Huwardas, *Beiträge zum griechischen und gräkoägyptischen Eherecht der Ptolemäer- und frühen Kaiserzeit*, 44. The closest parallel to our text appears to be P. Oxy. 266 (96 A.D.). Cf. B. G. U. 975 (45 A.D.).

The execution of a formal contract was not required in order to effect a legal divorce. For this the act of separation was sufficient. Therefore, as a *fait accompli*, the divorce itself furnished the motive rather than the substance of the agreement which was customarily made by husband and wife upon their separation. The repayment of the dowry was the essential feature of such contracts, which assume accordingly the form of receipts (cf. P. Oxy. 906. 10, note). For a discussion of ancient divorce procedure in the light of the papyri see E. Levy, *Der Hergang der römischen Ehescheidung*, 106 ff.

(Ἔτους) ? Αὐτοκράτορ]ος Τίτου Καίσαρος Οὐεσπασιανοῦ Σεβαστοῦ, Φαῶ[φι
   .., ἐν γραφείῳ
Ἀρ]σινοΐτου νομοῦ. ὁμολογεῖ Ἁρᾶισις Πετεσ[ούχου ?
   ὡς ἐτῶν
ἐβδομήκοντα ? τρ]ιῶν οὐλὴι σιαγόνι ἀριστερᾷ μετὰ κυρίου τ[
   τῆς θ]υγατρὸς αὐτῆς Ἡροΐδος ἀνδρὸς Νείλου τοῦ [ὡς ἐτῶν
5 οὐλῆι   ] κάτωι ἐξ ἀριστερῶν τῶι γενομένωι [αὐτῆς ἀνδρὶ Θουῶνι
   ὡς ἐτῶ]ν ἐβδομήκοντα ἐξ οὐλῆι γόνατι ἀριστερῶ[ι ἀπέχειν παρ'
   αὐτοῦ τὴν ὁμολογ-
οῦσαν παραχρῆ]μα διὰ χειρ[ὸς ἐ]ξ οἴκου ἀργυρίου δραχμ[ὰς
   φερν]ὴν ἣν ὤφιλεν ὁ Θουῶνις τῆι Ἁρᾶισι κα[τὰ συγγραφὴν συνοικεσίου
τὴν τετελειω]μένην διὰ τοῦ αὐτοῦ γραφείου τῶι ε (ἔτει) . [
10   ]ν καὶ συγχ[ωρεῖ ἡ Ἁρᾶισις ?
   ] διὰ τὸ συνῆρ[θαι τὴν συμβίωσιν
. . . .

1. A date early in the fourth year of Titus' reign (81 A.D.) is unlikely, though not altogether impossible. Titus died on the 13th of September in that year. News of his death would have required not more than three or four weeks to reach the Fayum. Unless, therefore, this document was penned very early in Phaophi (Sept. 28-Oct. 27), it is improbable that it was written in 81 prior to the announcement of the accession of Domitian.
2. Ἁρᾶισις. Cf. Ἁρᾶισι (line 8). Doubtless the same as Ἁρᾶσις. αι does not often replace α (whether long or short) except in the final syllable (cf. Mayser, *Grammatik*, I, 121). But iota adscript is consistently (with the exception of ἀριστερᾷ, line 3) employed in this text. Note especially οὐλῆι (lines 3, 6) and κάτωι (line 5). Its irrational use within a proper name is thus not altogether surprising. W. Döllstädt (*Griechische Papyrusprivatbriefe in gebildeter Sprache aus den ersten vier Jahrhunderten nach Christus*, 11-12) comments upon the frequent retention of iota adscript in personal names, especially in the case of persons of high rank.
3. ἐβδομήκοντα? τρ]ιῶν. The age of Haraisis is purely conjectural. She may, of course, have been considerably younger than Thouonis. Indeed, the motive for the divorce may have been occasioned by a marked discrepancy in their ages. But of this there is no evidence, and it is perhaps safer to assume that husband and wife were of approximately the same age. κυρίου. Possibly the paternal uncle of Heroïs, that is, the brother-in-law of Haraisis.
6. οὐλῆι. For the spelling see Mayser, *Grammatik*, I, 125. Cf. P. Ryl. 154. 3, 4.

31. DEED OF DIVORCE

8. φερν]ὴν ἦν ὤφιλεν. Cf. τὴν ὀφιλη[μένην] . . . φερνή[ν] (B. G. U. 975. 21-22).
Θουῶνις (= Θοῶνις). For ου in place of ο in Egyptian proper names see Mayser, *Grammatik*, I, 117.

9. ε (ἔτει) [. On the not improbable assumption that Heroïs was the daughter of Haraisis by Thouonis, possible dates for the execution of the contract of marriage are the fifth years of Nero (58/59), Claudius (44/45), and Caligula (40/41). A date in the reign of Vespasian would be much too late, for Heroïs was already married in 79 or 80. Of the letter following the symbol for ἔτει hardly more than a dot remains, making its identification impossible. Attention is attracted by the unusually long period of wedded life which preceded the divorce, extending perhaps to forty years. As a rule, both in ancient and modern life, divorces occur within the first few years after marriage. Cf. P. Oxy. 266 and P. Lips. 27, both of which disclose divorces terminating only two years of married life.

11. διὰ τὸ συνῆρ[θαι τὴν συμβίωσιν. Cf. P. Oxy. 266. 15-16 and P. Grenf. II. 76. 19. For the reading συνῆρ[θαι in preference to συνηρ[ῆσθαι (cf. M. Chrest. 293, introd.) see P. Teb. 809. 4, note. Although ρ has been dotted as a doubtful letter, the reading is almost certainly correct. The upper half of the letter has been broken off, but a considerable portion of the characteristic tail-stroke is clearly visible.

32. LOAN OF MONEY AND WHEAT

Garrett Dep. 7660.　　　13 × 11 cm.　　　Oxyrhynchus.　　　99 A.D.

An acknowledgment of a loan of 100 drachmas and 2 artabae of wheat to be repaid in Payni of the same year. Similar loans of money and wheat from this period are recorded in P. Teb. 388, P. Mey. 5, and B. G. U. 339.

 Ἡρᾶς ? Ἡρ]ᾶτος τοῦ Ἡρᾶτος μητρὸς Θα-
 ήσιος　?] τῆς Ὤρου τῶν ἀπ' Ὀξυρύγχ(ων)
 πόλεως] Πέρσης τῆς ἐπιγονῆς Παᾶ-
 τι ‸ α ‸ νιος τοῦ Ὤρου μητρὸς Σιν-
5 θοώνιος ἀπὸ τῆς αὐτῆς πόλεως χ(αίρειν).
 ὁμολογῶ ἔχειν παρὰ σοῦ διὰ χειρὸς
 ἐξ οἴκου ἀργυρίου Σεβαστοῦ νομίσματ(ος)
 (δραχμὰς) ρ, (γίνονται) (δραχμαὶ) ρ, καὶ μεμετρῆσθαι ἐξ οἴκου
 (πυροῦ) (ἀρτάβας) β, (γίνονται) (πυροῦ) (ἀρτάβαι) β, κεφαλαίου αἷς
              οὐδὲν τῷ
10 καθόλου προσῆκται, ἃς καὶ ἀποδώ-
 σω ἐν τῷ Παῦνι μηνὶ τοῦ ἐνεστῶτος
 τρίτου ἔτους Αὐτοκράτορος Καίσαρος Νέρουα
 Τραιανοῦ Σεβ]αστο[ῦ Γ]ερμαν[ικοῦ

3. Πέρσης τῆς ἐπιγονῆς. For the meaning and application of this legal fiction see Pringsheim, *Sav. Zeit.*, XLIV (1924), 396 ff., and Tait, *Archiv*, VII,

175 ff. More recent discussions of the problem are cited by Wilcken, P. Wurz. 11. 3, note.

4-5. Σισθοώνιος. For the name cf. P. Oxy. 49. 5 (100 A.D.) and P. Oxy. 257. 17-18 (94/95 A.D.).

33. LOAN OF WHEAT

Garrett Dep. 7547. 7 × 21 cm. Provenance unknown. 126 A.D.

An acknowledgment of a loan of 131 artabae of wheat negotiated between two brothers. The text exhibits several unusual features which distinguish it from other documents of a similar nature. In the first place, it is clearly stated that it is the purpose of the loan to defray the ἀρταβία on a plot cultivated by the borrower (lines 4-6). The purpose for which a loan is secured is rarely, if ever, stated in the acknowledgment, except in the case of loans of of seed-corn granted by the state. Our text appears to be unique in this respect.

No less unusual is the promise of the borrower to include the transportation fees (σακκηγία) in the repayment of the loan (lines 15-17). This too appears to be unique. The closest parallel may again be found among the contracts for the delivery of seed-corn (cf. P. Oxy. 1024, 25-37: ἅμα τοῖς τῆς γῆς δημοσίοις. See note to P. Hamb. 19. 19.).

It is also noteworthy that the loan is made on the written order or authorization (διαστολή) of a third party (lines 6-9). This again is reminiscent of the procedure involved in the granting of loans of seed-corn, which required a written authorization issued by the strategus or some other official to the sitologi of the local granary. It is not clear why such an order was necessary in the present instance.

The land cultivated by the borrower is described as an οἶκος. The use of this term suggests the association of the plot with an οἶκος πόλεως (cf. P. Hamb. 36, introd.), to which it may have belonged. Unfortunately the identity of the πόλις cannot be established, for the provenance of the text is uncertain.

   Φᾶσις Χαιρήμων[ος
   Πετερμούθῳ ἀδελφ[ῷ
   χαίρειν. ἔσχον παρὰ
   σοῦ ἐν χρήσι ὥστε
5 εἰς ἀρταβίαν οὗ γε-
   ωργῶ οἴκου, ἀκολού-
   θως ᾗ ἔσχηκα
   διαστολῇ παρὰ
   Καλοκαίρου, ἣν
10 καὶ ἀνέδωκα σοί,

33. LOAN OF WHEAT

πυρο[ῦ] μέτρῳ δ[ρό-
μῳ ἀρτάβας ἑ[κα-
τὸν τριάκον[τα
μ[ία]ν, (γίνονται) (πυροῦ) (ἀρτάβαι) ρλα,
15 ἃς [κ]αὶ ἀποδώσ[ω
σοὶ ἅμα τῇ σακ[κη-
γείᾳ . . . . χ . [. .
ἐν τῷ . . . . [. .
ἀνυπερθέτως.

20 (ἔτους) ι̅ Αὐτοκράτο[ρος
Καίσαρος Τραια[νοῦ
Ἁδριανοῦ Σεβ[αστοῦ,
μην[ὸ]ς Και[σαρείου
ιδ.

4. Read χρήσει.

2. Πετερμούθῳ. For the dative in —ῳ cf. Κολλούθῳ (P. Par. 54. 12, 24, cited by Mayser, *Grammatik*, I, 285).

4-5. ὥστε εἰς ἀρταβίαν. For the use of ὥστε without a verb see Mayser, *Grammatik*, II¹, 301-302. For the land-tax of one artaba per aroura see Wilcken, *Grundzüge*, 187-188, and S. L. Wallace, *Taxes in Roman Egypt from Augustus to Diocletian*, s. v. That the word is not used here loosely to refer to a loan of seed-corn at the same (and normal) rate is made unlikely both by the fact that the two contracting parties are brothers and by the fact that the loan is negotiated in Mesore. Distributions of seed-corn were regularly made at a later period in the year, commonly in Hathyr (see Schnebel, *Landwirtschaft*, I, 138-140).

17-18. The restoration of these lines is difficult. One would expect to find a reference to the month in which the repayment was promised, but the writing has been practically obliterated and nothing can be read with certainty. Parallels are wanting.

34. REPAYMENT OF LOANS

Garrett Dep. 7655.   7 × 15.5 cm.   Theadelphia.   144 A.D.

Horus acknowledges to Ecysis the receipt of an indefinitely stated sum which was owed to him by the latter. The text follows, in somewhat abbreviated form, the formula commonly found in such receipts (cf. P. Amh. 111-113). Unusual, however, is the indefinite statement of the amount involved in the payment (lines 14-17). This sum is described as being πάντα ὅσα ποτὲ ὤφειλεν ὁ Ἐκῦσις τῷ Ὥρωι κατ' ἐγγράπτους ἀσφαλείας. It is thus implied that Ecysis is here making settlement in full for various debts previously incurred by him, the sum of which could be determined from the respective contracts involved. For the form of such contracts see P. Oslo 39 (Theadelphia, 146 A.D.).

From the opening lines it is learned that this receipt was written in Theadelphia on the eighth of August, 144 A.D. It is evident from the form of the document that it was drawn up in the record-office (γραφεῖον) of that village. Especially significant in this respect is the objective formulation of the text (ὁμολογεῖ), coupled with the descriptive identification of each of the two parties concerned (cf. Mitteis, *Grundzüge*, 60 ff.). A detailed description of the management and operation of a γραφεῖον is furnished by a group of documents recently published by Boak (P. Mich. II, Part 1). Cf. Mitteis, *op. cit.*, 62 ff.

The text is incomplete owing to the loss of several lines at the bottom.

  Ἔτους ἑβδόμου Αὐτοκρατ[ορος
  Καίσαρος Τίτου Αἰλίου Ἀδριαν[οῦ
  Ἀντωνίνου Σεβαστοῦ Εὐσεβ[οῦς,
  Μεσορὴ ιε, ἐν Θεαδελφείαι τ[ῆς
5 Θεμίστου μερίδος τοῦ Ἀρσινοίτου νομοῦ. ὁμολογεῖ
  Ὧρος ἀπάτωρ μητρὸς Αὐγ-
  χεως ὡς ἐτῶν τεσσα[ρ]άκον-
  τα πέντε οὐλὴ δακτύλῳ μ[ι-
10 κρῷ χιρὸς ἀριστερ[ᾶ]ς Ἐκῦσι
  Πανεσνέως ὡς ἐ[τ]ῶν τριάκοντα πέντε οὐλὴ δακτύ-
  λῳ μικρῷ χιρὸς ἀριστερᾶς
  ἀπέχιν παρ' αὐτοῦ πάντα
15 ὅσα ποτὲ ὤφειλεν ὁ Ἐκῦσις
  τῷ Ὥρωι κατ' ἐγγράπτους
  ἀσφαλείας καὶ μηδὲν τὸν
  Ὧρον μηδὲ τοὺς παρ' αὐτοῦ
  ἐνκαλεῖν μηδ' ἐγκαλέσιν
20 τῷ Ἐκῦσι μηδὲ τοῖς παρ' αὐτοῦ ἀπὸ τῶν ἔμπροσθεν
  χρόνων μέχρι τῆς ἐνεστώ-
  σης ἡμέρας. Ὧρος ἀπάτωρ
  μητ[ρ]ὸς Αὐγχεως ἀπέ-
25 [χω παρὰ το]ῦ Ἐκύ[σεως] πάν-
  [τα ὅσα πο]τὲ [ὤφειλεν . . .

     5-6. αρσινοϊτου.

4. ἐν Θεαδελφείαι κ. τ. λ. For the omission of a specific reference to the γραφεῖον see Mitteis, *Grundzüge*, 61-62. Cf. P. Oslo 39. 4.

8. ὡς ἐτῶν κ. τ. λ. Owing to the difficulty of determining in many cases the exact age of the contracting parties, such approximations are not uncommon. So also in lines 11-12. Cf. Hasebroek, *Das Signalement in den Papyrusurkunden*, 26-27.

9. οὐλή. The nature and position of such οὐλαί are summarized by Hasebroek, *op. cit.*, 36 ff. It is noteworthy that both Horus and Ecysis have distinguishing marks on the little finger of the same hand. This coincidence may perhaps be attributed to the haste and inaccuracy of the notary. Cf. Hasebroek, *op. cit.*, 38-39.

16-17. Ὥρωι. The use of iota adscript at so late a date is worthy of note (cf. Φιλαδελφείαι, line 4). For its gradual disappearance beginning with the close of the second century B.C. see Mayser, *Grammatik*, I, 132-133. ὠφειλεν . . . κατ' ἐγράπτους ἀσφαλείας. Cf. P. Oxy. 1472. 15-17 and P. Lond. 336. 24-25 (= M. Chrest. 174).

19. ἐνκαλεῖν. For the failure to assimilate ν and κ see Mayser, *op. cit.*, I, 233-234.

35. Receipt for Payment of Debt

AM 8937.   9.5 × 4.5 cm.   Theadelphia.   About 161 A.D.

Only the opening lines of the following receipt have been preserved. Its provenance and approximate date are suggested by the occurrence of the name Ἀρετίων Νάσωνος. The identification of this individual with the πρεσβύτερος κώμης Θεαδελφείας of the same name, who appears in P. Mey. 4. 6, 25 (161 A.D.), is almost certain.

   Νεῖλος Μύσθου Ἀρητίωνι Νάσωνος δι(ὰ) τοῦ υἱοῦ Χαιρήμονος
   χαίρειν. ἀπέσχον παρὰ σοῦ τὸ ἐπι-
   βάλλον σοι μέρος ὧν ὀφείλει μοι
5 γυνηρων πρα . . . .
       .   .   .   .   .   .

36. Partnership Contract

AM 8943.   5 × 12 cm.   Provenance unknown.   195-197 A.D.

The conclusion of a partnership agreement drawn up by four individuals whose names are subscribed in lines 10-15. The contract possibly provides for the formation of a partnership between tax farmers (cf. λ[ο]γεύματα, line 1), or alternatively it may represent an agreement to lease and farm a plot of ground on a partnership basis. A date in the reign of Commodus subsequent to his acquisition of the titles *Arabicus* and *Adiabenicus* (195 A.D.) and prior to the accession of Caracalla (198 A.D.) is indicated by the regnal formula. The subscription was made by the second hand in large uncials.

```
                           ] ..λ[ο]γεύματα ποιησόμεθα
                        μέ]χρι συνκλεισμοῦ γενήμα-
        τος          κα]τὰ τὰ προκείμενα μέρη
                          ]να λήμματα μετὰ
    5                     ]αι ὡσαύτως κατὰ τὸν αὐτὸν
                          ]εν πᾶσι τοῖς διὰ τῆς μισθώ-
        εως            ] δικαίοις πᾶσι. ἡ κοινωνία
        κυρία ἔστω.  ⌊? Αὐτοκ]ράτορος Καίσαρος Λουκίου
        Σεπτιμίου Σεουήρου] Εὐσεβοῦς Περτίνακος
   10   Σεβαστοῦ Ἀραβικοῦ Ἀδι]αβηνικοῦ, Ἁθὺρ ιᾱ.  (Hand 2) Κολ-
        λοῦθο]ς Μαξίμου
        ὁμολογ]ῶ ὡς πρόκιται.
(Hand 1) ὁ δεῖνα τοῦ δεῖνος ὁμολογ]ῶ ὡς πρόκιται.  (Hand 3 ?) Ὡρίων Ξενο-
        φῶντος ? ὁμολογῶ ὡς] πρόκιται.  (Hand 4 ?) Δῖος Στεφάνου
   15   ὁμολογῶ ὡς πρ]όκιται.
```

37. Receipts for Payment of Rent on Leased Land

Garrett Dep. 7624.   25.5 × 8.5 cm.   Tanis.   255 and 256 A.D.   Plate IV.

The text is divided into two columns, in each of which a separate receipt is recorded. Both receipts record payments of rent (ἐκφόριον) made on a parcel of land situated near Tanis, a small village lying a few miles south of Arsinoïte Philadelphia. This land is further described as the κλῆ(ρος) Πτιαπ( ). Aurelius Heracleides, ex-cosmete of Alexandria, appears as lessor. Those to whom the land was leased are the Aurelii, Patron, Asoeis, and Atammon (cf. 29), these three farming the land on shares (ἐπὶ κοινωνίᾳ).

In the first of these receipts, dated on the eleventh of August, 255 A.D., the lessor acknowledges receipt of rent for the current year, 254/255. In the second a similar payment is recorded for the following year. Although in the case of the latter only the year (255/256) has been preserved from the date, this receipt should doubtless be assigned to the summer of 256, after the completion of the harvest. The amount of the payment is not definitely specified in the case of the first receipt. That it was approximately equal to the payment of 656½ artabae made in the following year is almost certain, for the continued validity of the lease is specifically affirmed at the close of the first receipt.

The relation of this document to a lease [1] in the same collection.(SB.

---

[1] It is worth noting in this connection that a small additional fragment of this

7474) has been already pointed out by Professors Van Hoesen and Johnson (*T. A. P. A.*, LVI [1925], 213 ff.). In both texts the same persons appear as lessor and lessees, and in both cases the land is leased on shares. Yet the editors of the lease decline to identify the land of the receipts with the land of the lease, pointing out (*op. cit.*, 217) that, whereas the lease is for a plot of βασιλικὴ γῆ situated ἐν τόπῳ Φθ.[ ] (line 4), the land mentioned in the receipts is described as the κλή(ρος) Πτιαπ( ), as shown above. The points of resemblance between the two texts are so remarkable, however, that it is difficult to accept the view that they are not related to the same parcel of land. Professor Johnson has himself suggested to me that Φθ may be an aspirated form of Πτ, and that the location of the two plots may thus be identical. A similar phenomenon is observable in the case of two pairs of names listed in Preisigke's *Namenbuch*, Πταρου[αο]ῦμος—Φθαρουαοῦμαι and Πταῦς—Φθάϋς (the accent should doubtless be identical). The likelihood that Φθ and Πτ are the initial letters of the same name is made almost certain by the unmistakable traces of an iota which follow Φθ. We thus have Φθι[ ] and Πτιαπ( ).

There remains the necessity of demonstrating that the land in both instances was from a κλῆρος. That such was in fact the case is strongly suggested by what has been said above. One would, therefore, expect to find a reference to the κλῆρος in the lacuna near the end of the fourth line of the lease. The editors have offered as a restoration ἐν τόπῳ Φθ.[. . λεγομένο]υ. A dot is not required under the final υ; although the letter is broken, the reading is certain. The genitive λεγομένου in place of the required dative in itself arouses the suspicion that the restoration is incorrect, and this suspicion is confirmed by the length of the restoration (10 letters). There is space in the lacuna for not more than 8 letters. The corresponding lacunae in lines 2, 3, 5, and 6 are supplied by 6, 7, 9, and 4 letters respectively. The gap in line 4 exceeds that in the preceding line by one letter at the most, whereas an additional letter has been lost from line 5. Requirements of space would be exactly satisfied by reading ἐν τόπῳ Φθι[απ( ) κλήρο]υ, thus supplying 8 letters in the lacuna (including the mark of abbreviation). No exact parallel can be cited, but there is a similar expression in B. G. U. 633. 6-7, with the order of the last two words reversed: ἐν τό(πῳ) κλήρου Μώρου λεγομένου.

Although it is hazardous to draw conclusions from restored passages, it would nevertheless appear that there is strong evidence in support of the

---

lease was discovered among the pieces belonging to Garrett Dep. 7627 (**29**), written almost certainly by the same hand. The fragment contains a few letters from lines 9 and 10:]πιτελου[(line 9),]υνκομιδ[(line 10). The two words of which these letters form a part (ἐπιτελούντων and συνκομιδῆς) had been correctly restored by the original editors.

contention that reference is made to the same parcel of land in the two documents. In the Roman period similar κλῆροι are not infrequently mentioned in connection with land which had been confiscated by the state and which was subsequently reclassified as βασιλικὴ γῆ (cf. Wilcken, *Grundzüge*, 303). It is not clear how Heracleides acquired this plot of crown land, but it may be safely affirmed that it was a portion of a large private estate. Private ownership is definitely indicated by expressions found both in the lease (ὑπαρχούσας σοι, line 4) and in the receipts (ὧν γεωργεῖτέ μου ἀρουρῶν, lines 5-6). The frequent difficulty of distinguishing between imperial and privately owned οὐσίαι has been pointed out by Oertel, *Liturgie*, 231, and Meyer, P. Giss. 101, introd. For the imperial οὐσίαι see especially Wilcken, *Grundzüge*, 298 ff.; Rostovtzeff, *Kolonat*, 119 ff., 180, 192 and *Gesellschaft und Wirtschaft im Römischen Kaiserreich*, II, 24 ff., 293 ff.; and P. Ryl. 168, introd.

Interesting parallels are furnished by the extensive Heroninus correspondence, a group of contemporary documents which throw much light upon the administration of the imperial (?) οὐσίαι at this period (cf. P. Flor. II, pp. 58-64). On the basis of such a comparison one may conjecture that Amaïs and Heroninus served as overseers (φροντισταί) of extensive estates situated near their respective villages, acting as agents for the wealthy absentee landlords, Aurelius Heracleides in the former instance, Aurelius Alypius and others in the case of the latter. It has been thought by many that the landlords appearing in the Heroninus documents leased rather than owned their estates, subletting the land to others (so Comparetti, P. Flor. II, p. 60; Oertel, *op. cit.*, 232; and Meyer, P. Giss. III, p. 98), a view which is accepted with some hesitation by Wilcken, *Archiv*, V, 437-438, who stresses the need of further evidence. Johnson (*Roman Egypt*, 214 f.), however, prefers the view that these estates were in reality privately owned and managed by privately employed φροντισταί. Included among the administrative duties of the φροντισταί was the obligation to collect for these landlords the revenues derived from the lands under their supervision (cf. Oertel, *op. cit.*, 233-234).

Wealthy citizens of Alexandria are known to have frequently assumed leases on land situated in the χώρα (cf. Rostovtzeff, *Kolonat*, 181-182). It is thus not surprising to find an ex-cosmete from Alexandria interested in a Fayum estate.

It is necessary in conclusion to establish for the lease the date 252 A.D. It is stipulated in line 5 (of the lease) that the term of the contract shall extend for a period of five years ἀπὸ σπ[ορᾶς τοῦ εἰ]σιόντο[ς] ? (ἔτους). Only a portion of the numeral is visible. A re-examination of the original confirms Wilcken's view (*Archiv*, VIII, 310) that the remaining stroke of the doubtful letter requires the restoration of either γ or ϛ. The former is the more likely reading in my opinion. On the assumption that the lease and the receipts are related to each other in the manner described above, one must assign the lease to the year 252, its term commencing with the third year of Gallus and Volusianus (252/253). The receipts thus cover payments of ἐκφόριον for the third and fourth years of the term of the lease (254/255 and 255/256).

COL. I

Αὐρήλιος Ἡρακλείδης κοσμητεύσας τῆς
λαμπ(ροτάτης) πόλεως Ἀλεξανδρέων διὰ
Ἀμᾶϊ φροντιστοῦ Τάνεως Αὐρη(λίοις)
Πάτρωνι καὶ Ἀσόει καὶ Ἀτάμμωνι μισθ(ωταῖς)
5 κλή(ρου) Πτιαπ( ) χαίρειν. ἀπέσχον
παρ' ὑμῶν τὸ ἐκφόριον ὧν γεωργεῖταί μου
ἀρουρῶν ἐπὶ κοινωνίᾳ περὶ κώ(μην) Τάνιν
ὑπὲρ τοῦ ἐνεστῶτος δευτέρου ἔτου[ς] πλήρης   254/255
κ[υ]ρίας οὔσης τῆς μισθώσεως καὶ ἐπερω(τηθεὶς) ὡμολ(όγησα).
10 Α[ὐρήλ]ι[ο]ς Ἡρακλείδης σεσημ(είωμαι) ὁς πρόκιται.
L β [τῶν] κυρίων ἡμῶν Οὐαλεριαν[ο]ῦ καὶ Γαλλιηνοῦ Σε⟨βασ⟩τῶ[ν] /,
Μεσορὴ ιε //.   11 August 255.

COL. II

Α[ὐ]ρή[λιος Ἡρακλείδης κοσμητεύσας] τῆς λαμπρο-
τά[της πόλεως τῶν Ἀλεξανδρέω]ν διὰ Ἀμᾶϊ
15 φρ[οντιστοῦ Τάνεως Αὐρηλίοις Π]άτρωνι
καὶ Ἀσ[όει καὶ Ἀτάμμωνι μισθ]ωταῖς κλήρου Πτ[ιαπ( )   χαίρ]ειν.
ἀπέσχον [παρ' ὑμῶν τὸ ἐκφόριο]ν ὑπ(ὲρ) ὧν
γεω[ρ]γε[ῖ]τ[έ μου ἀρουρῶν ἐπὶ κοιν]ωνίᾳ
20 περ[ὶ κώμην Τάνιν ὑπὲρ τοῦ ἐν]εστῶτος γ (ἔτους) //   255-256
επι[πυροῦ ἀρτάβας ἑ]ξακοσίας πεντή-
κον[τα ἓξ ἥμισυ πλήρης   ] γί(νονται) (πυροῦ) (ἀρτάβαι) χνςϛ /
αιτ[   ]—ταστου [[...]] χνςϛ / ὡς πρόκ(ειται).
25 L γ [τῶν κυρίων ἡμῶν Οὐαλεριανοῦ] καὶ Γαλλιηνοῦ Σεβαστῶν, 255/256
[month, day.   ]—
       3, 14. αμαϊ.   10. Read ὡς.

1. Αὐρήλιος Ἡρακλείδης. The possible identification of this Heracleides with an Arsinoïte strategus of the same name, who served under Gallienus after 260, has been suggested by Van Hoesen and Johnson, op. cit., 216. Cf. B.G.U. 244. 1. The latter may perhaps be the same as the Aurelius Heracleides who appears as senator and ex-gymnasiarch of Arsinoë in the sixth year of the same emperor (P. Lond. 1170. 265-266). It is

unlikely that any of these can be identified with the Aurelius Heracleides who is mentioned in the Heroninus correspondence, for the latter seems not to have been of high rank (cf. P. Flor. II, p. 62). κοσμητεύσας κ. τ. λ. Aurelius Appianus, whose relationship to Heroninus appears to have been analogous to that of Heracleides to Amais, had similarly held a high position in Alexandria. In P. Lond. 1226. 2-3 he is recorded as ex-exegete and senator.

9. κυρίας οὔσης τῆς μισθώσεως. As in P. Ryl. 184. 8-9 (214 A.D.). A longer variation of the same is found in P. Fay. 96. 19-20 (122 A.D.).

10. Although the signature is written in a hand different from that appearing in the body of the receipt, it is difficult to identify it with the signature appearing in line 18 of the lease. Cf. Wilcken, *Archiv*, VIII, 310.

12. Μεσορή. Payments of ἐκφόριον so long after the conclusion of the harvest are exceptional. The leases usually specify delivery in Payni, or at the latest in Epiph. Cf. Waszynski, *Bodenpacht*, 104-105. The terms of the present lease (SB. 7474. 13) are uncertain in this respect, owing to the condition of the text.

17. Preceding χαίρειν there is space sufficient for eight or nine letters, but this space was probably left vacant.

21-22. It is evident that only a very large plot would account for an annual rental of 656½ artabae. The terms of the lease specify the delivery of 3¾ artabae for each aroura of seed land (SB. 7474. 6). Figured on this basis the payment represents almost exactly the amount due on 175 1/16 arourae. Rates of from one to nine artabae are noted by Waszynski, *op. cit.*, 99.

38. ROMAN WILL

Garrett Dep. 7645a.   27 × 8 cm.   Hermopolis.   About 264 A.D.   Plate IV.

Very few wills of Roman form have been discovered among the papyri. Among these the text published below assumes a prominent position by reason of the new light it throws upon the form of the Roman *cretio* in a Greek translation. Our text is most nearly related to B. G. U. 326 (M. Chrest. 316) and P. Oxy. 907 (M. Chrest. 317), the former a Greek translation of a will drawn up in Latin, the latter an abbreviated copy of a Greek original of a Roman will. From neither of these texts can the exact form of the *cretio* be determined, owing to rather extensive lacunae. Our text not only supplies the words missing in these lacunae (see note to line 5), but furnishes in addition (lines 4-5) the provision that the *aditio* must be completed within one hundred days after the death of the testatrix, with the exclusion, however, of those days during which the designated heiress is ignorant of her appointment or incapable of making the *aditio*. We thus have the Greek equivalent of a *cretio vulgaris*. For a list of related texts see Kreller, *Erbrechtliche Untersuchungen*, 279 ff.

The date of the will is indicated approximately by a petition (30), in which Asclatarion, the mother of the testatrix, appears. Although the latter text is itself undated, there has been preserved on its verso (61) a small fragment of an account written in the year 264 A.D.

The testatrix, Aurelia Serenilla, also called Demetria, was evidently under *tutela*, for she required the authority of a κουράτωρ as well as of a κύριος in drawing up her will. For the distinction see Mitteis, *Grundzüge*, 248-250. Although she was, as a Roman citizen, under obligation to make her will strictly in accordance with the forms prescribed by the Roman civil law, yet as a citizen of Egypt she availed herself of the privilege of composing the text thereof in Greek, a concession extended to such persons by the emperor Severus Alexander (cf. SB. 5294. 12-14 and Mitteis, *Grundzüge*, 246-247).

The provisions of the will are only partially preserved. As heiress (κληρονόμος) Serenilla appointed her mother. Her sons (see note to line 4) are declared to be disinherited (ἀποκληρόνομοι). After this follows the *cretio*, of the form described above. Specific bequests of land are then made to the husband (and κύριος) of the testatrix, and in line 8 there appears to be a reference to a similar bequest made to her κουράτωρ. From the concluding portion of the will only a few scattered letters remain.

For the form of a Roman will composed in Greek see especially Kreller, *op. cit.*, 380-389, and Kraus, *Die Formeln des griechischen Testaments*, 86-90. Additional literature is cited by Meyer, *Jur. Pap.*, 66-67.

On the verso there are fragments of an unrelated account.

Αὐ(ρηλία) Σε]ρηνίλλα ἐπικαλουμέ[νη] Δημητρία Φιλιππιανοῦ τοῦ καὶ
Κοπρέου γε[νο]μένου βουλ(ευτοῦ) Ἑρμοῦ πόλ(εως) τῆς μεγάλης ἀρχαίας καὶ λαμ-
προτά]της μετὰ κυρίου Αὐ(ρηλίου) Ἑρμ[ίν]ου τοῦ κ[α]ὶ Ἀχιλλέως Εὐδαίμονος εὐθηνιάρχ(ου) τῆς αὐτῆς Ἑρμοῦ πόλ(εως) καὶ κουράτορος Αὐ(ρηλίου) Οὐαλερίου Λόγγου
οὐετρ]ανοῦ ἀπὸ τῆς αὐτῆς [Ἑρμ]οῦ πόλ(εως) διαθ(ήκην) ἐποίησεν γραφησομένην τε ὑπηγόρευσεν. Αὐ(ρηλία) Ἀσκλατάριον ἡ κα[ὶ] Κόπριλλα μήτηρ μου
κλη]ρονόμος μοι ἔστω. οἱ δὲ υἱοὶ ⟨οἱ⟩ ἐμοὶ ἀποκληρόνομοι ἔστωσαν. προσερχέσθω δὲ τῇ κληρονομίᾳ μου ἐν ἡμέραις ρ̄ ταῖς ἐπι-
5   σήμοις] μου ὅταν γνῷ καὶ δύνηται μαρτύρασθαι ἑαυτὴν εἶναί μοι κληρον[ό]μον. Αὐ(ρηλίῳ) Ἀχιλλεῖ τῷ καὶ Ἑρμίνῳ κοσμητ(ῇ) συμβίῳ μου
καταλεί]πω περὶ Ἰβιῶ[ν]α Πετεαφθὶ μαχί{ι}μων συντάξεων ἐκ τοῦ Ναυβη κλήρου ἀφ' ὧν ἔχω ἐν μίᾳ κοίτῃ ἀρουρῶ(ν)
......]   ς ἐξ[......]   ἀρ[ο]ύρα[ς π]έντε καὶ περὶ τὴν α[ὐτὴν] κώμην βίου κοινωνίας Ἀλίνης ἧς ἔχω ἀρούρας τρεῖς
......]...[..]τουμ[......]κα ν [........]...[.]ιος

κουρα[τ.] πιφη[..] . [....]β / ἧς οἰκῶ, τῷ δ' ἐπ' [ἐμ]οῦ
κουράτορι ευ οι

9 About 58 letters   ]δεν ζητηθησ[..] ου [.......]νο
10 About 54 letters   τῆς] αὐτῆς πόλ(εως) δοθῆ[ναι ....]ον
11 About 59 letters   ] μίαν τέταρτον [..............]ου

Traces of letters from two additional lines.

    . . . .
       2. λογ'γου.   6. ιβιω[ν]α.

2. Αὐρηλίου Ἑρμίνου τοῦ καὶ Ἀχιλλέως Εὐδαίμονος εὐθηνιάρχ(ου). This person, who is named here in the capacity of κύριος, is doubtless to be identified with Αὐρηλίῳ Ἀχιλλεῖ τῷ καὶ Ἑρμίνῳ κοσμητ(ῇ), the husband of Serenilla (line 5). The order of the two names, Herminus-Achilles, has become strangely reversed, however, to Achilles-Herminus, and it should also be noted that the office of eutheniarch has been changed to that of cosmete. It does not seem likely, in spite of these differences, that two different individuals are intended. One or the other office may have been written in error. It is also possible that Herminus held both offices simultaneously (cf. Oertel, Liturgie, 343). Or perhaps we should read εὐθηνιαρχ(ήσαντος). For another Ἑρμεῖνος ὁ καὶ Ἀχιλλεύς from Hermopolis see SB. 4298. 9-10 (204 A.D.). An Aurelius Achilles (from Hermopolis?) also appears in P. Lips. 57. 40 (261 A.D.)

Other instances of the participation of a κύριος in drawing up a woman's will are cited by Wenger, Stellvertretung, 179. In one case (P. Oxy. 104. 6) the testatrix is assisted, as here, by her husband. Much uncertainty prevails regarding the status of the κύριος. In legal transactions of a seemingly identical nature women are at times assisted by a κύριος and at times not. After a painstaking investigation of the papyrological evidence Wenger reached an essentially negative conclusion in this regard (op. cit., 174).

4. κλη]ρονόμος μοι ἔστω. There should be space for about five letters in the lacuna, as in the preceding lines, yet it seems impossible to suggest a letter or letters which might have preceded κληρονόμος. The tail stroke of ρ from the line above may have occupied the space of one letter. The article would be irregular in this construction. For its omission see Stud. Pal. I, p. 6, line 10. The latter text also has μου rather than μοι (cf. P. S. I. 696. 4), but our text shows that either word can be read in doubtful cases (cf. P. Oxy. 907. 4). οἱ δὲ υἱοί ⟨οἱ⟩ ἐμοὶ ἀποκληρόνομοι ἔστωσαν. This reading, if correct, corresponds to the Latin: Filius meus exheres esto (Gaius II. 127). The reading of each of the doubtful letters is strongly supported by the traces of these letters which remain. It is impossible to read οἱ δὲ λοιποὶ πάντες, as in B. G. U. 326. 7 and P. Oxy. 907. 4-5. It is surprising in the light of Just. Inst. II. 13. 1 (... 'filius meus exheres esto' non adiecto proprio nomine, scilicet si alius filius non extet) to find that filii are here not disinherited nominatim. And yet is must be remembered that in the case of a will made by a mother the exheredatio liberorum was not mandatory (Just. Inst. II. 13. 7). There existed in this instance neither the necessity of disinheriting the sons specifically nor of disinheriting them nominatim. The sons might have been disinherited inter ceteros (Gaius

II. 128) without voiding the will. No other instance of the *exheredatio* of specific persons is found in the papyri (cf. Kreller, *op. cit.*, 382). Following υἱοί a short stroke can be seen which may serve to indicate the unconscious omission of οἱ. It is not surprising that the writer accidentally omitted the article in view of the syllable which precedes. Can the loss of μοι before ἔστωσαν be accounted for in the same manner? In P. Oxy. 907. 5 we find ἀποκληρόνομοί μου ἔστωσαν, but elsewhere it is doubtful whether μου or μοι should be read (cf. B. G. U. 326. 7) and Stud. Pal. I, p. 7, line 24). Grenfell-Hunt would read μου in such cases (cf. note *ad loc.*). Yet, as explained above, either reading is admissable. We should thus perhaps read ἀποκληρόνομοι ⟨μοι⟩ ἔστωσαν.

5. προσερχέσθω ... ἐν ἡμέραις ρ̄ ταῖς ἐπισήμοις μου. A *cretio* with this provision does not occur elsewhere in the papyri. It corresponds closely to the Latin *cretio vulgaris: Titius heres esto cernitoque in diebus centum proximis quibus scieris poterisque* (Ulp. *Reg.* 22. 27). One hundred days seems to have been the usual period allowed for making the *aditio* (cf. Gaius II. 170). For the honors accorded the dead during the ἐπίσημοι ἡμέραι see P. Lips. 30, introd. ὅταν γνῷ καὶ δύνηται μαρτύρασθαι. The corresponding passage in B. G. U. 326. 8-9 can now be amended to read ὁπόταν [γνῷ καὶ δύνηται μα]ρ[τύ]ρασθαι. The lacuna in P. Oxy. 907. 5 should be restored in the same manner, considerations of space suggesting the substitution of ὅταν for ὁπόταν. A similar restoration is required in P. S. I. 696. 5-6. Our text thus confirms the reading μαρτύρασθαι first proposed by Kreller, *op. cit.*, 123. For the *testatio* cf. M. Chrest. 327. 5-10 (discussed by Kreller, *op. cit.*, 121-123).

6. μαχί{ι}μων συντάξεων. Doubtless to be construed with what follows as a partitive genitive. There is considerable evidence for γῆ μαχίμων in the Ptolemaic period, but in the Roman period references to such land are less numerous. Cf. P. Ryl. 202. 5 and see note *ad loc.* Our text proves the continued existence of such land in the Hermopolite nome in the third century A.D.

10. δοθῆ[ναι. The infinitive probably depends upon βούλομαι, which may have followed in the lacuna.

39. LEASE OF A MELON GARDEN

Garrett Dep. 7623a.   10 × 6.5 cm.   Provenance unknown.   3rd cent. A.D.   Plate VII.

The accompanying text shares with P. Hamb. 99 the distinction of being one of two extant leases of melon patches. Although but a fragment of the original document remains, it furnishes the interesting terms on the basis of which the lease was drawn. In addition to a cash rental fee amounting to three hundred drachmas, the lessee contracts to deliver daily to the lessor ten cucumbers, four melons, and four gourds during the months of Payni and Epiph, the delivery of the produce to commence with the harvesting of the crop. In the Hamburg papyrus only the payment of a cash rental is stipulated. The term of our lease is a single year (line 10).

The opening lines (1-3) appear to be wholly unlike the corresponding sections of other leases of garden land (cf. B. G. U. 1118-1120, P. Ross. Georg. II, 19, and P. Oxy. 1631). One would expect to find a reference to the location of the garden, but no satisfactory solution is apparent.

References to the culture of gourds are furnished by Schnebel, *Landwirtschaft*, I, 202-203.

```
           ] ατια[ . 'Αρ]τέμιδο[ς
ε[. . . . . . . . . .] καὶ Ἱέρωνος ἃ κατα-
α[. . . . . . . . . . ε]ἰς κατάθησιν
σικυρ[άτ]ων καὶ κο⟨λο⟩κύνθων, φόρου
5 ἀποτάκτου ἀργυρίου δραχ⟨μ⟩ῶν τρι-
ακοσίων καὶ ἡμερησίως ἀφ' ἧς
ἡμέρας ἐντρυκήσωμεν σικύρια
δέκα, κολόκοινθοι δ̄, πέπονες δ̄, τὸν
δὲ φόρον ἀποδώσω ἐν τῷ Παῦνι
10 κ]αὶ Ἐπε[ὶ]φ μησὶν τοῦ αὐτοῦ (ἔτους)
ἀ]νυπερ[θέτω]ς, τῶν τῆς γῆς δη-
μοσ]ί[ω]ν [ὄντων] πρὸς Ὠρίωνα
                 ] . . [
```

7. Read ἐντρυγήσομεν.

1. Alternatively one might read αγια or ωτια. The word cannot serve as antecedent for ἅ in the following line, for an additional letter must be supplied in the lacuna, probably σ or ν. The context is against referring Ἀρτέμιδος to the goddess.
2. The ε may be the initial letter of the name of the father, e. g. Ἑ[ρμοδώρου τοῦ], though the omission of τῆς would be irregular following the genitive.
3. The initial letter is almost certainly α. It is impossible to read either θ or σ.
4. σικυράτων καὶ κολοκύνθων. For the variety of spellings found in these words cf. Mayser, *Grammatik*, I, 101, 178, 188.
7. ἐντρυγήσομεν. The verb is rare and found only here in the papyri. Its application here to the harvesting of garden produce extends the significance of the word.

40. EMBANKMENT CERTIFICATE

AM 8911.   13 × 4.5 cm.   Theadelphia.   49 A.D.   Plate I.

The following certificate is an early specimen of a well-known type recording the completion of the five days of labor on the embankments (πενθήμερος) required annually of all who did not enjoy privileges of exemption from this service.

A large number of such certificates emanating from the Fayum have been assembled and tabulated by Oertel (*Liturgie*, 64 ff.), the earliest of which are dated in the year 49 A.D. Two certificates issued slightly later (51 and 63/64 A.D.) show striking differences in form, these changes representing a development toward the form which became practically stereotyped early in the following century. Oertel concludes that the middle of the first century marks not only the point of time at which this form of certification had its inception, but marks also the period in which the annual five-day embankment service itself was first introduced.

Our certificate, dated in the year 49, is thus of especial interest, inasmuch as it is one of the earliest specimens of its type. Most striking is its relation to the three other texts issued in the same year (P. Lond. 165, a-c). Not only are these certificates almost identical in form and size, but they are all signed by the same Dionysius, who doubtless served in the capacity of κατασπορεύς (cf. Wilcken, *Grundzüge*, 335, and Oertel, *op. cit.*, 188). It is further not unlikely that of the first and second hands in the present text either one or both may be identical with the corresponding hands in the London certificates.

In two important features our certificate will be found to differ from its companions. The place of service is described in the London texts as ἐν κληρουχίᾳ, but here it is stated as being ἐν τ(ῇ) Πλωτ( ). This expression, which is without exact parallel among the certificates of this class, is not unlike the enigmatical ἐν Συριω πλω( ) found in P. S. I. 51. 2 (63/64 A.D.). Cf., however, P. S. I. 1044, introd., where the reading is revised to ὑπ(ὲρ) Ἰσαρίω(νος) Πλω( ). The possible connection between these two expressions is strengthened by the fact that both texts refer to the service of citizens of the same village, Theadelphia. In the latter respect our certificate again differs from the three London texts, for the latter were issued to laborers from Socnopaei Nesus.

When studied in conjunction with P. Lond. 165, a-c, our text would thus seem conclusively to confirm the possibility suggested by Oertel (*op. cit.*, 189), that the κατασπορεύς may have had jurisdiction over more than one village. The texts cited by Oertel in this connection (B. G. U. 875 and P. Cairo Preis. 26) are separated by an interval of two years, whereas in the present instance the same official is shown to supervise the work of citizens of two different villages at two different places in the course of the same year.

Regarding the relation of the three hands found in these certificates Wilcken (*Archiv*, I, 146) has remarked that a plentiful supply of such certification forms was prepared in advance (cf. P. Goth. 1, introd.). After the completion of the embankment work it was thus in each case only necessary for a second hand to fill in the name of the laborer in question. The certificates were then signed by the κατασπορεύς who had supervised the work. In the present text the year and month were written by the first hand, a space having been left vacant in which the day was subsequently supplied by a second hand.

The nature and administration of the πενθήμερος are discussed by Wilcken, *Grundzüge*, 334 ff., and Oertel, *op. cit.*, 64 ff. See also P. Bour. 39, introd.

   ("Ετους) ἐνάτου Τιβερίου Κλαυδίου Καίσαρος Σεβαστοῦ Γερμανικοῦ
   Αὐτοκράτορος, ἐν μη(νὶ) Ἐπὶφ κ̄β̄, ἐν τ(ῇ) Πλωτ( ) ἠργ(άσατο) τὴν
          πενθ(ήμερον)

(Hand 2) Ἁθρῆς Ἁρθωνίου δεκανὸς ἀπὸ Θεαδε(λφίας).
(Hand 3) Διονύσιος σεση(μείωμαι).

 2. The final letter of Ἐπίφ was rewritten by the second hand, which also supplied the following numeral ($\overline{κβ}$).
 4. The signature is written in large semi-uncials (see Plate I).

41. Receipt for the Trades' Tax

AM 8916.   13.5 × 28 cm.   Philadelphia.   50 A.D.

A receipt recording the payment of 60 drachmas, 2 obols, 2 chalci in partial satisfaction of the trades' tax (χειρωνάξιον) assessed for the year 49/50 A. D. An additional payment of 3 drachmas, 3 obols is also recorded, evidently representing a subsequent installment of the same tax (see note to line 6). As is usual in the case of the χειρωνάξιον, the trade for which the tax was paid is not specified.

The receipt has been cancelled, the last three lines having been crossed out.

   Ἔτους δεκάτου Τιβερίου Κλαυδίου
   Καίσαρος Σεβαστοῦ Γερμανικοῦ Αὐτ[οκ]ρά[τ(ορος),
   Φαρμοῦθι. παρὰ Ἰσιδώρου ⟨τοῦ⟩ καὶ Μάρωνος τοῦ
   Μάρωνος ν(εωτέρου) χειρω(ναξίου) συντάξε(ως) τοῦ αὐτοῦ
 5 δεκάτου (ἔτους) Φιλαδελ(φίας) ἀργυρ(ίου) δρ(αχμὰς) ἑξήκοντα
   =χ^β, ∕ (δραχμαὶ) ξ=χ^β, ὁμ(οίως) (δραχμὰς) τρεῖς Γ, ∕ (δραχμαὶ) γΓ.

 3. Ἰσιδώρου ⟨τοῦ⟩ καὶ Μάρωνος. It is less difficult to suppose that the article has been inadvertently omitted and that the payments were made by a single individual, than to accept the reading of the text and understand joint payments by two individuals. Where payments by two or more persons were acknowledged by means of a single receipt, it was customary to record each payment separately (cf. W. O. 672). The otherwise inconsistent use of the patronymic supports the same conclusion, for it is omitted in the one instance, included in the other.
 4. χειρω(ναξίου). The provenance of the receipt might suggest payment by a weaver. The weaving trade is known to have flourished in Philadelphia, a tax register from the first century (P. Cornell 23. 38) recording no less than eighty-eight weavers residing in that village. Nothing can be deter-

mined from the amounts paid, and it is not certain that the two payments recorded here, totalling 63 dr., 5 ob., 2 ch. (= 64 dr. ?), represent payment in full. In Philadelphia the customary rate was 76 dr., but lower rates are also attested, including one of 64 dr. (B. G. U. 1616. 3). συντάξε(ως). This evidently refers to the total amount of the assessment for the year. Only partial payments are recorded in each instance. Cf. O. Meyer 8. 3, 9. 2-3 (ἀπὸ τῆς συντάξεως).

6. ὁμ(οίως). The reading of this word is uncertain, both letters being partially obliterated. The entry which follows represents almost certainly an additional payment of the χειρωνάξιον. If, on the other hand, the supplementary tax (προσδιαγραφόμενα) of 6¼% is intended, this has been miscalculated, an additional obol and 3 chalci being necessary to complete the required sum. Such supplements, moreover, are rarely found in receipts of this class (cf. Johnson, *Roman Egypt*, 537). It is even less likely that some other tax has been thus recorded.

42. Grain Accounts

AM 8923.   18 × 10.5 cm.   Oxyrhynchus.   93 A.D.   Plates V and VI.

The purpose of the following accounts is uncertain. That they are in some way related to the payment of land rentals may be inferred from the entries in lines 4 a-b and 5 a. It is evident that the accounts on recto and verso are, at least in part, directly related (see notes to lines 13-15, 18, 22), but the details are obscure. The lands for which payments are recorded were situated in various Oxyrhynchite villages. The payments on the recto were made by two women.

On the verso there is a duplication of entries in Cols. II and III, the debit entries in the one column appearing as credit entries in the other, and vice versa. Those in Col. II are arranged according to villages, those in Col. III according to the persons making the payments. Within the separate columns each entry is balanced by a corresponding debit or credit entry. A similar accounting device is found in P. Goodsp. 30 (see pp. 31 f.). It would be a mistake, however, to conclude that the ancients were familiar with the principles of modern double-entry bookkeeping. Cf. Grier, *Accounting in the Zenon Papyri*, 7 f.

The totals in Cols. II and III are exactly equal (115 art., 9 choin.), when allowance is made for the difference of 2½ art. noted in the margin of line 27, a difference occasioned by the fact that the scribe failed to post in Col. III the remainder of the entry found in line 26.

$\iota\beta$(ἔτους) Δομιτιανοῦ   92/93 A.D.
  Διονυσία Πετοσί(ριος ?)   Ἀθῦχ(ις) ∓— ιςχ$^\beta$[
  ἡ α(ὐτή), Παῦνι ς   —ϵχ$^\gamma$//[
4 ἡ α(ὐτὴ) Προταρ( ) Κλαυδίῳ Ἡρακλεί(δου), Παῦνι ς   —ιβ∟[χ^ς
a   ἀρου(ρῶν) ι, — ιαd, βασιλ(ικῆς)

b   dη, -:- adχ⁵, / -:- ιβLχ⁵
5   ἡ α(ὐτὴ) Ἐντεῖις Προτ(αρ ?) Ἡρακ(λείδη) Διονυ(σίου)
                    καὶ τῇ ἀδελ(φῇ)   -:- μδ[
a   ἑκατοστ(ῆς) Lχ⁵, ὀνηλ(ασίου) ϛ/χ⁵
6   ἡ α(ὐτὴ) Θμοι(νεψῶβθις ?), Θὼθ ις   -:- δLχ[⁵ ?
     Θοῶνις Ἁρπαήσι(ος) Ἀθῦχ(ις)   -:- sLχ[
            / 7 -:- πθdχᵃ
9 (Hand 2) π . . ε ιδ (ἔτους) ρκεή καὶ ἡ . d, / ρκεdή—   94/95 A.D.

VERSO
COL. I

10 (Hand 3)]χᵝ   14   ἀρο]υ(ρῶν) ι
            ]ζLd   βα]σιλικῆ(ς)
            ]χᵝ   ]αντι
13   ]καή)   17   ]s

COL. II

(Hand 2) Ἀθῦχ(ις) καὶ Πω( )   λγϛ/χᵝ
   // L Φίλω(ν) κδ, Θήδ(εσις ?) χᵟ, Κεφάλω(ν) θLχᵑ, ἴσ(ον)
20 Ἐντεῖι(ς)   οαχᵃ
   // L Διον(ύσιος) Ἀδμή(του) ν, Θήδ(εσις ?) Ἰακό(βου) καχᵃ, ἴσ(ον)
   Θμοι(νεψῶβθις ?)   δLχ⁵
   // Κεφάλω(ν) δLχ⁵
        / ρθdχᶿ
25 Ἀθῦχ(ις)
       Θῶνις Ἁρπ(αήσιος) sL
   λο(ιπαὶ) βd, Κεφάλω(ν) δd
        / ριεϛ/χᶿ

COL. III

        λόγος (πυροῦ)
30 // Διον(ύσιος) Ἀδμή(του)   ν
     L δι' Ἐντείε(ως)   ν
   // Θήδε(σις ?) Ἰακό(βου)   καή
     L Ἐντῑ(ις) καχᵃ, Ἀθῦχ(ις) χᵟ
   // Φίλων   κδ
35   Ἀθῦχ(ις) κδ
   // Κεφάλω(ν)   ιηLχᵟ
     Ἀθῦχ(ις) θLχᵑ, Θμοι(νεψῶβθις ?) δLχ⁵
        / ριγLχᶿ
39   Ἀθῦχ(ις) Θοῶ(νις) δd,   ἴσ(ον).

2. Ἀθῦχ(ις). Ἀθῦχις and Ἐντεῖις (cf. lines 5, 20) were villages situated in the
   Upper toparchy. Cf. P. Oxy. 1659. 14, 15 (note).

42. GRAIN ACCOUNTS

4. Προταρ( ). The name of a village is suggested on the analogy of the entries in lines 5 and 6. No village of this name is known, however. It does not appear possible to read πρότερ(ον) Κλαυδί(ου) κ. τ. λ., which might designate a payment on land formerly belonging to Claudius and now owned by Dionysia. Cf. 14. I. 8-9 (note). The letter preceding ρ is almost certainly α.

4 a–b. Posted in the margin opposite line 4 (see Plate V). The total found in line 4 evidently comprises these two items. The symbol for ¼ is of unusual form. Cf. line 11 (see Plate VI).

5. Ἐντεῖις Προτ( ). Payments for two villages are probably combined in the total given in this line. The omission of καί is surprising. Cf. line 18. See also note to line 4.

5 a. Posted in the margin opposite line 5. The ἑκατοστή is here figured at the rate of 1½%, the ὀνηλάσιον at the rate of 2%, both being calculated on the basis of the sum recorded in line 5. An artaba of 40 choin. is clearly indicated by the entries in lines 32-33, 36-39. For the ἑκατοστή computed at the rate of 1½% see P. Iand. 138, introd., and Johnson, *Roman Egypt*, 509. The ὀνηλάσιον (cf. P. Bour. 42. 9, 169) is evidently a local variant of the φόρετρον. Cf. Johnson, *op. cit.*, 511.

6. Θμοι(νεψῶβθις?). A village situated in the Eastern toparchy. Cf. P. Oxy. 1659. 55 (note).

9. ρκεή. This total (for the fourteenth year) may have been inserted here for the sake of comparison. Written by the same hand as Cols. II and III on the verso, this line might suggest a date in 94/95 A.D. for the latter, a possibility definitely precluded, however, by the close relationship in which the two accounts can be shown to stand. See note to line 18. The total given here does not agree with the total found on the verso (line 28), and has no apparent connection with that account. The fraction (⅛) has been written as in line 32 (see Plate VI).

13-15. These lines establish a definite connection between the accounts on the recto and verso (Col. I). The total in line 13 exactly corresponds to the sum of the entries in lines 2-3 (for the 40 choin. artaba see note to line 5 a). An entry of 21⅛ art. is found also in line 32 (Col. III). Lines 14 and 15 find their counterpart in line 4 a. The bracket at the end of line 13 may indicate a cancellation. Cf. 9. I. 1 (note).

18. The total in this line exactly corresponds to the sum of the three entries recorded on the recto, lines 2-4, definitely establishing a direct connection between the accounts on recto and verso (Cols. II and III). One would accordingly expect Ἀθυχ( ) καὶ Προ( ) in place of Ἀθυχ( ) καὶ Πω( ), but this reading seems impossible to establish. A similar correspondence between entries on recto and verso is seen in lines 6 and 22. And yet no such relation obtains between the entries in lines 5 and 20, and lines 7 and 26. The correspondence in the latter instance, though close, is not exact. Names and entries occur in each of these accounts which have no apparent counterpart in the other. The exact relation of the two accounts is thus uncertain. The totals, moreover, are quite disparate. For the relation of Col. I to the recto see note to lines 13-15. Col. I, it should be noted, was written by a different hand from that appearing in Cols. II and III.

19. ἴσ(ον). A term used by the scribe to indicate that the sum of the entries in this line exactly balances the corresponding entry in the preceding line.

Cf. lines 21, 39. No precisely similar use of the word is recorded elsewhere. Cf., however, P. Teb. 82. 6, note.

22. A corresponding entry seems to be found in line 6. See note to line 18.
29. λόγος (πυροῦ). Probably intended to serve as a heading to the entire account rather than to a separate column.
32. καή. Cf. line 13.
39. It is strange that this entry, though included in the total, should have been posted in the succeeding line. Evidently the total had been previously determined. The exact sum required to complete this total was then posted from line 27, leaving an unaccountable remainder of 2½ art. in the account in Col. II.

43. Receipts for Poll-Tax (λαογραφία)

Garrett Dep. 7615.   34 × 9.5 cm.   Arsinoë.   141 A.D.

In the following receipts acknowledgment is made to three half-brothers of the payment of twenty drachmas received from each of them on account of the λαογραφία for the year 140/141. As citizens of Arsinoë residing in the Syrian quarter they were relieved from the heavier burden imposed upon those who were not citizens of the metropolis, the latter being required to contribute double this amount (cf. Wilcken, *Grundzüge*, 189, and C. W. Keyes, *A. J. P.*, LII [1931], 263). In both cases small supplementary fees were collected. Payments at the rate of twenty drachmas were accompanied regularly, as here, by προσδιαγραφόμενα amounting to ten obols (cf. Keyes, *op. cit.*, 263).

The three receipts were written in parallel columns. A list of similar receipts is presented by Keyes, *op. cit.*, 263, note 2.

```
  Ἔτους δ Αὐτοκρά(τορος) Καίσ(αρος) Τίτου Αἰλίου
  Ἀδριανοῦ Ἀντωνίνου Σεβ(αστοῦ) Εὐσεβοῦς,
  Παχ(ὼν) ι̅ς̅, ἀριθ(μήσεως) Φαρμοῦ(θι), δι(ἔγραψε) Χαιρή(μων) Χαιρή(μονος)
                                           τοῦ Χαιρήμον(ος)
  μη(τρὸς) Διοδώρ(ας) λαογ(ραφίας) τετάρτου (ἔτους) Συρι(ακῆς)
5 (δραχμὰς) εἴκοσι, (γίνονται) κ, προσ(διαγραφομένων) χ(αλκοῦ) ὀ(βολοὺς)
                                           δέκα.

  Ἔτους δ Αὐτοκρά(τορος) Καίσ(αρος) Τίτου Αἰλίου
  Ἀδριανοῦ Ἀντωνίνου Σεβ(αστοῦ) Εὐσεβοῦς,
  Παχ(ὼν) ι̅ς̅, ἀριθ(μήσεως) Φαρμοῦ(θι), δι(ἔγραψε) Ἡρακ(λῆς ?) Χαιρή(μονος)
  τοῦ Χαιρή(μονος) μη(τρὸς) Ἀπία(ς) λαογ(ραφίας) τετάρτου (ἔτους)
10 Συρι(ακῆς) (δραχμὰς) εἴκοσι, (γίνονται) κ, προσ(διαγραφομένων) χ(αλκοῦ)
                                           [ὀ(βολοὺς) δέ]κα.

  Ἔτους δ Αὐτοκρά(τορος) Καίσ(αρος) Τίτου Αἰλίου
  Ἀδριανοῦ Ἀντωνίνου Σεβ(αστοῦ) Εὐσεβοῦς,
```

43. RECEIPTS FOR POLL-TAX (λαογραφία)   45

Πα[χ(ὼν) ι̅ς̅, ἀρι]θ(μήσεως) Φαρμοῦ(θι), δι(έγραψε) Διόδωρ(ος) Χαιρή-
(μονος)
τοῦ [Χαιρή(μονος) μη(τρὸς) Ἀπί]α(ς) λαογ(ραφίας) τ[ε]τ[άρτ]ου (ἔτους)
15 Σ[υρι(ακῆς) (δραχμὰς) εἴκοσι], (γίνονται) κ, προσ(διαγραφομένων) χ(αλκοῦ)
ὀ(βολοὺς) δέκα.

44. Receipt for Poll-Tax (συντάξιμον)

Garrett Dep. 7649.   11.5 × 7.5 cm.   Fayum.   141 A.D.

Receipt for 12 drachmas, 1½ obols, 2 chalci received in partial payment of the poll-tax (συντάξιμον) for the year 141/142, together with smaller sums paid on account of sundry other taxes. In the Arsinoïte nome payments of both λαογραφία and συντάξιμον were commonly accompanied by payments of these smaller taxes (cf. Keyes, *A. J. P.*, LII [1931], 266-267), the rates of which, with the exception of the pig-tax, varied from year to year (cf. P. Col. II, pp. 29-30). The poll-tax and pig-tax, on the other hand, were of fixed amount. The συντάξιμον is now identified with the λαογραφία, when the latter is paid at the rate of 40 + drachmas (cf. Keyes, *op. cit.*, 269, and P. Col. II, p. 39).

The grouping of the μερισμοί in pairs is unusual (see line 5). It should be noted that the amount paid (2½ obols) for the combination of δεσμοφυλακία and ποταμοφυλακία corresponds exactly to the amounts paid separately for these two taxes in 133/134 (P. Col. II, p. 14, line 3. See also p. 29 of the same work for additional references). The same correspondence does not obtain, however, in the case of the other pair. Assuming that the μαγδωλοφυλακία was paid at the rate of 3 obols, as in the Columbia accounts, the amount paid for φυλακία was 1 drachma, 2 chalci, a rate not found elsewhere for this tax. The pig-tax is paid at the rate of 1 drachma, 1 obol, a rate commonly found in the Fayum (cf. P. Princ. I, p. xix, and P. Col. II, p. 29).

A list of συντάξιμον receipts is furnished by Keyes, *op. cit.*, 264-265.

Ἔ[τ]ους πέμπτου Αὐτοκράτορος Καίσαρος Τίτου Αἰλίου
Ἁ]δριανοῦ Ἀντωνίνου Σεβαστοῦ Εὐσεβοῦς, μηνὸς
Χοιὰ]κ ς̅, διέγρ(αψεν) διὰ Διδ[ύ]μου καὶ μετόχ(ων) πρακ(τόρων) Ἥρων
Φάσειτ[ος
      ] ονος μητ(ρὸς) Θα[.....] συνταξί(μου) τοῦ αὐτοῦ ἔτους ἀργυρ(ίου)
5 (δρ.) δώ]δεκα (ὀβολ. ?) (ἡμιώβ.) (δίχαλκ.), (γιν.) [(δρ.)] ιβ (ὀβολ. ?)
(ἡμιώβ.) [(δίχαλκ.)], ὑϊ(κῆς) ⟨(δρ.)⟩ α (ὀβολ.), μα[γ(δωλο-
φυλακίας)] καὶ φυλ(ακίας) (δρ.) α (τριώβ.) (δίχαλκ.), δεσ(μοφυλακίας)
καὶ ποτ(αμοφυλακίας) (διώβ.) (ἡμιώβ.).

45. Receipt for Poll–Tax (λαογραφία)

Garrett Dep. 7648. 9 × 7 cm. Arsinoë. 174 A.D.

A receipt for 20 drachmas, 10 obols received as poll-tax (λαογραφία) from a resident of the Macedonian quarter of Arsinoë. Compare **43**.

Ἔτους ιδ̄ Αὐρηλίου Ἀντωνίνου Καίσαρος
τοῦ κυρίου Ἀρμενιακοῦ Μηδικοῦ
Παρθικοῦ μεγίστου, Μεσο(ρὴ) ιβ̄,
ἀριθ(μήσεως) Ἐπείφ, δι(έγραψε) Πωλίων
5 Ἥρων(ος) τ(οῦ) Παθερμουθ(ίου) μη(τρὸς) Ταεῦ(τος) ὑπ(ὲρ)
λαο(γραφίας) τεσσαρεσκαιδεκ(άτου) (ἔτους) Μακ(εδόνων)
(δραχμὰς) εἴκ(οσι), (γίνονται) ⟨(δραχμαὶ)⟩ κ′, προσ(διαγραφομένων)
χ(αλκοῦ) ὀβο(λοὺς) δέκα.

46. Account Recording Payments of Dike–Tax

Garrett Dep. 7678. 11 × 12 cm. Oxyrhynchus. 2nd cent. A.D.

An account recording the payment of the dike-tax (χωματικόν) by fifteen persons residing in various quarters in Oxyrhynchus. Payments of this tax were normally made at the rate of 6 drachmas, 4 obols at this period (see note to P. Ryl. 194. 3). The most recent discussion of the χωματικόν is presented by Mlle. Préaux, O. Wilbour, pp. 43-44. Cf. Johnson, *Roman Egypt*, 580.

The year for which the payments were made is not recorded, unless it is to be found in the enigmatic sixteenth line (see note *ad loc.*). For a similar account of money payments by various individuals see P. Oxy. 392.

χω(ματικοῦ) Ἱπποδ(ρόμου) Πετεσ(οῦχος) Παπο(ντῶτος) ϛϝ
χω(ματικοῦ) Ἱπποδ(ρόμου) Παποντ(ῶς) Ἁρπαή(σιος) ϛϝ
χω(ματικοῦ) Ἱπποδ(ρόμου) Ἁρπαῆσι(ς) Ἀρσιή(σιος) ϛϝ
χω(ματικοῦ) Δρό(μου) Γ(υμνασίου) Γλαυκίας Πτολ(εμαίου) μη(τρὸς)
5   Κλεοπά⟨τ⟩ρα(ς) καὶ Σαραπ(ίων ?) ἀδε(λφὸς) ιγ
χω(ματικοῦ) Κρη(τικοῦ) Ἀκῶρ(ις) Σατύρο(υ) μη(τρὸς) Ἀρσεῖτ(ος) ϛϝ
χω(ματικοῦ) Κρη(τικοῦ) Σαραπ(ίων ?) Ὥρο(υ) μη(τρὸς) Σινθ(οώνιος) ϛϝ
χω(ματικοῦ) Ἄνω Παρ(εμβολῆς) Διόσκ(ορος) Διοσκ(όρου) μη(τρὸς) Τανεν-
    (τήριος) ϛϝ
χω(ματικοῦ) Κρη(τικοῦ) Ἀπόλ(λων) Κόμω(νος) μη(τρὸς) Ταποτάμω(νος) ϛϝ
10 χω(ματικοῦ) Θο(ήριδος) Κλεόπα{ρ}τρ(ος) Διδύμου ϛϝ
χω(ματικοῦ) Πλ(ατείας) Διονύ(σιος) Ἐπιτυγχ(άνοντος ?) μη(τρὸς) Ε..[..]
    ϛϝ
χω(ματικοῦ) Δρό(μου) Γ(υμνασίου) Ἀσκλ(ᾶς) Ὡρίω(νος) μη(τρὸς) Ἡ-
    ρᾶτ(ος) ϛϝ

46. ACCOUNT RECORDING PAYMENTS OF DIKE-TAX

χω(ματικοῦ) Ποι(μενικῆς) Σύρος Διοδ(ώρου) μη(τρὸς) Διονυ(σίας)   ϛϝ
χω(ματικοῦ) Ἰβιοτ(αφείου) Ἡρᾶς Τρύφωνος   ϛϝ
15 χω(ματικοῦ) Δρό(μου) Θοή(ριδος) Κέρδ(ων) Ἀπόλλ(ωνος ?) Ἀρθώσι(ος) ϛϝ
    σα . . . ιε.

8. Τανεν(τήριος). Perhaps the same woman who appears in P. Oxy. 91. 3 (187 A.D.).
10. χω(ματικοῦ) Θο(ήριδος). Perhaps Θο[ή(ριδος)] should be read. Both words appear to have been written as an afterthought, for they are found in the margin at the left of the text. χω( ) was written opposite line 9, and Θο( ) just beneath it in the following line. For the almost certain identification of the ἄμφοδον Θοήριδος with the ἄμφοδον Δρόμου Θοήριδος see Rink, *Strassen- und Viertelnamen von Oxyrhynchus*, 33.
11. Ἐπιτυγχ(άνοντος). Or Ἐπιτυγχ(άνου). Both names are listed by Pape, *Griechische Eigennamen*, s. nn.
14. Ἰβιοτ(αφείου). No quarter of this name is otherwise known, but that it may be identified with the ἄμφοδον Ἑρμαίου is suggested by P. Teb. 88. 53, where the burying-place of the sacred ibises is called a Hermeum.
16. The few letters in this line are more than usually cursive. A total would appear to be indicated by ιε, which may refer to the number of persons (fifteen) from whom payments were received. A figure indicating the total sum (100 drachmas) received from these persons can hardly be identified, however, in the letters which precede. A date may perhaps be concealed in this line. The third letter strongly resembles the customary abbreviation for ἔτους (L). There may thus be a reference to a total for the first(?) year.

47. RECEIPT FOR POLL-TAX (λαογραφία)

AM 8932 (verso).   16.5 × 16 cm.   Philadelphia.   2nd cent. A.D.

A receipt for 44 drachmas paid in several installments in settlement of the poll-tax (λαογραφία). Although the reading of the name of the tax is uncertain, the purpose of the payments seems clearly indicated by the sums involved. As in P. Mil. 11, no mention is made of the small extra fees (2 chalci and a half-obol) usually paid in connection with the poll-tax. Cf. Keyes, *A. J. P.*, LII [1931], 267 f.

The receipt has been written on the verso of a letter (69).

Ἔτους εʹ, [. . .] , [δ]ιέγρα(ψεν) Ἀιῶνι
Ον[. . .]ιου( ) ὁ [κ]αὶ Ἄριος ὑπ(ὲρ)
μ . [. . . .]κ[.]α ( ) εἰ(ς) λαογρ(αφίαν) τοῦ
αὐ(τοῦ) ε (ἔτους) κώ(μης) [Φ]ιλαδε(λφίας) δραχ(μὰς)
5 τέ[σσα]ρ[ας, / ϛ] δ, Χοιὰκ ϛ δ,
  Τῦ[β]ι ϛ η, Φ[α]ρμοῦθι ϛ η,
  Παχὼν ϛ δ, Παῦν[ι] ϛ η,
  ὁμο[ίω]ς Με[σο]ρὴ ϛ η.

1. αἰῶνι.
3 εἰ(ς) λαογρ(αφίαν). Cf. P. Mil. 9. 4, note.

48. Receipt for τέλος μόσχου θυομένου

Garrett Dep. 7630.   10 × 12 cm.   Fayum.   206 A.D.

Owing to its imperfect state of preservation, the present text adds little to our knowledge of the tax imposed upon calves offered for sacrifice. Cf. B. G. U. 356, 383, 463, P. Lond. 472, P. Fay. 244, and P. Teb. 307. Much has been lost, including the name of the village in which the sacrifice was offered. As in P. Teb. 307. 9, the amount of the tax appears to have been 20 drachmas, although it should be noted that in the latter text the tax is described as δεκάτη μόσχων, rather than as τέλος μόσχου θυομένου, as here. S. L. Wallace, *Taxes in Roman Egypt*, s. v., argues, however, for the probable identity of the two taxes. Our text would tend to support this conclusion, although the reading of the crucial passage (lines 4-6) is largely conjectural and to be accepted as evidence with caution. For an exhaustive discussion of this tax the reader is referred to Mr. Wallace's forthcoming work (*op. cit.*, s. v.).

It is of interest to note that in the present instance the tax was collected a day in advance of the sacrifice. A small seal which originally accompanied the receipt has been lost, leaving a hole near the bottom of the papyrus.

Ἔτου]ς ιδ/ Λουκίου Σεπτιμίου Σεουήρου Εὐσεβοῦς
Περτίνα]κος καὶ Μάρκου Αὐρηλίου Ἀντωνίν[ου
Εὐσεβοῦς Σεβ]αστῶν καὶ Πουβλίου Σ[ε]πτιμίου
Γέτα Καίσαρος Σ]εβαστοῦ, Παχὼν δ/. [διεγρ(άφησαν)] (δραχμαὶ ?)
                                              εἴκοσι
5   Αὐρηλ(ίῳ) Ἀπίω]νι νο(μάρχῃ) Ἀρσινοΐ(του) (διὰ ?) Σαραπίωνο[ς]
    ...[..].[.].
    ὑπὲρ τέλους μ]όσχου θυομένου αὔριον ἐν κώ(μῃ)
    .... ὑ]πὸ Ὀνησίμου Ἀμερ[ί]μνου [.] υ( ).

5. Ἀπίω]νι νο(μάρχῃ). Payment of the δεκάτη μόσχων is made to the same individual in P. Teb. 307. 6 (208 A.D.). For the remarkable term of office of Apion, extending over a period of 15-20 years, see Oertel, *Liturgie*, 166-167.

6-7. ἐν κώ(μῃ) [?]. In favor of identifying this village with Σοκνοπαίου Νῆσος is the fact that the tax on sacrificial calves is described as τέλος μόσχου θυομένου only in receipts emanating from that source, a fact pointed out to me by Mr. Wallace. Yet, as my informant has suggested, the evidence is supported by only a very few texts. It may be significant that no other text among the lot purchased by Mr. Garrett in 1924 can be shown, so far as I know, to have come from Socnopaei Nesus.

7. At the end of this line there is probably some reference to Onesimus' place of origin.

49. Tax Receipt

Garrett Dep. 7669.   5.5 × 7.5 cm.   Provenance unknown.   217 (?) A.D.

A receipt recording the payment of 3/16 artaba of barley to three ἀπαιτηταί κριθῆς Συριακῆς, together with a supplementary charge of 1/128 artaba. The nature of the payment is uncertain. Collectors of " Syrian barley " are not otherwise attested.

    Αὐρήλιοι Ἰούλιος καὶ Ἰάσων
    καὶ Ἀντίπατ(ρος) ἀπαιτητ(αὶ) κριθ(ῆς) Συρι-
    ακῆς Δράκοντι καὶ ὡς χρη-
    ματ(ίζει) ἔσχαμεν παρὰ σοῦ ἀπὸ τῶν
5 ἐπ' ὀνόματ(ος) Αὐρηλίου Διοσκόρου
    κ(ρι)θ(ῆς ?) ἡ ι$\overline{\varsigma}$, γ(ίνεται) ἡ ι$\overline{\varsigma}$, χο( ) ρκή.
    (ἔτους) κε Ἀντωνίνου τοῦ κυρίου
    Σεβαστοῦ, Φαρμοῦθι $\overline{\beta}$.
    ιθ (ἔτους ?) [
10 κ (ἔτους ?) [
    [........] σχα
    . . . .

2-3. κριθ(ῆς) Συρι|ακῆς. If the reading is correct, this is the only reference in the papyri to Syrian barley. For Syrian wheat see Thompson, *Archiv*, IX, 207 ff., who argues for the identification of such wheat with the πυρὸς τρίμηνος of the Zenon papyri. κυριακῆς is an alternative reading, though not so well supported by the original. Cf. κυριακὸς οἶνος (P. Oxy. 1578. 7).

6. κ(ρι)θ(ῆς). This reading is very doubtful. The original shows ⌐θ. A sixteenth of an artaba would be an unusual fraction (cf. Wilcken, *Grundzüge*, lxix). χο( ). Cf. P. Teb. 346. 4, note. It does not seem possible to read χο (for διχοινικία). In the numeral at the end of the line there is no stroke over the ρ to mark the fraction. χορ( ) μή is also possible.

50. Receipt for ἀννῶνα στρατιωτῶν

Garrett Dep. 7687b.   9 × 10.5 cm.   Oxyrhynchus.   255 A.D.   Plate VII.

Receipt for one hundred drachmas paid to the ἀπαιτηταί of the Western toparchy on account of the ἀννῶνα στρατιωτῶν. Payment is made by Aurelius Bitharion, a high-priest. Most difficult to explain is the reference to the estate of Ptolemy (line 9), represented by its overseer, Thonius. It would appear that in some manner the responsibility for the collection of this tax devolved upon the estate. The payment is almost certainly an *adaeratio* (cf. W. O. I, pp. 155 f.). Such requisitions became very burdensome in the third century. See Johnson, *Roman Egypt*, 621 f.

Γ (ἔτους) τῶν κυρίων ἡμῶν   255/256 A.D.
Οὐαλεριανοῦ καὶ Γαλλιηνοῦ
Σεβαστῶν, Χοιάκ. διέγρα(ψεν)
ἀπαιτηταῖς λιβὸς τοπαρχ(ίας)
5 ὑπὲρ ἀννώνας στρ(ατιωτῶν) (σπείρας) ᾱ ἱ(ππικῆς)
Αὐρήλιος Βιθαρίων ὁ καὶ
Εὐδαίμων ἀρχιερεὺς
δραχμὰς ἑκατόν, γ(ίνονται) (δραχμαὶ) ρ.
οὐσία Πτολεμαῖς δι' ἐμοῦ
10 Θώνιος βουλ(ευτοῦ) ἐπιτ(ρόπου) ε . . . ι( ).

3. Χοιάκ. For the spelling see P. Strassb. 57. 22 and Mayser, *Grammatik*, I, 110-111. The omission of the day of the month is probably the result of an oversight.
4. ἀπαιτηταῖς. Sc. ἀπαιτηταῖς ἀννώνας. Cf. P. Oxy. 1192. 3-4 (280 A.D.), where, however, these officials appear to have made collections in kind rather than in money, as here. Payments of the annona were usually received by ἐπιμεληταί. Cf. Wilcken, *Grundzüge*, 361-362. λιβὸς τοπαρχίας. This toparchy is frequently mentioned in Oxyrhynchite papyri, a fact which suggests Oxyrhynchus as the provenance of the present text.
7. ἀρχιερεύς. The higher priests enjoyed immunity from the λαογραφία, but not from other taxes. Cf. Otto, *Priester und Tempel*, II, 246-250.
9. οὐσία Πτολεμαῖς. An otherwise unknown estate. For the spelling see Mayser, *op. cit.*, I, 148, 260.

51. CUSTOM-HOUSE RECEIPT

AM 8953.   4 × 5 cm.   Philadelphia.   3rd cent. A.D.

Numerous receipts recording the collection of customs fees on commodities transported from one nome to another have already been published. The custom-houses, as one would expect, seem to have been located in villages situated near the border of their respective districts. Thus, in the case of the Fayum, such offices are known to have been located in Bacchias, Dionysias, Caranis, Philadelphia, and Socnopaei Nesus, villages situated on the northern boundary of the nome, facing the desert.

Three different fees are recorded for the Fayum, the $\bar{ρ}$ καὶ $\bar{ν}$ (ἑκατοστὴ καὶ πεντηκοστή), the ἐρημοφυλακία, and the λιμὴν Μέμφεως, the nature of which has been discussed in considerable detail by Fiesel, *Nach. Ges. d. Wiss. Gött.* (phil.-hist. Kl.), 1925, 57 ff. According to Fiesel the $\bar{ρ}$ καὶ $\bar{ν}$ represents a basic charge of 3% levied in all cases, whereas the ἐρημοφυλακία and the λιμὴν Μέμφεως were surcharges of similar amount, the former being applicable to loads entering or leaving the Fayum via a desert route, the latter to loads brought into or taken out of the Fayum along roads connecting this district with the harbor at Memphis. But for a different interpretation of the evidence see Wallace, *Taxes in Roman Egypt*, s. v., and Johnson, *Roman Egypt*, 591 f. Our receipt records the payment of the λιμὴν Μέμφεως on a small shipment of dates being exported from the Fayum through the custom-house in Philadelphia.

For a more complete discussion of the mode of collection and registration of such payments the reader is referred to Fiesel, *op. cit.*; Wilcken, *Grundzüge*, 190 f., and *Archiv*, XI, 136 f.; Clauson, *Aegyptus*, IX, 240 ff.; and Meyer, *P. Hamb.* 76-78, introd. More recently the available material has been considerably augmented by the publication by Boak (*Soknopaiou Nesos*, 23 ff.) of several receipts recording the payment of taxes of the same type. Cf. Welles, *Am. Jour. Arch.*, XL (1936), 287 f.

A small hole (about one centimeter in diameter) located in the lower margin indicates the loss of the seal which originally accompanied the text. Such seals were frequently affixed to receipts of this character, their omission being occasionally noted by the phrase χωρὶς χαρακτῆρος. Cf. Fiesel, *op. cit.*, 75 and B. G. U. 1595, introd. For the nature and use of seals in the ancient world see Dölger, *Sphragis*; Pieper, *Aegyptus*, XIV (1934), 245-252; and Boak, *op. cit.*, 24 f.

Although the date of the text must remain uncertain by reason of the impossibility of ascertaining the reign to which the fourth year (line 5) should be assigned, the character of the hand suggests a date late rather than early in the third century.

   Τε]τελ(ώνηται) διὰ πύ(λης) Φιλαδελ(φίας) λιμέ-
   νος Μέμφεως Αὐρή(λιος)
   ...... ἰξάγων ἐπὶ ὄνῳ
   ἑ[νί], ᾱ, φοίνικος (ἀρτάβην) μίαν,
  5 ᾱ. (ἔτους ?) δ/, Ἐπεὶφ τρίτῃ καὶ εἰ-
   κάδι, κγ̄. ... ═

3. Read ἐξάγων.

3. It is quite impossible to restore the name at the beginning of the line. The first few letters in every line have been almost completely obliterated.
6. Analogous texts afford no parallels which might aid in the interpretation of the three letters which follow the date. Perhaps a signature.

52. Tax Accounts

Garrett Dep. 7676. 12 × 18 and 6 × 11 cm. Provenance unknown. 3rd cent. A.D.

Two fragments apparently from tax accounts. Little remains but a list of names. In the first fragment there is also found a list of cash entries from a preceding column. These entries are in varying amounts and perhaps represent both partial and complete payments of the ἀριθμητικόν, together with a small surcharge. This is especially suggested by the amount of the entry in line 10 (16 dr., 3½ ob., 2 ch.), although it must be admitted that this does not correspond exactly to any payment of ἀριθμητικόν recorded elsewhere. For this tax see P. Ryl. 213. 22, note, and Wallace, *Taxes in Roman Egypt*, s. v.

The occurrence of several names having the prefix Σεν- suggests a provenance in Upper Egypt. Such names are particularly common in the ostraca.

On the verso of both fragments there are small sections from money accounts.

FRAG. 1

```
                              Ε[
                              [
        ]  ϛ[                Σενπανεχά[τ]ου Πανεχάτου [
     ]διαν  ϛ  β[            Σενψενενούπιος Παγχ[
5    ]  ϛ  sϛ[                     τος Ψενο[
     ]ινεβθ  ϛ  δ[.] ό [     Θαμίνιος Ἀρεμίφιος καὶ [
     ]    ϛ  sϛ  ό χ°        Σενταςνῶς Μ   ε [
     ] .  ϛ  θϝ  ό χ°           δ         [.]   [
     ]    ϛ  θϝ  ό χ°        Θεραίτιος Ψενγήριος
10   ]ιος ϛ  ιsϛ  ό χ°       Ψηρίφιος Ψενοσίριος
     ] .  ϛ  aϛ  ό χγ        Πανεχάτου Πουρανούπιος
          ]ϛ  ό χ°           Σεναρεμίφιος Ὥρου
          ]  ό χ°            Τεβῶς Φατρείους καὶ Σενπανεχπαστι[
          ]  ό χγ            Σενπετεμεί(νιος) Τανεχάτιδος Πετ[
15        ]  ό [χ]γ          Θαμίνιος Ψανσν[ῶτος
```

FRAG. II

```
        ] νομενο[
     ]χια ἔχει ἐπιβο[λὴν ?
     Βάσσου τοῦ καὶ Κολαίν[ου
     Ἀπολλωνίου Ἀπολλωνίο[υ
20        Νίγερος    [
     ἐκτὸς βορινῆς πλαστῆς [
     αιαν [.]ε( ) ἐν τῷ τῶν τόπ(ων) κω    [
          ]ειν[.. κ]ώμης  ϛ [
          ] ιος ὁμοίως      [
25   Πανίσκου Δημητρίου καὶ Α[
     Θαμίνιος Ἄπιτος         [
          ]ιθοερου [......]   [
```

11. χγ. Cf. lines 14 f. A payment of 3 chalci is only theoretically possible. Only one coin of smaller denomination than the obol is known to have circulated in Egypt, this coin having a value of 2 chalci. Cf. Johnson, *Roman Egypt*, 432.

53. Tax Accounts

AM 8915.   31 × 23 cm.   Philadelphia.   56 and 57 A.D.

Two summarized accounts of disbursements made by the bank in Philadelphia during the years 55/56 and 56/57 A. D. The entries are recorded by months, the nature of those in the first column being uncertain, whereas those in the second column cover withdrawals of money to effect payment of the dike-tax (χωματικόν). These monthly disbursements may represent payments of taxes by the bank for an estate out of funds credited to the account of the latter, such payments being made for workmen employed on the estate. The accounts were probably drawn up by the owner or manager of the estate.

The entries recorded in the first column (lines 2-13) add up to a total of 399 dr. 4 ob., being in exact agreement with the total indicated in line 14. The balance (361 dr., line 15) remaining after the deduction of this sum was evidently computed from an original balance of 760 dr. 4 ob., which, however, appears nowhere in the account. From the second balance there was further subtracted the sum of 93 dr. 1 ob., leaving in the account an indicated final balance of 267 dr. 5 ob., which sum seems to have been recorded in line 16.

The figures in the second column do not correspond exactly to the total (700 dr.) entered by a second hand in line 30, unless the sum of 27 dr. 5 ob. is read in line 21, a reading which is very uncertain. It should be noted in this connection that all of the entries represent simple multiples of the customary amount (6 dr. 4 ob.) paid on account of the dike-tax, with the exception of those found in lines 21, 24, and 27. Moreover, the last of these exceptions is rather apparent than real, for the sum of 83 dr. 2 ob. clearly includes a half payment of the tax. The entries in lines 21 and 24 are thus irregular. In the case of the latter the reading is well established, and so it is possible that a similarly irregular entry may have been recorded in line 21. The balance of 1103 dr. 1 ob. (line 30) is obtained by deducting 700 dr. from the original sum of 1803 dr. 1 ob. found in line 17.

The text was one of a large number discovered on the site of the ancient Philadelphia in 1921. Although the second (line 17), third, and fourth (line 12) years can be referred to the reign of either Claudius or Nero, a date in the latter's reign is to be preferred. Fragmentary farm accounts pertaining to the second and third years of Nero are found on the verso.

Col. II (recto) appears to have been drawn up after the close of the second year (line 29), and it may be conjectured that the earlier of the two accounts on the verso was prepared not long afterwards. Col. II occupies a position near the center of the papyrus. Col. I, apparently written a year later (line 12), was inscribed in the copious margin which had been left vacant at the left. The accounts on recto and verso were written by different hands.

Col. I

  L τράπεζα
  Ἀθύρ   ∫ μβ
  Χοίαχ   ∫ ιαϝ
  Τύβη   ∫ η⁻
5 Μεχ(ίρ)   ∫ γϝ
  Φαμε(νώθ)   ∫ ιηϝ
  Φαρμοῦθ(ι)   ∫ λβϝ
  Παχώ(ν)   ∫ λγϝ
  Παῦνει   ∫ ξηϝ
10 Ἐπείφ   ∫ πβϝ
  Μεσορή   ∫ νδϝ
  μη(νὸς) Σεβαστ(οῦ) δL ὑπ(ὲρ) γL ∫ κθ
  Φαῶφι   ∫ ιδ
    (γίνονται) ∫ τϟθϝ
15 λοιπὲ   ∫ τξα
  ἀφ' ὧ(ν) οὐσιῶ(ν) ∫ ϟγ⁻, λοι(παὶ) ∫ σξζ[ϝ

Col. II

  ὑπόστασις χωματικ(οῦ) β (ἔτους)   ∫ Ἀωγ⁻
  L τράπεζα
  Φαῶφι   ∫ ϛϝ
20 Ἀθύρ   ∫ ϛϝ
  Χοίαχ   ∫ κ[ζ]ϝ
  Τύβη   ∫ κ
  Μεχ(ίρ)   ∫ λγ=
  Φαμενώθ   ∫ ρβ−
25 Φαρμοῦθ(ι)   ∫ ρπ
  Γερμανικ(είου)   ∫ κ
  Παῦνει   ∫ πγ=
  Ἐπ[εί]φ   ∫ σιγ=
  Μεσορή   ∫ ϛϝ
30 (Hand 2) (γίνονται) ∫ ψ (Hand 1) λοιπ(αὶ) ∫ Ἀργ⁻

15. Read λοιπαί.

12. Σεβαστ(οῦ). Cf. Γερμανικ(είου) (line 26). The occurrence of these honorary names (representing Θώθ and Παχών respectively) furnishes no clue as to

53. TAX ACCOUNTS

the date of the text. Both of these names are attested as early as the reign of Claudius. Cf. O. Mey. 36. 5 and O. Brüss. 7. 8.

13. This payment, like that recorded in the previous line, was doubtless made in arrears for the account of the third year.

54. Wage Account

Garrett Dep. 7679. 14 × 29.5 cm. Provenance unknown. Early 1st cent. A.D.

An account arranged by months recording small payments of wheat, presumably as wages, to five individuals whose names recur regularly. With a few exceptions these payments are in quantities of two artabae per person monthly, totalling ten artabae, or slightly less, for each month. Workmen ordinarily received an allowance of only one artaba per month (cf. Johnson, *Roman Egypt*, 301). Perhaps the larger sums found here include a similar allowance for the wife of each workman. One of the laborers seems to have been employed in irrigation work (cf. lines 13, 20, 27).

Col. I

```
    .]  Ἁρμίεις
   ...] . . . . [
   .......] . [..]ευ
    Ἀθὺρ]    ι [
 5  Ἁρμίεις Ὠρίων(ος) (πυρ.) (ἀρτ.) β
    Ἐ]σοῦρ[ις] Ὠρίων(ος) (πυρ.) (ἀρτ.) β
    Ἀθ]ην[ώτω]ρος [Καρι( )] (πυρ.) (ἀρτ.) β
    Μυσ]θᾶς Βα[λανί(ου) εἰ]ς
    Φ]αῶφι καὶ Ἀθὺρ (πυρ.) (ἀρτ.) δ
10  Ἀνίκητος (πυρ.) (ἀρτ.) ς
    εἰς ἄρτωις εἰς Φρύν( )
    ὥστε  επαριτης (πυρ.) (ἀρτ.) β
    Ὠρίων λώγ(ῳ) πωτ(ισμοῦ ?) (πυρ.) (ἀρτ.) β
        (γίνονται) (πυρ.) (ἀρτ.) κ
15  Χοίακ
    Ἁρμίε[ι]ς Ὠρίων(ος) (πυρ.) (ἀρτ.) β
    Ἐσοῦρις Ὠρήω(νος) (πυρ.) (ἀρτ.) β
    Ἀθηνώτωρος Καρ( ) (πυρ.) (ἀρτ.) β
    Μυσθᾶς Βαλανί(ου) (πυρ.) (ἀρτ.) β
20  Ὠρίων λώγ(ῳ) πωτ(ισμοῦ ?) (πυρ.) (ἀρτ.) β
        (γίνονται) (πυρ.) (ἀρτ.) ι
    Τῦβι
    Ἐσοῦρις Ὠρίων(ος) (πυρ.) (ἀρτ.) β
    Ἁ]ρμίας Ὠρίων(ος) (πυρ.) (ἀρτ.) β
25  Ἀθηνώτωρος Καρι( ) (πυρ.) (ἀρτ.) β
```

Μυσθᾶς Βαλανί(ου) (πυρ.) (ἀρτ.) β
Ὠρίων λώγ(ῳ) πω(τισμοῦ ?) (πυρ.) (ἀρτ.) β
    (γίνονται) (πυρ.) (ἀρτ.) ι
Μεχίρ
30 Ἀρμίες Ὠρίων(ος) (πυρ.) (ἀρτ.) β
Ἐσ]οῦρι(ς) Ὠρίων(ος) (πυρ.) (ἀρτ.) β
Ἀ]θηνώτωρος (πυρ.) (ἀρτ.) β
Μυ]σθᾶς Βαλανί(ου) (πυρ.) (ἀρτ.) β
    (γίνονται) (πυρ.) (ἀρτ.) [η]
35 Φαμενώθ
Ἀρμ[ί]εις Ὠρίων(ος) (πυρ.) (ἀρτ.) β
Ἀθηνώτωρος Καρι( ) (πυρ.) (ἀρτ.) β
Ἐσ[ο]ῦρις Ὠρίω(νος) (πυρ.) (ἀρτ.) β
Μυσθᾶς Βαλανί(ου) (πυρ.) (ἀρτ.) β
40   (γίνονται) (πυρ.) (ἀρτ.) η

Col. II

Φαρ[μοῦθι]
Ἀρμ[ίεις Ὠρίων(ος) (πυρ.) (ἀρτ.)] β
Ἐσοῦ[ρις Ὠρίων(ος)] (πυρ.) (ἀρτ.) β
Ἀθηνώτωρ[ος] (πυρ.) (ἀρτ.) β
45 Μυσθᾶ[ς] Βαλανί(ου) (πυρ.) (ἀρτ.) β
ὥστ' Ὠρ(ίωνι) (πυρ.) (ἀρτ.) αLd
⟦ει⟧ (γίνονται) θLd
Παχών
ὥστε εἰς ἄρτωις
50 εἰς Πρύν( ) (πυρ.) (ἀρτ.) ζ
ὥστ' Ὠρ(ίωνι) αLd
    (γίνονται) ηLd
ἀπὼ τῆς θέσιως
ἧς τέτωκέ μαι
55 Ἡρᾶς
μέδρ(ῳ) μτλ (γίνονται) (πυρ.) (ἀρτ.) κδL
μέδρ(ῳ) δετάτῳ
ἐπωλικῷ
ὁμωίω(ς)
60 διωος σιτω
(πυρ.) (ἀρτ.) ϙ δLd χαρκῷ
μέδρῳ
χιρισταῖς.

11, 49. Read ἄρτους.   13, 20, 27. Read λόγ(ῳ) ποτ(ισμοῦ).   50. Read Φρύν( ).
  53. Read ἀπὸ, θέσεως.   54. Read δέδωκέ μοι.   56, 57, 62. Read μέτρῳ.

54. WAGE ACCOUNT

57. Read τετά⟨ρ⟩τῳ.   58. Read ἐ⟨μ⟩πορικῷ.   59. Read ὁμοίω(s).
61. Read χαλκῷ (?).

11. ἄρτωις (= ἄρτους). For ου > ωι see Mayser, *Grammatik*, I, 138. Cf. line 49. Φρυν( ). Doubtless a proper name, rather than φρίν(ους) (*toads*). Cf. line 50.

56. μτλ. The reading is almost certain. Possibly for μ⟨ε⟩γ⟨ά⟩λ(ῳ)?

58. ἐπωλικῷ (= ἐμπορικῷ). Cf. SB. 7341. 17 (μέτρῳ τετάρτῳ [ἐ]υπόρων τῷ τοῦ Ἡρακλέ[ους]). The loss of μ before a labial is a common phenomenon (Mayser, *ibid.*, 190), likewise the substitution of λ for ρ (Mayser, *ibid.*, 188). Alternatively one might suggest reading (πεντα)πωλικῷ [= (παντο)-πωλικῷ], although it is not likely that the writer would have been so ignorant of the etymology of the word.

60. διωος. Possibly for διμνῶος (*of two months*). Cf. P. Ryl. 183. 7. No similar instance of the dropping of μν is attested, however. For the various forms assumed by this consonant combination see Nachmanson, *Glotta*, IV (1913), 245-248. It does not appear possible to read δικιος (= Δίκαιος?).

61. χαρκῷ (= χαλκῷ?). For λ > ρ see Meisterhans-Schwyzer, *Grammatik der attischen Inschriften*, 83, 9 (and note 713).

55. Alphabetical List of Names

Garrett Dep. 7640 (verso).   6.5 × 33 cm.   Oxyrhynchus.   1st (?) cent. A.D.

Possibly a list of poets, although Laertes, Licinnus, and Lysander are unknown. Written in two columns in large uncials. For the text on the recto see **24**.

Λυκόφρων   Μενα
Λαέρτης
Λικίννος
Λοίσανδρος

4. Read Λύσανδρος.

1. Μενα. The writer, for some unknown reason, left this name incomplete. Perhaps he started to write Μένανδρος.
3. Λικίννος. For Λυκίνος? Cf. Lat. *Lucinus*.

56. Account

AM 8929.   10.5 × 13.5 cm.   Provenance unknown.   153/154 A.D.

Fragment of an account listing sales and purchases. A few letters from another column written in a different hand are visible at the left. On the verso there is a small section of a grain (?) account, the cash equivalent of each entry being computed in drachmas.

. . . .

]..[
κειμένων (?) Καμοκ[

τοῖς λόγοις ἠγορασ[
τῶν κτηνῶν τῆς οὐσί[ας
5 ρου καὶ καλλιμόρφο[υ
ἐπράθη κριθὴ ἐπὶ τοῦ αὐτ[οῦ
καὶ φακὸς ἐκ (δραχμῶν) κβ [
(ἔτους) ιζ Ἀντωνίνου [Καίσαρος τοῦ κυρίου, month, day.

7. φακὸς ἐκ (δραχμῶν) κβ. The price here recorded as paid for an artaba of lentils (ἐκ is occasionally used with reference to sales and purchases to indicate the total price paid, but it more commonly has distributive force, as may be assumed here. Cf. Mayser, *Grammatik*, II², 347 f.) is abnormally high. Cf. Johnson, *Roman Egypt*, 313. Wheat and lentils were considered of approximately equal value at this period, an official conversion ratio of 15 : 19 being indicated by P. Col. 1 recto 6 (cf. P. Col. II, p. 164). The price of wheat rarely exceeded 8 drachmas during the second century (cf. Johnson, *op. cit.*, 311). It may thus be more than a coincidence that in a tax receipt (W. O. 1587) dated in the same year (Sept. 153) a price of 24 drachmas is indicated for wheat, corresponding closely to the price recorded here for lentils. The extreme scarcity of grain and food stuffs suggested by these unusually high prices may have been an important contributing factor leading up to the serious revolt which is known to have broken out in Egypt in the course of that year (153/154). Cf. W. Chrest. 19, introd.

57. Soldier's Expense Account

AM 8933.   12.5 × 21 cm.   Provenance unknown.   2nd cent. A.D.

Included in the following account, which may have been drawn up by the treasurer of a cavalry squadron, are expenditures for arms, clothing, and implements for the use of a person whose name has been lost, and disbursements to the concubine of a certain Antonius, as well as for the support of the latter's wife, mother, and children. The name of a third party appears in the opening line, but the nature of the entry is uncertain. The large sums involved in the account suggest that the payments were made out of officers' allowances. Only the higher (equestrian) officers, moreover, were permitted to marry during their term of enlistment, this regulation remaining in effect until the close of the second century (cf. Lesquier, *L'armée romaine d'Egypte*, 278, and Parker, *The Roman Legions*, 237 f.), although at a somewhat earlier date an exemption from this restriction was granted also to subordinate officers (cf. Mitteis, *Grundzüge*, 283). For military accounts cf. Johnson, *Roman Egypt*, 670 ff.

After the subtraction of the sums recorded in lines 1-5, amounting to over 1080 drachmas, there remained in the account a balance of 1 talent 3988 drachmas. Further outlays reduced this sum to 1 talent 3300 drachmas, the closing balance.

57. SOLDIER'S EXPENSE ACCOUNT

Ten additional lines at the head of the text are represented by only a few scattered letters.

```
        . . . . . . . . .
       παυλυτ[..]  εἰς Τιβερ[ε]ίνου σκ    ʃ  [
       κ[α]ὶ [.....] ερμ       υτ  [.]  ʃ τπ
       τιμὴ κατηδια τῶν ὅπλων ἱππ[ι]κῶν
       κα[ὶ ἱ]ματίων καὶ σκευῶν      ʃ χ
5      καὶ [.....] [....] νου       ʃ ρ
       γίνον[τ]αι ἀργυρίου τάλαντον ἓν
       καὶ δραχμὰς τρισχιλίας ἐνακοσίας
       ὀγδοήκοντα ὀκτό.
       ἐκ τούτων ἐδαπανήθη εἰς φωκάριν
10     τοῦ Ἀντωνίω                   ʃ τ
       καὶ εἰς διατροφὴν τῶν παιδίων καὶ τῆς
       γυναικὸς καὶ τῆς μητρὸς αὐτοῦ ʃ τπη
       γίνονται ἀργυρίου τάλαντον ἓν καὶ δρα-
       χμαὶ τρισχίλιαι τριακόσιαι.
```

7. Read δραχμαὶ τρισχίλιαι κ. τ. λ.   9. Read φωκάριον.   10. Read Ἀντωνίου.
11. τρο of διατροφήν written above line in small letters.

1. σκεύη (?).

9. φωκάριν. Probably for φωκάριον (= φωκαρία), an assumption both finding support in B. G. U. 600. 20 (φωκαρίου) and confirming the correctness of the form there attested, concerning the accuracy of which doubts have been raised (cf. BL. II², 19). For the neuter singular in -ιν cf. Mayser, *Grammatik*, I, 260. The cognate form, φωκαρία (Lat. *focaria*), is found in B. G. U. 614. 13. Cf. Meyer, *Der römische Konkubinat*, 97 ff.

58. List of Names

Garrett Dep. 7671a (verso).   9 × 16.5 cm.   Provenance unknown.   2nd-3rd cent. A.D.

Portion of a column containing a list of names. Traces of additional writing are visible beyond a broad margin at the left. The occurrence of the name Κλεοχάρης (line 10) should be noted, a name not found in Preisigke, *Namenbuch*. Cf. Pape, *Eigennamen*, 676.

On the recto there is a fragment of an account relating to land. Only the ends of the lines remain. Three hands can be distinguished.

```
       Ἀπίων Ἀπί[ων(ος)] τοῦ [καὶ
       Διογένης Διογέ(νου) τοῦ [καὶ
       Θαμοῦνις Ἁρπ( ) Δη( ) [
       Χαιρήμων Σωσικλέου[ς
5      Χαιρήμων Φειδίππ[ου
```

Διδυμάριον Ἐπ [
Διογένης Ὀκ [
Ἡρακλείδης Ἡρακ[λείδου (?)
Ἱέραξ Ἀπόλλων[ος
10   Κλεοχάρης [
    [....] [

3. Δη( ). Probably in the dative case.

59. List of Names

Garrett Dep. 7697 (verso). 9 × 11 cm. Provenance unknown. 2nd-3rd cent. A.D.

A short list of names written on the verso of a small piece of papyrus cut off from a larger piece on which an account (or list of names) had been previously inscribed. Only the beginnings of six lines are preserved on the recto.

Τύρων [Παμ]ίνιος (?) Τύρωνος
Ἰσίδωρο[ς Π]αμίνιος
Παμμίας υ(ἱὸς) Θαυβά⟨σ⟩θιος Παγχ( )
Ἐσοῦρις υ( ) Αἰλουρᾶς
5   Ἀνοῦπις ὁ κ(αὶ) Ἀνουβίων
Ἑρμείων Ἑρμείωνος Π πω
Εὐδαίμων Ἀπάρτωνος
Φιβίχις Εὐδαίμονος
Πτολεμαῖος Βελλῆους Παι ( )

4. υ( ). Not ὁ κ(αί).

60. Account

Garrett Dep. 7675a.   14.5 × 7.5 cm.   Provenance unknown.   2nd-3rd cent. A.D.

A fragmentary record of miscellaneous expenditures, including the payment of taxes.

Col. I

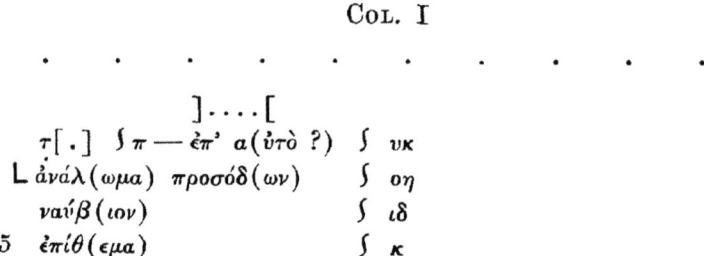

    ]....[
τ[.] ͵π — ἐπ' α(ὐτὸ ?) ͵ υκ
ⳉ ἀνάλ(ωμα) προσόδ(ων)   ͵ οη
   ναύβ(ιον)   ͵ ιδ
5 ἐπίθ(εμα)   ͵ κ

(γίνονται) ἐπ' α(ὐτὸ ?) ⧸ ριβ
⧸θ ⧸ υκ, (λοιπαὶ) ⧸ τη, ὧν κωλ( ) ⧸ ρ, (λοιπαὶ) ση
καὶ (πυροῦ) (ἀρτάβη) 𝈪χδ

COL. II

ι ⧸ ρξδΓ καὶ σ[ίτου ?
10 ἀνθ' οὗ ἑξῆς ἔλασσον [⧸ νζ
   (λοιπαὶ) ⫽ τῶν ὅλ(ων) ⧸ ρζ[Γ ?
καὶ λαχανοσπ(έρμου) τῶν ποτισθ(έντων ?) [ἀρτάβας ς]
ἐκ ⧸ κ ⧸ ρκ, (γίνονται) ἐπ' α(ὐτὸ ?) ⫽ [
   καὶ θέρμου τὸ ε[

On the verso:
15] ͞ϛ κ ( ) ιε (ἔτους)   207/8 (?) A.D.

2. ἐπ' α(ὐτό ?). Possibly for ἐπὶ τὸ αὐτό. Cf. lines 6, 13.
7. ⧸θ. Perhaps θ(έματος). Cf. P. Oxy. 1145. 2 ff.
9. Above the drachma sign a portion of an alpha is visible, belonging evidently to the preceding line. Not as in line 7.
12–13. The price indicated here for vegetable seed is in line with prices recorded elsewhere. Cf. Johnson, *Roman Egypt*, 313.

61. ACCOUNT

Garrett Dep. 7645b (verso).   16.5 × 7.5 cm.   Hermopolis.   264 A.D.

The interest of this account lies in its date, from which the dates of **30** and **38** can be approximately determined. The account covers receipts and expenditures from the year 263/264, these being arranged in separate columns, from each of which only a small portion has been preserved.

Π(αρὰ) Αὐρηλίο[υ ....]ου
λόγ(ος) λημ(μάτων) καὶ ἀν[αλ(ωμάτων) τῶν ἀπό] ε' Χοιὰκ ἕως λ'
Παχὼν καὶ ἀπὸ [λ' Π]αχὼν τοῦ ἐνεστῶτ(ος) ια (ἔτους)
τοῦ κυρίου ἡμῶ[ν Γ]αλλιηνοῦ Σεβαστοῦ
5 ⌊ [λημ(μάτων) ..]τ χ [   ]
   [   ]
          ]μου ἐποικ [
       ]   /⧸ τ [
       ] .... /⧸ ϙς[

COL. II

10 ⌊ ἀναλ(ωμάτων)
στρατιώτῃ ἀπὸ Πέλα [

τέκτονι ποιήσαν[τι
τῷ α(ὐτῷ ?) βαλόντι τ[
ι̣ο̣υ̣ς ὡ̇ς τ(οῦ) α' ε'[
15 παν[ή]γυριν καὶ π[
τῷ α' φοίνικα [
τὸ βουλευτήριον
] υτο [

Traces of two additional lines.

. . . .

62. ACCOUNT

AM 8952.   4 × 6 cm.   Provenance unknown.   3rd cent. A.D.

Fragment of an account bearing the heading λόγος χρυσί[ων], in which there are listed expenditures for soldering, a libation cup, birds, and bronze. In view of the heading it is posssible that small metal statues of birds are intended in line 4.

Λόγος χρυσί[ων
τιμῆς κολλή(σεως ?) τε[
καὶ ὑπ(ὲρ) σπονδ(είου) καὶ θ [
τιμῆς ὀρνίθων [
5 Σαρᾶτι ἱεροψά[λτῃ
τιμῆς χαλκοῦ [
μνῶν [
ἄλ(λος) τιμῆ(ς) χαλκο(ῦ) α[
μενο( ) ὑπ[ὲρ

5. Σαρᾶτι. For the nickname see Mayser, *Grammatik*, I, 253.

63. LIST OF NAMES (?)

Garrett Dep. 7890b.   10 × 14 cm.   Oxyrhynchus.   3rd-4th cent. A.D.

A text of uncertain nature referring to a list of names of persons who were apparently accused of stealing seed-corn from a wheat-field. The names of those farming the field are appended.

Of chief interest are the occurrence of the new word κλεπτοσπορία, and the use of the expression παχύνοντα κότ(ον), a phrase which recalls a similar juxtaposition of the two words in Aeschylus, *Supplices*, 616-618.

The κώμη Σύρων referred to in line 5 is probably the Oxyrhynchite village of this name, for the natives from whom this text was purchased came from

63. LIST OF NAMES

Behneseh, the modern site of the ancient metropolis of the Oxyrhynchite nome.

```
         ὀνόμ(ατος ?) Οὐάλεντος Α[.] [.....] ρ[
                                        πραιπ(οσίτου).
   ζητούμενα ὀνόματα
   κλεπτοσπορίας ἕνεκεν
5  κώμης Σύρων
   σι[τ(ικῶν)]    (ἀρουρῶν) δ',
   ἐπὶ δὲ τὰ ὀνόμ(ατα) τῶν γεωργ(ούν)τ(ων)
   Πατερηοῦς
   Ἀπολλώνιος ἐπικαλούμ(ενος) Οὐάλενς
10 καὶ τὸν σκυτέα τὸν παχύν-
   οντα κότ(ον) τῶν πρεσ(βυτέρων ?)
```

64. ACCOUNT

Garrett Dep. 7670a. 11 × 8 cm. Provenance unknown. Late 3rd cent. A.D.

Fragment of a money account. Broken on all sides. The figures at the left are from a preceding column and are separated from the following column by a 2 cm. margin. Traces of an account are also discernible on the verso.

```
   ]ʃ[        (Hand 2)  [.] [...] [
   ʃ]φμ·              Σαραπάμμων Θωνίου    [
   ʃ]οϵLd·            Ἰσίδωρος Σαραπάμμωνος [
   ]ʃ ρι·             Τιμόθεος Ἀλεξάνδρου   [
5  ]ʃ τοδ·            Δωρόθεος Ἀλεξάνδρου   [
   ]ʃ ρι·             Παῦλος Ἀκύλλου       [
   ]ʃ κ·              Πεκύλλος Διονυσίου    [
```

3. ϊσιδωρος.

65. LETTER

AM 8914. 9 × 22 cm. Provenance unknown. 40 (?) A.D.

A letter addressed to Dionysius by Nemesion, a large portion of which has been made unintelligible by extensive lacunae. The recipient is requested to pass on certain instructions to a tenant farmer relative to his work, including the admonition to fertilize the soil with manure whenever necessary. The rest is obscure. An entire line may have been lost between lines 6 and 7.

    Νεμεσίων Διονν[σ]ίωι
    τῶ[ι] ἀδελφῶι χαίρειν.
    ἐπέντειλαι τῶι γεωργῶι
    περὶ τῶν ἔργων. κοπρηγεί·
5 τωι καθ' ἡμέραν ἐὰν χρεί-
    αν ἔχη . . . [
        ]α . τοσ[
    ἐ[π]ιέναι πρὸς πασθα [
    τε χάριν τῶν ταυρικῶν ἐὰν
10 περὶ χαλκῶν πο αλ [
    ξαι αὐτῶι ἕως καταβῶι
    καὶ λωιεαρ ποδ[ι]σθήτωι τὰ
    ἐκεῖ ἕως ὅτου καταλάβῃ
    εαν ἀπὸ τῆς ἀριθμήσεω[ς.
15   ἔρρωσο.
    (ἔτους) δ Γα[ΐ]ου Καίσαρο[ς] Σε[βαστοῦ]   39/40
    Γερμανικοῦ, Μεσ[ο]ρ[ὴ] κγ.

On the verso:
Διονυτᾶι . . . . [

12. Possibly ⟨ἕ⟩λωι. Or perhaps λ⟨άβ⟩ωι. Cf. P. Teb. 37. 21-22 (ἕως καταβῶ καὶ λάβωι).
18. Διονυτᾶι. Cf. Διονυ[σ]ίωι (line 1). For the formation of nicknames in -ᾶς see Mayser, *Grammatik*, I, 252-254 (additional literature cited p. 252, note 1).

66. LETTER

AM 8925.   7 × 5 cm.   Provenance unknown.   1st cent. A.D.   Plate II.

A small fragment of a letter conveying urgent instructions to pass on a certain order, in case the flood does not get beyond the writer, and to send irons for the oxen. The spelling ἀγκέλλις (for ἀγγέλλεις) is worthy of note (lines 1-2); likewise the division of πλήν (πλ/ήν) at the end of line 2, and the use of this word with the subjunctive in place of the customary construction with τοῦ c. inf.

    ἐντάχιον ἀγκέλ-
    λις πυῖν ταχὺ πλ/
    ὴν γένητε τὸ ὑδ-

ωρ ἐπάνο μου καὶ
5 πέμψε μυ ἐντάχ-
ιον τὰ σιδήρια τῶν
βοῶν. ἐπιδέδο-
κα χαλκὸν τὸ τέ-
[λος ?

. . . .

1-2. Read ἀγγέλλεις ποιεῖν.   3. Read γένηται.   5. Read πέμψαι μοι.

67. LETTER

AM 8927.   13 × 7 cm.   Provenance unknown.   1st-2nd cent A.D.

A short letter addressed to Dionysius by his sister (?) Theano, in which she reports concerning a certain man about whom information was evidently desired. The closing formula is noteworthy.

The text of this letter, together with a brief commentary, has been published by Professor S. H. Weber (*T. A. P. A.*, LVI [1925], xlii).

Θεανὼ Διονυσίῳ [τῶ]ι ἀδελφῶι
πλεῖστα χαίρειν. περὶ οὗ μοι ἐδήλωσας ἀνθρώπου οὐχ εὕραμεν τί ἤ-
νυσεν καὶ αὐτὸς δὲ ἐξῆλθεν πρός σε.
5 ἔρρωσο ἀσπαζόμενός μου λείαν τὰ
τέκνα. πάλιν ἔρρωσο. Φαρμοῦθι κϛ.

On the verso:
Διον(υσίῳ)   ╳   ἀδελ-
              φῷ.

. . . .

68. LETTER

Garrett Dep. 7622.   10 × 22 cm.   Provenance unknown.   2nd (?) cent. A.D.

In the following letter, only the concluding portion of which remains, the writer refers to a small financial transaction apparently just completed by him in behalf of the addressee. He promises to devote his careful attention to the further commands of the latter. There follow in conclusion a number of salutations, from the nature of which one may conclude that the two correspondents were closely acquainted with each other.

Only two or three letters remain of the address on the verso.

```
. . . . . . . .]μι[
'Αλεξα]νδρείας [
. . . . .]κα αυτη[
. . . .] δη [.]σι[
5  . . . .]ωηφαιοσ . . . [.]αι[. . .] . . σε [
(δραχμὰς) κδ, τὰς δὲ λοιπὰ[s] (δραχμὰς) ιβ τω [. . .] . . ου . . . ἐ-
βαλόμην. περὶ ὧν ἐὰν θέλῃς γράφ[ε
μοι πεπεισμέ[ν]ος ὅτι πάντα τὰ κε-
λευόμενά μο[ι] ὑπὸ σοῦ προθυμότα-
10 τα ποιήσω. ἄσπασαι τὴν ἀδελφήν
σου καὶ Θαῆσιν [κ]α[ὶ .]τπιν καὶ τὴν θυγα-
τέρα αὐτῆς καὶ Ἄγαθον καὶ Μερκούλιο[ν
καὶ] [.]σερ[. . .]ιον Π[άμ]φιλον καὶ Ἀρχίβιον
κα]ὶ Ἰσίδωρον κ[αὶ] Ἀπολλώνιον τ[ὸ]ν μέ[γαν.
15   ἐρρῶσθαί σε εὔχομ(αι), φίλτατε, πανοικεὶ
εὐτυχ[ο]ῦντα.
```

7. περὶ ὧν ἐὰν θέλῃς κ. τ. λ. The use of ἐάν in conditional relative clauses in place of ἄν, though seldom found in texts from the early Ptolemaic period, became increasingly common with the passage of time. Cf. Mayser, *Grammatik*, II¹, 261, 263. For a briefer formulation of the same promise see P. Oxy. 743. 38-40 (καὶ σὺ δὲ ὑπὲρ ὧν ἐὰν θέλῃς γράφε μοι καὶ ἀόκνως ποήσω).

10-14. For multiple salutations in private letters cf. P. Mich. Inv. 346 (cited by Winter, *Life and Letters in the Papyri*, 86-87).

15. πανοικεί. The use of this word is discussed in detail by W. Döllstädt, *Griechische Papyrusprivatbriefe in gebildeter Sprache aus den ersten vier Jahrhunderten nach Christus*, 15-16.

69. Letter

AM 8932 (recto).   16.5 × 16 cm.   Philadelphia.   2nd cent. A.D.

Concluding portion of a private letter. A few scattered letters and words can be distinguished from the ends of lines in a preceding column. In adding the closing formula (lines 5-7) the writer greatly reduced the size of his hand. The formula itself is unusual. Cf. P. Oxy. 1766. 16-17. For the more commonly used phrases occurring in closing salutations see Exler, *A Study in Greek Epistolography*, 74-77.

On the verso there is a tax receipt (cf. **47**).

Col. II

```
μοι εἰς τὴν γεουχίαν οὐκ οὖ-
σαν πόρρωθεν τῆς Φιλαδελ-
φίας. πειράσομαι δὲ ἐπὰν
```

ἐκεῖ γένῃ συντυχεῖν σοι πρίν
5 με καταπλεῦσαι. ἐρρῶσθαί σε
εὔχομαι, κύριέ μου ἀδελφέ, πανοικεὶ
εὐτυχοῦντα καὶ διὰ παντὸς εὐδοξ[ο]ῦντα.
〚. .〛

1. γεουχίαν. A new word evidently referring to a parcel of land cultivated by ἀ γεοῦχος. The dotted letters have been practically erased, but the remaining traces support the readings given.

70. Letter

Garrett Dep. 7689.   13 × 19 cm.   Provenance unknown.   2nd-3rd cent. A.D.

In a letter to Ammonius, Eumelus urges his correspondent to receive the mother of Dioscorus, in the event that she comes to him, and to deliver to her the rents of certain lands. He asserts emphatically that this is not the purpose of her visit, and then explains that she will come up the river to him as an accommodation, in order that he may be spared the necessity of making a journey in the opposite direction, and that no one may be inconvenienced on his (Eumelus') account. After commending Ammonius upon the manner in which he has rendered a report to the tax-collectors, Eumelus concludes his letter by extending greetings from himself and others to the members of Ammonius' household as well as to the family of a mutual acquaintance.

The text exhibits a number of interesting orthographic phenomena, to which reference is made in the notes. The address which originally stood on the verso has been almost entirely obliterated.

Εὔμηλος Ἀμμωνίῳ τ[ῷ] τιμιωτάτῳ φίλῳ πολλὰ
χαίρειν.
πρὸ μὲν πάντων εὔχομαί σε ὑ⟨γ⟩ιαίνειν καὶ τὸ προσκύνη[μά
σου ποιῶ παρὰ τῷ κυρίῳ Σαράπιδι. καλῶς ποιή-
5 σις, ἀδελφέ, ἐὰν ἀναβῇ πρὸς σὲ ἡ μήτηρ Διοσκόρου, συνλαβέσται αὐτὴν καὶ δοῦναι αὐτῇ τὰ τῶν ἀρουρευδίων
〚α τα η[. .] ν〛
ἐκφόρια. μὲ τοὺς πάντας θεοὺς οὐκ ἵνεκε τούτου
ἀνάβη, ἀλλὰ εἶνα ἀκατάπλο[κ]όν σε ποι⟨ή⟩σῃ καὶ μηδείς
10 σοι κόπον παρέχῃ εἴνεκ' ἐμοῦ, καὶ ἀπὸ τῶν ἐνοικίων
ἤτι ἔδωκας τοῖς πράκτορσιν λόγον αὐτῇ ἀρετῖ.
ἀσπάζομαι τὰ ἀβάσκοντά σου τέκνα καὶ τὴν
σύμβιόν σου καὶ πάντας τοὺς ἐν οἴκῳ κατ' ⟨ὄν⟩ομα.
ἀσπάζεται ὑμᾶς Διόσκορος καὶ Σαραπιάς.
15 ἀσπάζου Κᾶτιν καὶ τὴν σύμβιον αὐτοῦ καὶ τὰ τέκνα α(ὐτοῦ).

4. σαπιδι. 8. εκφοριων corrected to εκφορια, and τας to τους. 12. A double space separates this line from the line above. A similar space separates lines 2-3.

3. ὑ⟨γ⟩ιαίνειν. For the disappearance of γ between vowels see Mayser, *Grammatik*, I, 163-164.

4-5. ποιήσις. For the substitution of ι for ει, and of ει for ι (cf. είνα, line 9), see Mayser, *ibid.*, 87 ff.

5-6. συνλαβέσται. For the failure to assimilate ν before λ see Mayser, *ibid.*, 233 ff. For σθ > στ see Mayser, *ibid.*, 179. ἀρουρευδίων. The unusual substitution of ευ for ι should be noted.

8. μέ (= μά). For ἄ > ε see Mayser, *ibid.*, 58. In view of this substitution of ε for accented ᾰ, it is strange that Eumelus retained unaccented ᾰ in the case of Σαράπιδι (line 4) and Σαραπιάς (line 14), two words in which the weakening of α to ε is unusually common. Cf. Mayser, *ibid.*, 56-57. οὐκ ἵνεκε. Cf. εἴνεκ'. line 10. For the disappearance of the aspiration see Mayser, *ibid.*, 202-203, and cf. 100. 7.

9. ἀνάβη (= ἀνέβη). For the omission of the syllabic augment see Mayser, *ibid.*, 333. ποι⟨ή⟩σῃ. For the omission of η following οι see Mayser, *ibid.*, 83. Yet cf. ποιήσις (lines 4-5).

10. εἴνεκ'. Cf. ἵνεκε, line 8. εἴνεκε for ἔνεκα appears to be without parallel (cf. Mayser, *ibid.*, 241 f.). For ε > ει before consonants see Mayser, *ibid.*, 73.

11. ἤτι (= ἤδη). For δ > τ see Mayser, *ibid.*, 176-177. For the relation of η and ι see Mayser, *ibid.*, 82 ff. Cf. ἀρετί (= ἀρετῇ) at the end of the line.

71. Letter

AM 8950.   13 × 16 cm.   Provenance unknown.   3rd cent. A.D.

A letter referring to a dispute concerning the payment of 5500 drachmae. By reason of the condition of the text the details are obscure, but it appears that the obligation was in some manner connected with the performance of the *cosmeteia*.

On the verso a second hand has penned a brief eulogy of some one who cannot be identified. Only the opening lines are printed, the rest being fragmentary.

       Χαίροις Χαιρήμονι τιμιώτατε.
τοσαῦτα διηνέχθην πρὸς τὸν πρύτανιν ἕνεκεν
τῆς διαγραφῆς, ἔγραψας γὰρ διαγραφῆναι (δραχμὰς) Ἐφ,
ἀλλ' ἐπὶ ὅλον τάλαντον ἤτουσαν. ἠρκέσθην
5 ἐπὶ τοῦ παρόντος (δραχμαῖς) Ἐ, ἀλλ' ἐπεὶ παρόντος
Ὠριγένους πάλιν πολλὰ τοῦ γυμνασιάρχου
ὁ μὲν Ἡλιόδωρος ἡδέσθη με, προσενεχθέν-
τος αὐτῷ Σατορνείλου, παρῆν γὰρ καὶ ὁ φίλος μου, μόνος δὲ ὁ πρύτανις ἀντέστη μοι
10 ὡς ἀκοῦσαι καὶ λέγειν, ὁ γὰρ δεκάδαρχος

71. LETTER

πάνυ γε ετείμα καὶ Ὠριγένης τοσα[ῦ]τ[α]
παρὼν εἶπεν οἷα σ[.....]   [4-6
μόγις ἐγὼ ὑπέστην ἀ[ποδοῦναι ? δραχμὰς
χειλίας εἰς τὴν ιγ̄ α α[....]αι[...]μεν
15 ἀ]νεχώρησε ὡς εν[...] [...]οι [..] [.] χ..
.. αιτ αραμ   χάρις καὶ τῶν ο-
.] εκλ   Πομπηιανὸς τάλαντον καὶ [(δραχμὰς)] Ἐφ
ἔτι ὀφείλει καὶ ἔτι κατέχεται το[6-7
. ὅλον διδόντος οὕτως ὑπὲρ τῶν ἐκκειμ[έ-
20 νων ἐν σοὶ ὑπὲρ ἧς ἐξετέλεσας κοσμητεία[ς].

In margin at left:

ἀσπάζομαι τὰ παιδία καὶ τὴ[ν σύ]μβιον   ω[..]/.
ἐρρῶσθ[αί σ]ε εὔχομ(αι).

1. Read Χαίρημον.   4. Read ᾔτησαν.   13. ὑπεστην.   19, 20. ὑπερ.

Verso

(Hand 2) Τῆς φύσεως τὸ εὐσυνείδητον καὶ τῶν
τρόπων τὸ σπουδαῖον ἐκ πολλοῦ
25 μὲν ἀκούων νῦν δὲ ἔργῳ [.] μα-
θὼν ἤσθην. συν μαι χαίρων καλ-
ω[.] ο τὸν φίλον καθλη νος
τὰ .... κομισθέντα μοι γράμματα πτεραι ἀνέγνων ἅπερ προλα-
30 [β.......]...................

. . . .

1. Χαίροις Χαιρήμονι τιμιώτατε. This comparatively infrequent form of the praescript is discussed by Exler, *A Study in Greek Epistolography*, 67-68. Cf. Olssen, *Papyrusbriefe aus der frühesten Römerzeit*, 3, note 3. Here there seems to be a confusion of formulae, for the dative, Χαιρήμονι, has supplanted the vocative, Χαίρημον.

72. LETTER

AM 8949.   8 × 11 cm.   Provenance unknown.   3rd cent. A.D.

From the opening lines of the following letter it is apparent that the writer is giving instructions to make preparation for an impending visit of his steward. Pack animals are to be loaded with chaff and barley and despatched to the principal harbors. The rest is uncertain.

The writer should possibly be identified with the Aurelius Lucadius who was a resident of Hermopolis in 266 A.D. Cf. Stud. Pal. V. 52-56. iii. 3-6 and 73. 3-5. The identity is suggested by the association of Lucadius in each case with an ἐπίτροπος.

In the margin (line 14) there is an interesting reference to a χωματεπιστάτης, an official attested only here, but doubtless holding an office equivalent to that of the χωματεπείκτης. The latter is attested only for the fourth century.

    Λευκάδιος Εὐπόρῳ χαίρειν.
    ἐπειδὴ ὁ κύριός μου ἐπίτρο-
    πος ἐπιδημεῖν μέλλει τοῖς
    ὅρμοις ἀνάγκην ἔσχον
5   γράψαι [σο]ι ἵνα πάμπολλα
    κτήν[η] γεμώσας ἄχυρον
    καὶ κριθὴν σ . . . . ε ης
    ἐπὶ τοὺ[ς] ὅρμους τοὺ[ς μ]ε-
    γάλους π . . . . [. .] . .
10 κη παρὰ πατ [. . . .]σ
    οξωμονμη[
    . . . ν τὰς ἀννώνας.
    ἔρρωσο.

In margin at left:

    τὸν χωματεπιστάτην δι[. . . . . . .]λειχον[. . .] . τὴν
15   πενθήμερον [. .] . . . . . [

    4. αναγ‾κην.   5. ινα.

6-7. ἄχυρον καὶ κριθήν. The accusative with verbs of *filling* and *loading* is uncommon, but cf. γεμιζούσῃ τῇ θυγατρὶ ὕδωρ (sc. τὴν ὑδρίαν) (Paus. III. 13. 3).

73. LETTER

Garrett Dep. 7686.   12.5 × 16.5 cm.   Provenance unknown.   3rd cent. A.D.

A letter from Aphunchis to Augarus bearing greetings and unintelligible instructions to despatch a boat (?) to the writer without delay.

    Κυ]ρίῳ μου ἀδελφῷ Αὐγάρῳ Ἀφύγχις
      πολλὰ χαίρειν.
    πρ]ὸ μὲν πά⟨ν⟩των εὔχομαί σε ὁλοκλη-
    ρε]ῖν πα[ρ]ὰ τῷ κυρίῳ θεῷ. ἀλ⟨λ'⟩ ὅρα, κύριέ
5   μου, μὴ] ἀμελήσῃς το σε ταχέως μοι
    πέμπ?]ειν. [ἔ]τι ἡμέρε εἰσὶν τοῦ βαλεῖν
    τὰ πλ]οῖα εἰς ποτ⟦α⟧αμὸν ε, ἵνα κατα-

73. LETTER

γάγ ?]ωμεν τὸ πλοῖον εἰς Λο [..]
..] [..] ἐπεζήτησά τε εἰ πα[...]ικα
10 τὴ]ν ὁδὸν καὶ ἐν ἐτύμῳ αὐτὸ ἀφίω
μ]έχρη οὗ μοι παραγένῃ. ἀλ⟨λ'⟩ ὅρα μή
μοι κατάσχῃς δύο με⟨τὰ⟩ σοὶ ἐνταῦθα
.[...].[..]. ι εἰς δαπάνην ἔχω καὶ μ [.] ι συντά-
⟦συν[.]⟧
.ξειν σειμεῖα. ἀσπάζωμε τὸν ἀδελφὸν
15 Ἀλ[έ]ξα⟨ν⟩δρον καὶ τὸν ἀδελφὸν Μάκρο[ν]
καὶ ...] καὶ Εἰσσὰκ καὶ ὅλον τὸν οἶκόν σου
κα]τ' ὄνομα ἐ⟨ρ⟩ρέσθαί σε εὔχομε πολλοῖς χρόνοις.

12. σοι corrected from σει.

4. παρὰ τῷ κυρίῳ θεῷ. To be construed with ὁλοκληρεῖν, rather than with εὔχομαι. Cf. Ghedini, *Lettere Cristiane*, 95. That it cannot be confidently inferred from this phrase that the writer was a Christian is shown by Ghedini, *ibid.*, 8-9, 95-96.
7. ἔ ἵνα. Perhaps εἶνα should be read. Cf. 70. 9.
10. ἀφίω. A thematic form of ἀφίημι. Cf. Mayser, *Grammatik*, I, 354 (note 2). The subjunctive form, ἀφιῶ, is an alternative possibility, although the verb appears to be governed by εἰ in the preceding line.
12. A period is perhaps required after σοί.
17. ἐ⟨ρ⟩ρέσθαι (= ἐρρῶσθαι). The substitution of ε for ω is remarkable. For o > ε see Mayser, *ibid.*, 94-96.

74. LETTER

Garrett Dep. 7670b.   7.5 × 11 cm.   Provenance unknown.   About 300 A.D.

Fragment of a letter in which the writer first petitions his correspondent to show him the same respect and good will which he has received from others. He then gives instructions concerning some wine, but the details are lacking.

Χαίροις Παποντῶ,
Πτολεμαῖος σὲ ἀσπ[άζ(ομαι).
ὥσπερ ἐν οἷς τῷ ἀδελφ[ῷ
Διογένει παρεθέμην τ[ε
5 οὕτως τοτὲ ἐνέδειξαν
πρὸς ἐμὲ πᾶσαν εὔνοιαν
καὶ τ[ει]μὴν καὶ ὡς οὖν νῦν
δεηθεὶς θελήσεις καὶ αὐτὸς
τὴν αὐτὴν ἴσην εὔνοιαν

10   καὶ τειμὴν πρὸς ἐμὲ ἐν-
     δείξ[ασ]θαι. ε . . . κατὰ τὸν
     ἴδιον [τ]οῦ Παύλου οἶνον ἐφ' ἑ-

     . . . .

     On the verso:

          Παπουτῶιτι ✕ φιλ[τάτῳ
(Hand 2 ?) π(αρὰ) Πτολε(μαίου) προαιρέτῃ
15   γραιπ . . . .
                          9. ἰσην.   12. ἴδιον.

1. χαίροις. For this familiar form of address cf. Exler, *A Study in Greek Epistolography*, 35, 67-68, and Ghedini, *Lettere Cristiane*, 60. See also P. Iand. 12. 1. note.
2. Πτολεμαῖος σὲ ἀσπάζομαι. Cf. P. Lond. 144. 2 (for revised reading see Preisigke, BL., 266).
3. For ἐν οἷς = ἐν ᾧ see Liddell-Scott-Jones, s. v.
13. Παπουτῶιτι. It is difficult to account for the iota in the penult. *Iota adscriptum* is rarely, if ever, found at so late a date. Cf. Ἰναρῶιτος, as read by Kenyon in P. Lond. 50. 2 (Wilcken, U. P. Z. 116. 2, prefers, however, to read Ἰναρώυτος). Perhaps Παπουτῷ[ι should be read in line 1. For the use and meaning of the cross which frequently appears in the address see Ziemann, *De epistularum Graecarum formulis sollemnibus quaestiones selectae*, 281-282.

75. HOROSCOPE

Garrett Dep. 7668.   14.5 × 20 cm.   Provenance unknown.   138-161 A.D.

The concluding portion of the horoscope of a certain Ophellius born during the reign of Antoninus Pius (138-161 A.D.). An entire column in which the position of the heavenly bodies was recorded appears to have been lost. In the column which remains the location of four degrees (κλῆροι) is noted, together with explanatory observations. The exact date of the birth cannot be determined.

A complete list of horoscopes is presented by Sprey, P. Iand. 88, introd. For the dating of P. S. I. 22. 1-10 cf. Goodrich, *Archiv*, XII, 67 f.

     μοιρῶν] κ̄ᾱ οἴκῳ Κρόνου ὁρίοις Ἀφροδείτης.
       ὁ κ]λῆρος τῆς τύχης εὑρέθη Καρκίνῳ μοιρῶν ῑγ οἴκῳ Σε-
     λήνης ὁρίο]ις Ἑρμοῦ. οὗτος σημαίνει μέτρον τῆς τύχης.
       ὁ κλ]ῆρος ὁ τοῦ δαίμονος εὑρέθη Αἰγόκερῳ μοιρῶν κ̄ζ οἴκῳ
5   . . . .] . οὗτος σημαίνει τὸν περὶ ἤθους καὶ ἀγωγῆς τρόπον.
       ὁ κλῆρος ἔ]ρωτος εὑρέθη Ταύρῳ μοιρῶν δ̄ οἴκῳ καὶ ὁρίοις Ἄ-
     ρεως. οὗτος σημαίν]ει τὸν περὶ θέσεως καὶ συστάσεως
     τόπον. ὁ κλῆρος] τῆς ἀνάγκης εὑρέθη Κριῷ μοιρῶν ς̄ οἴκῳ Ἄρεως
     ὁρίοις . . . . . οὗ]τος σημαίνει τὸν περὶ ἐκχθρῶν καὶ παντὸ[ς] λαπ θου

75. HOROSCOPE

```
10      ............]τος.   ἕξετε πᾶν περὶ τοῦ οἰκοδεσπό-
        του ........] ἀστέρων ψῆφον ἐπικρατοῦντας πάντων δὲ
        ............]μι   ἀστέρων τὸν τοῦ Ἑρμοῦ ἀστέρα ἐσχηκότα
        ........] η [....]οσκο[..] τὸ τῆς οἰκοδεσποτείας βραβεῖον ἔσχατα
        ........]δεδει μῆνας ιγ μεθ' οὓς παρῆλθε τὸν σινωτικὸν
15   κλιμακτ]ηρικὸν ὅρον καὶ γείνεται ἡ ὑπόστασις ἀπὸ τοῦ οἰκοδε-
        σπότου.]           δι[ευτύχ]ει.
```

(Hand 2)   γένεσις Ὀ]φελλίου [(ἔτους)] Ἀντωνίνου [Κ]αίσαρος τοῦ κυρίου
.... ἀσ]τροθ[έσις] ὥρας ζ νυ[κτ]ός.

76. EROTIC INCANTATION

Garrett Dep. 7665.   8 × 14 cm.   Provenance unknown.   3rd cent. A.D.

Numerous magical papyri of an erotic nature have already been published. Among these may be cited the following texts reprinted by Preisendanz in his collection of magical papyri (*Papyri Graecae Magicae*): nos. 15, 16, 17a, 19a, 32, 32a, 39, and O 2.

The acrostic arrangement of magical words is frequently found in such texts. Cf. P. Gr. Mag. 17a, 19a, 33. The words used in the present instance appear to be new. Magical symbols somewhat similar to those found in line 11 are reproduced in P. Gr. Mag. II, pp. 170-171.

A lock of hair was originally affixed to the papyrus, a trace of which still remains. For the use of hair in magical papyri see Preisendanz, *Sexual-Probleme*, IX (1913), 614-615.

```
    .κο]αχαμφωνχωωθψαχε
        κοαχαμφωνχωωθψαχ
        οαχ[α]μι[φ]ωνχωωθψα
            αχαμφωνχωωθψ
5              χαμφωνχωωθ
                αμφωνχωω
                  μφωνχω
                    ιφωνχ
                      φων
10                      ω
```

(magical symbols, about ten in number)

ἄξον τὴν Πτολεμαίδα ἣν
ἔτεκεν Ἑλένη τῷ Πτολε-
μαίῳ ὃν ἔτεκεν Διδύ-
15   μη. πύρωσον τῆς αὐτῆς τὸ

```
            ἧπαρ καὶ τὸ πνεῦμα καὶ τὴν
            καρδίαν καὶ τὴν ψ[υ]χὴν ἕως
            ἂ]ν ἐκπηδήσασ[α
            ἐλ]θῃ ἡ Πτολεμ[α]ὶς ἣν ἔτε-
    20      κεν Ἑλένη πρ[ὸς] τὸν Πτολεμαῖον
            ὃν ἔτεκεν Διδ[ύ]μη, ἤδη, ταχύ.
```

14. ετε[....]κεν.   18. A short line.

1. The use of Egyptian magical formulae was not confined to that land. A magical phrase almost identical with phrases appearing in papyrus texts has been identified in a maledictory inscription (on lead) recently discovered in Athens. Cf. G. W. Elderkin, *Hesperia*, V (1936), 43-49. Names of probable Egyptian origin occurring in this inscription suggest that in this instance the phrase was employed by an Egyptian residing in Athens. It cannot therefore be inferred that the use of Egyptian magical formulae was widespread among native Athenians.

17-19. ἕως . . . ἔλθῃ. Cf. P. Gr. Mag. 19a. 51.

77. Petition to the Prefect

Garrett Dep. 7636.   13.5 × 22.5 cm.   Oxyrhynchus.   Early 4th cent. A.D.

The approximate date of this petition is assured by the hand and suggests the possible identification of Aurelia Isarion (line 7) with a woman of like name who appears in P. Oxy. 1206 (335 A.D.). The details of the petition remain obscure, but it appears that the *patria potestas* (line 4) of the petitioner (?) is in some manner connected with the question at issue. For the jurisdiction of the prefect in such cases see Reinmuth, *The Prefect of Egypt from Augustus to Diocletian* (*Klio*, 34. Beiheft), 108-109.

Only the right half of the text has been preserved, the papyrus having been divided along a vertical fold. The text may have been complete when discovered, for the two halves could easily have become separated and thus have found their way into different collections. The probable interest of the complete text inspires the hope that the remaining portion may some day come to light.

```
                        τῷ διασημοτά]τῳ ἐ[πά]ρχῳ Αἰγύπτου
    παρὰ                ο]ἰκοῦντος ἐν τῇ λαμπρᾷ καὶ λαμπροτάτῃ
    πόλει τῶν Ὀξυρυγχιτῶν    ]εν τῷ πρ[ὸ]ς τὸν ἄνδρα τῆς συμβιώσεως
                        ἐ]ξουσίαν τῷ ἀνδρὶ κατὰ τὰς περὶ τῶν
    5                   ]μαι μηδένα λανθάνειν μάλιστα
                        ]υν εἰκότως καὶ αὐτὸς ἐρώμενος τὴν
                Αὐρή]λια Ἰσάριον πρὸς ἣν πάντα απλοη
                        ] λετην τῷ καὶ παιπαιδοποιῆσθαί με ἐξ αὐ-
    τῆς         τοι]γαροῦν αὐτὴν ἐκ τῆς τῶν ἡμετέρων
```

77. PETITION TO THE PREFECT

10   ] καὶ μέχρι αὐτοῦ τούτου πρίασθαι οἰκίαν
ἀμφόδου Δρό]μου Γυμνασίου παρὰ Αὐρηλίας Βησοῦτος
      ]ντος ἑαυτῆς συντάξασθαι ἐμοῦ κατὰ τοῦτο
      τ]ῶν γραμματείων ἀλλὰ πρὸς τὴν τῶν νο-
      ] κυρουμένην γῆν ὅτι καὶ παρὰ τοῦ
15   ] τῆς ἀξιώσεως βιβλία ἀνατείνω τῷ
      ] δι' εὐεργετικωτάτης σου ὑπογραφῆς ἐπι-
      ]τας ὁμολογήσω.   εὐτυχεῖ.
ἐπ]ίδοσιν.

7. ἰσαριον.   18. επ]ιδιξιν has been altered to επ]ιδοσιν.

78. PETITION TO THE *Proximi* OF A CITY

Garrett Dep. 7690.   13 × 14.5 cm.   Provenance unknown.   6th cent. A.D.

The beginning of a petition to the *proximi* of an un-named city in which the appellant seemingly complains that, although he has released a certain Acous, son of Apollo, in the presence of seven witnesses, he has not yet received in return the sum of 2 carats. Acous had perhaps completed a term of service in lieu of the interest on a loan contracted by his father. For such contracts, known as παραμοναί, see Schönbauer, *Sav. Zeit.*, LIII (1933), 435 ff., and Westermann-Hasenoehrl, P. Col. III, p. 38, who cite additional literature on the subject. A list of παραμοναί is supplied by Zambon, *Aegyptus*, XIII (1933), 653.

Φλαουίοις Σαραπάμμωνι καὶ Σερήνῳ
τοῖς αἰδεσίμ(οις) πρωξίμ(οις) ταύτης τῆς πόλεως
      π(αρὰ) Φιλοξένου ἀπὸ τῆς αὐτῆς.
αὐτίκ' ἀπήλλαξα πρὸς Ἀπόλλων⟨α⟩
5   τὸν υἱὸν Ἀκοῦτα ἐπὶ ἑπτὰ μαρτύρων
    ἱκανῶν καὶ μετὰ πολλὰς ἡμέρας
    τῆς ἀντικαταλλαγῆς καὶ ἔτι
..] [...] ων μοι δύο κεράτια ὑπὲρ
                          ] της εν
10   ]ενων προ
               ] πᾶσι (?) ἔχω (?)
               ]ριν παρ κ τω

1. φλαουιοις.   2. υιον.   3. ικανων.   4. απηλλαξα.   8. υπερ.

79. DIVISION OF AN INHERITANCE

Garrett Dep. 7667.   19 × 8.5 cm.   Oxyrhynchus.   326 A.D.

An agreement between three brothers to divide an inheritance received from their father. The details of the agreement are hopelessly obscured by the loss of about 35 letters from the end of each line, as well as by the loss of the concluding lines. The papyrus was folded vertically into six sections, two of which, at the extreme right, became detached along a fold and were thus lost.

Agreements of this nature are not uncommon, a list of the more important texts being presented by Mitteis, *Grundzüge*, 270 (cf. Kreller, *Erbrechtliche Untersuchungen*, 77, note 4). This material is carefully analyzed by Kreller, *ibid.*, 75 ff. For additional literature see Meyer, *Jur. Pap.*, 176.

The term regularly applied in the papyri to such agreements is διαίρεσις. The use of the Attic equivalent, διάλυσις, has been hitherto confined to texts from the late Byzantine period (cf. Kreller, *op. cit.*, 78). The present text thus provides the earliest occurrence of this term as applied to divisions of inheritances.

Ὑπατείας τῶν δεσποτῶν ἡμῶ[ν Κ]ωνσταντίνου τοῦ Σ[εβ(αστοῦ) τὸ ζ] καὶ
  Κωνσταντίου [τοῦ ἐπιφανεστάτου Καίσαρος τὸ α, month, day.
Αὐρήλιοι Ὡρίων καὶ Εὐδαίμων [καὶ] Εὐλόγιος οἱ τρῖς ἐκ πατ[ρὸς Δ]ιονυσίου
  Διοσκουρί[δου   ὁ προ-]
δηλούμενος ἡμῶν πατὴρ Διον[ύσιο]s τὸν βίον διεξῆλθεν, ἡμῖς δὲ οἱ τούτου
  πέδαις [εὐ-]
τρεπίσαι ἡμᾶς ἀποσχέσθαι τῆ[ς] πρὸς ἀλλήλους φιλονηκείας καὶ διάλυσιν
  ηκε [
5 ἔδοξεν [ἡ]μᾶς τοὺς τρῖς ἐπὶ τῶν ἐ[α]υτῶν μερῶν τὴν διάλυσιν ποιήσασθαι πρὸς
  ἑα[υτοὺς   Ὡρίωνι ?]
καὶ Εὐδαίμωνι ἀργυρίου τάλαντα [ἑβ]δομήκοντα πέ⟨ν⟩ται πρὸς τὸ ἔχιμ μαι
  τοῦ μέρ[ους
ἀρουρῶν τὰς μὲν οὔσας ἐπ' ὀνόμ[α]τος τοῦ πατρὸς περὶ κώμην Σενέπτα
  . [πα-]
ραχωρὶν ὅσων ἐὰν ἦ ἡμῖς δύο τε Ὡρίων καὶ Εὐδαίμων πρὸς τὴν τρίτην [
τοῦ ἐκδικουμένου ὑφ' ἡμῶν μέ[ρο]υς ἥμισυ μέρος, ὅσον ἐὰν ἐπὶ δὲ τῶν
  ἀρουρ[ῶν
10 σ . . . [. . . . .] . . . . αιτ[ca. 25 letters]ν ἥμισου προσωπ[
                              ]ερισ συ . [

3. Read παῖδες.   6. Read ἔχειν με.   7–8. Read πα/ραχωρεῖν.

6. πέ⟨ν⟩ται (= πέντε). For the dropping of ν before a dental see Mayser, *Grammatik*, I, 191. ἔχιμ μαι (= ἔχειν με). ν is frequently assimilated before μ. Cf. Mayser, *ibid.*, 230.

8. ὅσων ἐάν. See **68**. 7, note.

80. Order for Payment of Money

Garrett Dep. 7643.   12.5 × 8.5 cm.   Oxyrhynchus.   About 337 A.D.

An order from Aphthonius to pay twenty talents to a wool-merchant for some purpose connected with the landlord's house. The same person issues a similar order in P. Oxy. 92. Our text can be dated approximately from the latter (see Preisigke, BL., p. 315). Aphthonius appears also in P. Oxy. 1303.

Although the text on the verso is poorly preserved, enough remains to show that it is related in some manner to that on the recto. It is not unlikely that Ἐφελίῳ (line 6), the overseer, is identical with the Ophellius to whom the order is given in P. Oxy. 92. The reading Ὀφελλίῳ is definitely excluded.

Π(αρὰ) Ἀφθονίου.
ἀπὸ λόγ(ου) ὧν παρέχις ἀργυρίων π[αράσχες
Ἀσίνῳ Ἀρσᾶ ἐριεμπ[ό]ρ[ῳ   8-12   τὴν
γεουχικὴν οἰκίαν ἀργυρίου [τάλαντ-
5 α εἴκοσι. σεσημίωμαι.

On the verso:

(Hand 2 ?) Ἐφελίῳ προνοητῇ χαί(ρειν).
λογ   [...] παρέχις εἰς λόγ(ον) ..

Traces of letters visible in an additional line.

81. Repayment of a Loan

Garrett Dep. 7677a.   9 × 11.5 cm.   Oxyrhynchus.   344 A.D.

Receipt for the repayment of a mixed loan of wheat and money. Both the quantity of wheat and the exact amount of money involved cannot be determined, owing to the loss of words at the ends of lines 13 and 15.

Traces of three completely illegible lines on the verso.

Ὑπα]τείας Φλαου[ίων Λεοντίου
ἐπ]άρχου τοῦ ἱεροῦ π[ραιτωρίου
καὶ Σ]αλουστίου κόμιτος, [month, day.
Αὐρ]ήλιος Τιθοῆς Τ[ιθοῆτος

5 ἀπὸ] τῆς Ὀξυρυγχιτῶν [π]όλεως
γέρ]διος τὴν τέχνην δι' ἐμοῦ
τ]ῆς γυναικὸς |Σο]φίας
Α]ὐρηλίῳ Κολλ[ούθῳ 4-8 letters
ἀ]πὸ τῆς αὐτῆς [πόλεως
10 χαίρειν. ὁμολ[ογῶ ἀπέχειν
παρὰ σοῦ εἰς λ[όγον τῶν ὑπὸ
σοῦ χρεωστ[ουμένων
σί]του ἀρτάβας [6-10 letters
μ]όνας καὶ [τάλαντα
15 ἓ]ξ καὶ δραχμ[ὰς χιλίας. ?
κυ]ρία ἡ ἀποχ[ὴ δισσὴ γραφ(εῖσα), ?
κ]αὶ ἐπερωτ[ηθεὶς ὡμολό-
γησα] ωτη [

82. DIALYSIS

AM 8961.   30 × 111.5 cm.   Lycopolis.   481 A.D.

The complete text of this dialysis has already appeared in three separate publications. Following its initial publication by H. B. Dewing (*T. A. P. A.*, LIII [1922], 113 ff.) it was reprinted, with minor alterations, by Bilabel (SB. 7033) and again by Ensslin (*Rh. Mus.*, LXXV [1926], 422 ff.), detailed commentaries being contributed by both Dewing and Ensslin (cf. *Sav. Zeit.*, XLVI [1926], 344 ff. and L [1930], 198 f.). But, as has already been explained (*T. A. P. A.*, LXV [1934], l-li), a re-examination of the original makes possible a drastic revision of the opening lines and justifies the publication once more of this portion of the text.

The revision principally involves the more precise location of a sizable fragment which was assigned by previous editors to an uncertain position between lines 5 and 12. It is now apparent that this fragment contains portions of lines 6-8. Moreover, the lines which were formerly numbered 12-15 can now be identified as the ends of lines 6-9. Thus in its revised form the text runs continuously through lines 5-10, there being no lacuna between lines 5c and 12 as previously assumed. Line 10 of the revised text corresponds accordingly to line 16 as designated by previous editors.

The revised text of lines 1-18 is presented below.[1] In addition other revisions are noted separately as they occur in lines 19 ff., chief among these

---

[1] Several new readings suggested by Mr. H. I. Bell in 1924 (in a letter to Professor Dewing) have been confirmed (with slight modification in two instances) in the course of this study. These include: π[οιοῦσιν πρὸς ἑαυτο]ύς (3); κ[αθολικῆς] (4); [τοῦ τῆς ε]ὐλαβοῦς [μνήμης] (6); [τοὺς προγεγρ]αμμένους (9); ἐγκειμέν[οις] τῇ ἀπο[σταλ]ίσῃ παρ' αὐτ[ῶν] (11); πρὸς τ[ὸν αὐ]τόν (25); σκιωδόν (38).

being the addition of line 94 and the inclusion of the docket found on the verso. To facilitate reference to these scattered revisions (lines 19 ff.) the original line numbers, as given by Dewing, have been retained. The position of lines 6 ff. in the revised text can be readily determined, however, by subtracting six from the older line numbers.

℣

Τοῖς μετὰ τὴν ὑπατείαν τοῦ δεσπότου ἡμῶν Φλ(αουίου) Ζήνωνος τοῦ αἰωνίου Αὐγούστου
   τὸ γ̅///, Φαρμοῦθι ᾱ///, τετάρτης ἰνδικτί(ονος), ἐν Λύκων πόλει τῇ λαμπρᾷ.
[ταύτ]ην π[οιοῦνται πρὸς ἐαυτο]ὺς τὴν κοινὴν ὁ[μο]λ[ογ]ία[ν τ]ῆς διαλύσεως ἐκ μὲν τοῦ ἑνὸς
[μέρους Κῦρ]ος θεοφιλέστατος [ἐπίσ]κοπος τῆς κ[αθολικῆς Λ]υκοπολιτῶν ἁγίας τοῦ θεοῦ
5 [ἐκκλησίας] καὶ Δανιήλι[ος καὶ 'Αρείων ε]ὐλαβ(έστατοι) πρ[εσβ(ύτεροι) οἱ τρ]εῖς ὁμογνήσιοι [ἀδ]ε[λ]φοὶ
[ἐκ πατρ]ὸς το[ῦ τ]ῆ[ς] εὐλαβοῦς μ[ν]ήμης [Βησᾶ, ἐκ δὲ θατέρου Θεόφιλος] 'Απόλλωνος
[διάκονος] τῆς αὐτῆ[ς ἁ]γίας τοῦ θεοῦ ἐκκλη[σίας. ὁμολογοῦμεν ἀλλήλοις τ]ὰ ὑπο-
[τεταγμένα. χ]αίρειν. μικρῷ πρότερον ὁ προσημ[ανθεὶς Θεόφιλος καταλαβ]ὼν τὸ μέγα
α[ὐγου]σταλιανὸ[ν διὰ λιβέλλου αἰτι]άσε[ως ᾐτιάσατο τοὺς προγεγρ]αμμένους
10 Κῦρον τὸν θεοσεβ(έστατον) ἐ[πίσκοπον καὶ Δανιήλιον καὶ 'Αρείωνα τοὺς ε]ὐλαβ(εστάτους) π[ρ]εσβυτέρους
ἐπὶ φανεροῖς κεφαλαίοις τοῖς καὶ ἐγκειμέν[οις] τῇ ἀπο[σταλ]είσῃ παρ' αὐτοῦ ἐντεύξει,
καὶ διαλελάληται Κῦρον μὲν τὸν θεοφιλέστατον ἐπίσκοπον καταλαμβάνοντα
τὸ μέγα ἐκεῖνο δικαστήριον τὰς προσούσας αὐτῷ ἐκθέσθαι δικαιολογίας,
εἰ μὴ ἕλοιτο πρὸ δίκης ἐπιλύειν τὰ ἐναγόμενα, Δανιήλιον δὲ καὶ 'Αρείωνα τοὺς
15 εὐλαβ(εστάτους) αὐτοῦ ἀδελφοὺς ἐξ ἀντιρρήσεως πα[ρ]ὰ Μακαρίῳ τῷ [ἐλλ]ογιμωτά⟨τῳ⟩ συνηγόρῳ
τοῦ Θηβαίων φόρου δικάσασθαι. καὶ τούτων δ[ιαλελαλημένων ὁμο]λογία συντέθηται
μεταξ[ὺ] Θεοφίλου [το]ῦ προγεγραμμένου [διακόνου καὶ] Δανιηλίου καὶ 'Αρείωνος
18 τῶν εὐλαβ(εστάτων) ἐν τῇ α[ὐτ]ῇ [ἡμ]έρ[ᾳ ....]ο [.....ἐ]ν Λ[ύκω]ν [πό]λει, καθ' ἣν ὡμολόγησαν
κ.τ.λ.
25 προθεσμίας ἀπαντῆ[σα]ι πρὸς τὸ[ν α]ὐτόν.
- 38 σκιωδόν. Read σκιωτόν. Cf. P. Oxy. 921. 15, note.
68 εἴς τε πρόσωπον εἴς τε πρᾶγμα.

70 ὑ[π]εναντίον.
86 διάκονος.
87 ταύτη[ν] ⟨τὴν⟩ διάλυσιν (no room in lacuna for τήν).
90 Κολλοῦθος.
91 Αὐρήλιος Διονύσιος Σοῖτος μαρτιρῶ.
92 Αὐρήλιος Ἰοβῖνος Ἀκώριος.
93 μαρ[τυρῶ] τῇ διαλύσει ἀκούσα[ς] παρὰ τῶν διαλυσαμένων. (signature in shorthand?). ℞ Αὐρήλιος Βησᾶς.
94 .... μαρτυρῶ τ]ῇ δ[ι]αλύσει ἀκούσας [παρὰ τῶν διαλυσαμένων] [. . .].
95 Docket on verso. ℞ κοινὴ διάλυσ(ις) Κύρου θεοσεβεσ(τάτου) ἐπισκ(όπου) κ[α]ὶ [ἑ]τ[έ]ρων ἀδελφ(ῶν) κ[αὶ] Θεοφί[λου].

83. Declaration of Payment of Money out of a Deposit

Garrett Dep. 7887a.   16 × 17 cm.   Oxyrhynchus.   5th cent. A.D.

A statement addressed by a secretary to a certain unnamed count certifying apparently that a payment of 4 solidi, less 16 carats, weighed in accordance with the private standard of the Oxyrhynchites, has been made from his deposit to a woman whose name has been lost, leaving a balance of 16 carats on deposit.

Χ Μ Γ

]ο( ) κόμμε(τι) Ὀλύμ-
πιος σκρινιάριος
χαίρειν.   ἐκ τῆς σῆς] θέσεως ἐκ τῶν τεσ-
σάρων νομισμάτων
] Ἡρακλέους διὰ Θεο-
δώρου τοῦ αὐτῆς
5 συμβίου ?   νομίσματα τέ]σσαρα παρὰ κεράτια
δεκαὲξ ἰδιωτικῷ
ζυγῷ Ὀξυρύγχων, (γιν.) νο(μ.) δ π(αρὰ) κερ( ) ιϛ ἰδιωτι]κῷ ζυγῷ Ὀξυρύγχων, ὡς λοιπάζεσθαι
κεράτια δεκαὲξ   ]α καὶ πρὸς σὴν ἀσφάλειαν ταύτην
πεποίημαι τὴν ἀπόδειξιν ?   καὶ βεβαι]ῶ ὡς πρόκειται. †

2. κομμ ∫. Read κόμε(τι).   3. νομισματων.   5. ἰδιωτικω.
7. πρὸς σὴν ἀσφάλειαν. For the omission of the article cf. P. Oxy. 2003. 11. Cf. 94. 3-4.

84. Sale of a House

Garrett Dep. 7887b.   16.5 × 17.5 cm.   Provenance unknown.   5th (?) cent. A.D.

The conclusion of a contract for the sale of a house together with the appurtenances thereof. The vendors, Serenus and Euphemia, acknowledge receipt of the purchase price, the amount of which appears to have been stated differently by the two vendors (cf. lines 7 and 12). The two statements might be harmonized by reading ἑ[κατὸν δεκαπέντε κ. τ. λ.] in line 7 and by restoring ἑκατόν at the end of line 11. But 115 gold solidi would represent a remarkably high price for a house. In a well preserved analogous text (P. Lond. 1722, reprinted by Hunt-Edgar, *Select Papyri*, 30) from the year 573 A.D. the sale of a rather large house is recorded at a price of only 18 solidi. Moreover, on the assumption that the correct restorations have been supplied for the lacunae at the ends of lines 4 and 5, there would not be sufficient space for more than about 9-11 letters in the corresponding lacuna in line 7. The same objection can be raised against reading νομισμάτια ϵ [κερ(άτια) ιϵ κ. τ. λ.] in line 7 (with the corresponding restoration in line 11). Perhaps each vendor included in his declaration only that portion of the purchase price which fell to his lot individually. If such was the case, the vendors received a total of 21 solidi for their property.

Although Serenus wrote his own acknowledgment in crude uncials, it would appear that Colluthus (line 13) wrote on behalf of Euphemia. The names of the witnesses have been lost at the bottom.

On the verso there is an extensive Coptic fragment.

```
         .   .   .   .   .   .   .   .   .   .
    φιωο( ) [        ]μενο( ) παρ[
    εἰς πάντα τ[ὰ προγ]εγραμμέν[α] τ[
    φ     ιειν ὡμολογήσαμεν. ⊢. (Hand 2) Σερ[ῆνος τοῦ δεῖνος
    πέπρακα ἅμα Εὐφημίᾳ [τὴν προκει-
5   μένην οἰκίαν ὁλόκληρον σ[ὺν χρηστηρί-
    οις καὶ ἀπέσχον ἅμα [αὐτῇ      ?
    χρυσοῦ νομισμάτια ἑ[ξ ? καὶ βεβαι-
    ῶ ὡς πρόκ(ειται) {καὶ} πληρωθ[εὶς τὴν τιμήν. ?
(Hand 3) Εὐφημία Ἰωάννου μονάζουσα ἡ προκε[ιμένη πέπρακα
10  τὴν προκειμένην οἰκίαν ὁλόκληρον σὺν χρ[ηστηρίοις καὶ ἀπέσ-
    χον ἅμμα αὐτῷ τὰ τῆς [τιμῆς            χρυσοῦ νομισμάτια]
    δεκαπέντε κ[αὶ β]ε[βαιῶ τὴν πρᾶσιν ὡς πρόκειται. ?        ]
    Κολλοῦθος Ἀμ[        ἔγραψα ὑπὲρ αὐτῆς γράμματα μὴ εἰδυίας ?]
    τὴ]ν πρ[ᾶ]σ[ιν    ]κ [
```

85. SALE OF A SLAVE

Garrett Dep. 7658.   17 × 24.5 cm.   Provenance unknown.   5th (?) cent. A.D.

Fragment of a contract giving the terms of a sale of a slave. Of especial interest is the reference to the acquisition of a peculium (line 13). For a better preserved contract of the same nature cf. P. Lond. 251. On the verso there is found a fragment of an apparently unrelated account.

. . . .

Traces of letters from three lines, then:

ἢ μέτοχοι [.] . [..] . . . πεχ[
αὐτοῦ α   ημερ   [
δικαίῳ ἀνεμποδίστω[ς
ἐφ' ἅπερ πεπραμέν[α
5 ους ἐπελεύσεται ει[
Ἰωάννης οὐ τέκνα [οὐ   οὐ κληρονόμοι
ο]ὐ διάδοχοι οὐ διακ[άτοχοι
ο[ὐ τῷ μέλλοντι χρ[όνῳ
τὸν οἵῳ δήποται τ[ρόπῳ, τὸν δὲ καὶ ἐπελευσόμενον ?
10 ἢ ἀντιποιησόμενον [
τινι χρώμενον κ [τοῦ πεπρα-
μένου δούλου ἢ κατα[
ἐπικτήσασθαι πεκούλ[ιον
Ἰωάννης καὶ τέκνα [καὶ   καὶ κληρονόμοι
15 καὶ διάδοχοι καὶ δι[ακάτοχοι
ἀποστήσωμ[ε]ν καὶ ἐ[κδικήσομεν παραχρῆμα τοῖς
οἰκίοις αὐτῶν δαπ[ανήμασι   ἀπο-
στήσωσ[ι]ν ἀλλ' ὁ πε[πραμμένος ?
 . . . . σιν τοτε [

. . . .

6, 14. ϊωαννης.   10, 12. ῆ.

86. ORDER FOR DELIVERY OF OIL

Garrett Dep. 7889a.   14 × 5.5 cm.   Provenance unknown.   6th (?) cent. A.D.

An order from Joseph, a senator, addressed to Phoebammon, an oil manufacturer, instructing him to deliver two xestae of oil to the servants of Aconis, a *tractator*. The nearest parallels appear to be B. G. U. 960 ff. (= P. kl. Form. 888 ff.).

The five letters preceding the signature seem to have been written in shorthand.

86. ORDER FOR DELIVERY OF OIL

Φοιβάμμωνι ἐλαιουργ(ῷ) Ἰωσὴφ βου(λευτής).
παράσχ(ου) τοῖς παιδαρ(ίοις) Ἀειώνιος
τρακ(τευτοῦ) (ὑπὲρ) ἀναλ(ώματος) ἐλαίου ξέστας δύο, γί(νονται) ἐλ(αίου)
(ξέσται) β.
Φαρμοῦθι κ̄ᾱ, ἰνδ(ικτίονος) α⁄⁄. . . . . . signature.

On the verso:

5 ξ(έσται) β.

1. ιωσηφ.

87. LOAN WITH SURETY

AM 8966.   8.5 × 15 cm.   Oxyrhynchus.   612 A.D.

An acknowledgment of a loan of three solidi from Aurelius Phib, doorkeeper of the Church of St. Theodore, to Aurelius George, from the estate of Great Taruthinus in the Oxyrhynchite nome. The contract was drawn by Serenus, who appears as surety for George.

† Ἐν ὀνόμ]ατι τοῦ κυρίου καὶ δεσπ(ότου)
Ἰησοῦ] Χριστοῦ τοῦ θεοῦ καὶ σωτῆρ(ος)
ἡμ]ῶν, βασιλείας τοῦ θειοτάτου
καὶ εὐσεβ(εστάτου) ἡμῶν δεσπ(ότου) μεγίστ(ου)
5   εὐεργ(έτου) Φλ(αουίου) Ἡρακλείου τοῦ αἰων(ίου)
Α]ὐγούστου καὶ Αὐτοκρ(άτορος) θ(?) ἔτους
δευτέρου, Τῦβι λ, ἰνδ(ικτίονος) ιε.
Αὐρήλιος Γεώργιος υἱὸς Φοιβάμμωνος
μητρὸς Ἴσιδος μετ' ἐγγυητοῦ
10 ἐμοῦ Σερήνου υἱοῦ Σουροῦτος
μητρὸς Ἴσιδος ἑτέρας
ὁρμώμ(ενος) ἀπὸ κτήμ(ατος) Μεγάλ(ου)
Ταρουθίνου τοῦ Ὀξυρυγχίτου
ν[ο]μοῦ Αὐρηλίῳ Φὶβ θυρουρῷ
15 τοῦ ἁγίου Θεοδώρου υἱῷ
Ἀπφου⟨ᾶ⟩ ἀπὸ τῆς Ὀξυρυγχ(ιτῶν) πόλ(εως).
ὁμολογ[ῶ ἐσ]χηκέναι παρὰ σοῦ
ἐντεῦθεν ἤδη χρυσοῦ νομισ(μάτια)
τρία ἰδιωτικῷ ζυγῷ, γί(νεται) χρ(υσοῦ)
20 νο(μισμάτια) [γ] ἰδιω(τικῷ) ζυγῷ, ἃ κ[αὶ ὁμολογῶ
[ἀποδοῦναί σοι κ.τ.λ.   ]

On the verso:

22 † γρ]α(μμάτιον)
Αὐρηλίου Γ]εωργίου υἱοῦ Φοιβάμμωνος μετ' ἐγγ[υητοῦ κ.τ.λ.

8. φοιβαμμω. ^νος 9, 11. ἴσιδος. 10, 15. υἰω. 14. θηρουρω corrected to θυρουρω.

1-6. For the dating formulae under Heraclius see Bell, *Byz. Zeit.*, XXII (1913), 395-405. See especially p. 403 for the formula used at Oxyrhynchus. Nothing similar to the enigmatic θ( ) (line 6) appears in other documents from this reign. It is impossible to read Αὐτοκρά(τορος). The θ stands relatively high in the line and seems to mark an abbreviation.
12-13. κτήμ(ατος) Μεγάλ(ου) Ταρουθίνου. Cf. P. Oxy. 135. 13-14.
14-15. θυρουρῷ τοῦ ἁγίου Θεοδώρου. Cf. P. Oxy. 141. 3-4.
16. The omission of χαίρειν is noteworthy.

88. ACCOUNT OF ARREARS OF WINE

Garrett Dep. 7682b.   12 × 5.5 cm.   Oxyrhynchus.   5th cent. A.D.

A statement showing arrears of wine, amounting to 13½ cnidia (?), to be collected from two vine-dressers residing in the village of Nesus Leucadiou.

Ἔχθ(εσις) οἴν(ου) ἐποικ(ίου) Νήσου Λευκαδίου ∫ ἰνδ(ικτίονος)
π(αρὰ) Κοσμᾶ ἀμ(πελουργοῦ)   (κνίδια ?) εL
π(αρὰ) Ἀνοῦπ ἀμ(πελουργοῦ)   (κνίδια ?) η
γί(νεται) οἴν(ου) (κνίδια ?) ιγL.

89. RECEIPT FOR POLL-TAX (διαγραφή)

Garrett Dep. 7681a.   15.5 × 4.5 cm.   Provenance unknown.   6th cent. A.D.

Receipt for 3½ carats paid on account of the poll-tax (διαγραφή).

† Δέδωκ(εν) ὄνο(μα ?) ὡς Διοσκόρου (ὑπὲρ) Φοιβάμ[μω]ν[ο]ς
(ὑπὲρ) διαγραφ(ῆς) β ἰνδ(ικτίονος) χρυσοῦ κερ(άτια) τρία ἥμισυ,
γί(νεται) κ(ερ.) γL (μόνα ?),
καὶ ἑτοίμως ἔχω ἐνεγκεῖν σοι ἐντάγι(ον) τοῦ ὑποδέκτ(ου) τῆς
πόλ(εως) καὶ ἀναλαβεῖν τὸ ἐμόν. † Πέτρος δι ( ) στοιχεῖ μοι.

4. δι ( ). The reading διάκ(ονος) appears to be excluded.

90. RECEIPTS FOR μερισμός

Garrett Dep. 7623b.   8 × 4 cm.   Kerkesoucha Orous.   6th-7th cent. A.D.

This and the following receipt (91) were written by the same hand and issued to the same person in different months of the same year. Among

90. RECEIPTS FOR μερισμός

analogous receipts are P. kl. Form. 607 and 834. The μερισμός at this period was a general term denoting the tax quota. Cf. Preisigke, *Fachwörter*, s. v. In the present instance it was paid in unequal installments of 22¼, 14, and 3⅜ (cf. 91) carats.

† Ἀθὺρ ις, μερ(ισμοῦ) τρίτης ἰνδ(ικτίονος) Κερκεσούχω(ν)
Ὄρρους Μακαρίου Κερέκου κερ(άτια)
εἴκοσι δύο τέταρ(τον), (γίνεται) κβδ΄, μό(να) προσάπαξ.
† δ(ι᾽) ἐμοῦ Γεωργίου σὺ(ν) θ(εῷ) γρ(αμματέως). † /ξ
5 † Χοι(ὰκ) κγ, ὁ αὐτ(ὸς) κερ(άτια) δεκατέσσαρ(α), [(γίνεται)] ιδ μό(να)
προσάπαξ. † δ[(ι᾽)] ἐ[μο]ῦ [Γεωργίου σὺ(ν) θ(εῷ) γρ(αμματέως). † /ξ ?]

1-2. Κερκεσούχ(ων) Ὄρρους. That the name of this village was Κερκεσούχα Ὄρους (not Κερκεσούχων Ὄρος) is demonstrated by Boak, P. Mich. II, p. 6.
4, 7. At the end of these lines there is a signature (?) in shorthand resembling in shape the letter ξ as printed in the text, and with a diagonal introductory stroke. Cf. 91. 5.

91. RECEIPT FOR μερισμός

Garrett Dep. 7616.   6.5 × 6 cm.   Kerkesoucha Orous.   6th-7th cent. A.D.

Written by the same hand and issued to the same individual as 90.

† Μεχεὶρ ς, μερισμοῦ τρίτης ἰνδ(ικτίονος)
Κερκεσούχω(ν) Ὄρρους Μακαρίου
Κερέκου κερ(άτια) τρία τέταρτ(ον)
ὄγδο(ον), γί(νεται) (κεράτια) γδ΄η΄, μό(να) προσάπαξ.
5 † δ[(ι᾽)] ἐμοῦ Γεωργίου σὺ(ν) θ(εῷ) γρ(αμματέως). ξ

5. For the symbol at the end of the line see note to 90. 4, 7.

92. RECEIPT FOR POLL-TAX (ἀνδρισμός)

Garrett Dep. 7620.   7.5 × 14 cm.   Provenance unknown.   6th-7th cent. A.D.

This receipt for the payment of poll-tax (ἀνδρισμός) is similar to P. Lond. 1745-1750. There are differences in the formula, however, especially in lines 3-4, where the meaning of the abbreviations is uncertain. Nothing analogous to this receipt appears among the texts published in P. kl. Form. The present text records the payment of a sixth of a solidus.

† Θὼθ ι, ἔσχ(ον) διὰ Σουῖρος
ἀνδηρμὸς δεικάτης
ἰ(ν)δ(ικτίονος) ἀρ(ί)θ(μιον) ς΄ ἕκτον ἀ(πὸ) μη(νὸς)
Πα(ῦνι). Φοι(βάμμ)ω(ν) παῖ(ς ?) στοιχε(ῖ). †

2. Read ἀνδρισμόν.

2. ἀνδηρμός (= ἀνδρισμός). An interesting example of the metathesis of ρ. Cf. Mayser, Grammatik, I, 189-190.
3. ἀρίθμιον. Sc. νόμισμα. For the difference between νομίσματα ἀρίθμια and νομίσματα ἐχόμενα see P. Lond. IV, pp. 84-86.

93. Receipt for ἐμβολή

AM 8967.   10.5 × 5 cm.   Hermopolite (?) nome.   7th cent. A.D.

Receipt for thirty artabae of wheat collected for the ἐμβολή, or land-tax (cf. Wilcken, Grundzüge, 235, 371, P. Lond. IV, p. xxvi, and Hardy, *The Large Estates of Byzantine Egypt*, 19).

† Ἐμβολ(ῆς) ἀπὸ χω(ρίου) Μοιρῶ(ν) ὀκδόεις ἰνδ(ικτίονος)
δι(ὰ) Ἰωάννου τόπ(ο)υ Ἐρεμίας σίτου ἀρτάβας
τριάκοντα μοδί(ῳ) σωλ(ηνικῷ ?), γί(νονται) σί(του) ἀρ(τάβαι) λ
μοδί(ῳ) σωλ(ηνικῷ ?).
ἐγρά(φη) μη(νὸς) Ἐπὶφ ιβ, ἰνδ(ικτίονος) η. Βίκτωρ ος στοι[χεῖ].

1. Read ὀγδόης.   2. τοπ̄ (cf. P. kl. Form, p. 236). ερεμίας. Read Ἰερεμίου (?). Cf. P. Oxy. 1137. 5.   4. ἴβ. Read ὥς (?).

3. μοδ(ίῳ) σωλ(ηνικῷ ?). Measured in the *tubular* modius measure. For the word see P. Oxy. 1002 (cf. Preisigke, BL.).

94. Receipts for δημόσια

Garrett Dep. 7613.   25 × 6 cm.   Provenance unknown.   7th cent. A.D.

Two receipts written by the same hand but issued to different parties. The first of these records the payment of $2^{7}/_{24}$ carats on account of the δημόσια. The second receipt is badly mutilated, but it may be assumed that it too records a payment (16 carats) of δημόσια. Either the land-tax in particular or the public taxes in general may be intended (cf. P. Lond. 1740, introd.).

†
† Τόπ(ος) Ἑρμαίων(ος) ἀ(πὸ) τῶν κλ(ηρονόμων).   † Κολλοῦθος ὦ καὶ
Στέ(φανος) ἐδεξάμην καὶ ἐπληρ(ώθην) παρὰ σοῦ (ὑπὲρ) δημοσί(ων) ἕκτης ἰνδ(ικτίονος)
(ὑπὲρ) τρίτου μέρ(ους) χρυσοῦ κερ(άτια) δύο ἕκτον ὄγδοο(ν), γί(νεται)
κ(εράτια) β ̄ϛ̄η̄, καὶ πρὸς
ὑμετέρ(αν) ἀσφάλεια(ν) πεποίημαι τ(ὴν) ἀπόδειξ(ιν) ὡς πρόκιτ(αι).

5   † Κολλοῦθος ὢ καὶ Στέφ(ανος) /ι·

Fragment of second receipt (at left):

ἀπὸ] Ἀμμωνίου ῥιπ(αρίου)
ἐδεξάμην καὶ] ἐπληρ(ώθην) παρὰ σοῦ
κερ(άτια)] δεκαέξ, γί(νεται) κ(εράτια) ις,
καὶ πρὸς ὑμ. ἀσφ. πε]ποίημαι τὴ(ν) ἀπόδειξ(ιν)
10 ὡς προκ. (?). Κολλοῦθος] ὁ καὶ Στέφ(ανος) ⸏.

1. τοπ ερμαιων. No sign of abbreviation appears after either word.   1, 5. Read δ.

3-4. πρὸς ὑμετέρ(αν) ἀσφάλεια(ν). For the omission of the article cf. P. Oxy. 2003. 11, 2005. 11-12, 2009. 4. Cf. 83. 7.

95. INVENTORY OF STOLEN PROPERTY

AM 8956.   19 × 31 cm.   Provenance unknown.   4th (?) cent. A.D.

A list of articles left behind at her death by a certain Tloulla, and subsequently seized by her former husband, Paul. The inventory was prepared by the father of the decedent doubtless as a preliminary step in obtaining redress on account of the loss of a portion of the dowry. Several new words occur, some of them of Coptic or doubtful derivation.

⳨ Γνῶσις φανερῶν σκευῶν καταλειφθέντ(ων)
παρὰ τῆς μακαρίας μου θυγατρὸς
Τλούλλας λημφθέντων βιαίως
παρὰ τοῦ αὐτῆς ἀνδρὸς Παύλου
5   οὕτως·
χρυσοῦ————————————νο(μ.)   ιβ ⸏ =
βρεκτήριον χαλκ(οῦν)————α
κάδος—————————————α
τκουσου—————————————α
10 τήγανα————————————β
ἄμαξαν πατητικὴν—————α
ἐργαλιδίων σιδηρ(είων)   νο(μ.) α[
..[..]....[.].[.]κωτ [
λωδίκιον πορφ(υροῦν)   α
15 κιβῶτιν   ᾱ
ἕλκεστον ὀριχαλκ(οῦν)—————α
κρεμουριν   ᾱ
ἱμάτια   τέσσ[αρα
μαφόρια   β̄

20 στρῶμα σαλάχινον――――――――ā
    λαμπάδιον―――――― [
    ἁλισίδιν ἤτοι ἐνώτι[ον] πτυχί[α

6. ιβ.   15. κωριτιν altered to κιβωτιν. Read κιβώτιον.   18. ιματια.
22. Read ἁλυσίδιον.

3. Τλούλλας. A name derived from the Coptic word for *girl* or *daughter*. Cf. Heuser, *Die Personennamen der Kopten*, 63.

3–4. λημφθέντων βιαίως παρὰ τοῦ αὐτῆς ἀνδρός. *Forcibly taken by* (rather than *from*) *her husband*. The preposition almost certainly expresses agency here, as in line 2. For the use of παρά in place of ὑπό cf. Mayser, *Grammatik*, II², 484 ff.

20. στρῶμα σαλάχινον. (?). Cf. στρώματα σ ικιανα (P. Oxy. 921, 3).

96. Wage Account

AM 8965.   31.5 × 30.5 cm.   Oxyrhynchus.   551/552 or 566/567 A.D.   Plate VIII.

The following account is one of a large number of documents relating to the wealthy Apion family, whose estates were located principally in the Oxyrhynchite nome. What is known of this family has been set forth by Spohr, P. land. 48, introd.; Grenfell-Hunt, P. Oxy. 1829. 24, note; and Hardy, *The Large Estates of Byzantine Egypt*, 25-37.

The present account was rendered to Flavius Apion II evidently by the same John, who, as pronoëtes, issued a report of receipts from the estates under his supervision three or four years earlier (P. Oxy. 2019), for in both instances we find the phrase λόγ(ος) λημμ(άτων) καὶ ἀναλωμ(άτων) γενομ(ένων) δι' ἐμοῦ Ἰωάννου, to which is added in the case of the latter υἱοῦ Φιλοξένου προν(οητοῦ) προστ[άτο]υ οἰκ(ων) Τερύθεως καὶ Θεαγέν[ου]ς κ[αὶ Εὐτ]υχιάδος καὶ ἄλλ(ων) ἐξωτικ(ῶν) τόπων. In our Princeton text John presents to his master a list of wage payments (ὀψώνια) made to "Egyptian slaves, women, and others." These payments were all made in wheat, in amounts varying from three to twelve artabae, computed in the *cancellus* standard, the capacity of which has been shown by Grenfell-Hunt (P. Oxy. 1910. 15, note) to be equal to forty choinices. An artaba of wheat per month commonly served as a food allowance, that is, twelve artabae per year, the maximum total found in Col. I.

It is difficult to explain the purpose of the references to "receipts and expenditures" which appear in the margins of recto and verso, unless it be assumed that the present account was but one of several submitted by the writer, the general nature of which was best described in that manner. One is also at a loss to account for the double entries in lines 4-19 (double rations?), as well as for the list of names on the verso, which duplicates in part the list on the recto, with the possible omission, however, of the amounts of the payments (see note to lines 69-76). The solution of these difficulties might be sought in the fourfold entry in lines 83-84, where σχιδαρ( ) evidently stands for σχεδάρ(ιον). On the assumption that the list on the verso was but a preliminary *rough draft*, to which the writer subsequently referred in composing a definitive account on the recto, the correspondences between the two lists and the duplication of entries in lines 4-17 (cf. the corresponding duplication, lines 55-61 and 70-76) would be readily intelligible. But this explanation accounts neither for the duplicate entry in line 19, nor for the numerous entries on the recto (especially in Col. II) which find no counterpart on the verso. It is, moreover, apparent that the entry in line 69 has been copied, for there is no reference to Papnouthius in the lines which precede. And it is to be noted also that the list on the verso (lines 66 ff.) does not contain the three names which have been erased on the recto (lines 24-26). Thus it is on the whole more probable that the account on the verso has been copied from the recto than the reverse, though the purpose of the duplications on the verso is not apparent.

In addressing Apion reference is made by John to his consular rank (ἀπὸ ὑπάτων ὀρδιναρ(ίων)). It is known that Apion II held the high office of *consul ordinarius* in 539 A.D., and that he died between 577 and 579 (cf. Hardy, *op. cit.*, 32-34). The fourteenth and fifteenth indictions to which reference is made in the present text must, therefore, represent either the years 550/551, 551/552 or the years 565/566, 566/567.

The document appears to be complete except for the loss of the right hand portion of the second column on the recto, containing the concluding letters of a few names and the amounts of the payments. Although there are traces of letters in one spot along the upper edge of the recto, it is unlikely, by reason of the size of the papyrus sheet, that anything has been lost at the top.

RECTO

COL. I

⳨ Βρέ(ουιον) ὀψωνίων παιδαρ(ίων) Αἰγυπτ(ίων) καὶ γυναικ(ῶν)
   καὶ ἄλλ(ων) ἐπὶ τῆς ιε ἰνδ(ικτίονος), οὕτως·
   βρέ(ουιον) ὀψωνίων παιδαρ(ίων) Αἰγυπτ(ίων)·
   Φιλοξένῳ μειζοτέρ(ῳ)   σίτου κ(αγκέλλῳ) (ἀρτ.) ιβ
5 Φιλοξένῳ μειζ(οτ)έρ(ῳ)   σίτου κ(αγκ.) (ἀρτ.) ιβ
   τῷ αὐ(τῷ) ὑπὲρ παραμυθ(ίας)   σίτου κ(αγκ.) (ἀρτ.) ιβ
   τῷ αὐ(τῷ) ὑπὲρ παραμυθ(ίας)   σίτου κ(αγκ.) (ἀρτ.) ιβ
   Φοιβάμμωνι πατρ(ὶ) αὐ(τοῦ) ἀπὸ μειζοτέρ(ων) σίτου κ(αγκ.) (ἀρτ.) ιβ
   Φοιβάμμωνι πατρ(ὶ) αὐ(τοῦ) ἀπὸ μειζ(οτέρων)
10 Ἰακὼβ υἱῷ τοῦ αὐ(τοῦ) Φοιβάμμωνος   σίτου κ(αγκ.) (ἀρτ.) ιβ
   Ἰακὼβ υἱῷ τοῦ αὐ(τοῦ) Φοιβάμμωνος

Σερήνο ἀπὸ μειζοτέρ(ων)   σίτου κ(αγκ.) (ἀρτ.) ιβ
Σερήνῳ ἀπὸ μειζοτέρ(ων)
Βίκτορι υἱῷ τοῦ αὐ(τοῦ)   σίτου κ(αγκ.) (ἀρτ.) ϛ
15 Βίκτορι υἱῷ τοῦ αὐ(τοῦ)
Μαρίνῳ υἱῷ Λέοντος   σίτου κ(αγκ.) (ἀρτ.) ιβ
Μαρίνῳ υἱῷ Λέοντος
Χρυσερῶτι Μαύρ(ου)   σίτου κ(αγκ.) (ἀρτ.) δ
Χρυσερῶτι Μαύρ(ου)
20 Ἄννι ἀδελφ(ῷ) τοῦ αὐ(τοῦ)   σίτου κ(αγκ.) (ἀρτ.) ϛ
Ὑπατίᾳ θυγατρ(ὶ) Βίκτορος ἀπὸ μειζοτέ(ρων)   σίτου κ(αγκ.) (ἀρτ.) ϛ
Ἀρκαδίᾳ ἀδελφ(ῇ) αὐ(τῆς)   σίτου κ(αγκ.) (ἀρτ.) ϛ
Γεωργίᾳ ἀδελφ(ῇ) αὐ(τῆς)   σίτου κ(αγκ.) (ἀρτ.) ϛ
⟦Ἀπφουᾶ ἄπα Σίωνος   σίτου κ(αγκ.) (ἀρτ.) ιβ⟧
25 ⟦ἄπα Σίωνος υἱῷ αὐ(τοῦ)   σίτου κ(αγκ.) (ἀρτ.) ιβ⟧
⟦Φιλοξένᾳ ἀδελφ(ῇ) ἄπα Σίωνος   σίτου κ(αγκ.) (ἀρτ.) γ⟧
Ἀνδρέᾳ Μηνᾶ ρουας   σίτου κ(αγκ.) (ἀρτ.) ιβ
Φοιβάμμωνι υἱῷ αὐ(τοῦ)   σίτου κ(αγκ.) (ἀρτ.) γ
Παπνουθίῳ ἀδελφ(ῷ) Ἀνδρέου   σίτου κ(αγκ.) (ἀρτ.) ιβ
30 Σερήνῳ υἱῷ Παπνουθίου   σίτου κ(αγκ.) (ἀρτ.) ιβ

In margin at left, written at right angles:

31 † λόγ(ος) λημμ(άτων) καὶ ἀναλωμ(άτων) γενομ(ένων) δι' ἐμοῦ Ἰωάννου.

Col. II

Ἴσιδι θυγατρ(ὶ) τοῦ αὐ(τοῦ) Πα[πνουθίου
Πετρωνίᾳ θυγατρ(ὶ) τοῦ αὐ(τοῦ) Πα[πνουθίου
Πετρωνίᾳ θυγατρί [
35 Μαρίᾳ γαμ(ετῇ) τοῦ αὐ(τοῦ) Παπν[ουθίου
Παπνουθίῳ Μηνᾶ τοῦ Ἀν(δρέου ?) [
Γεωργίῳ υἱῷ τοῦ αὐ(τοῦ) [
Μηνᾷ πλακουντᾷ υἱῷ τοῦ αὐ(τοῦ) [
Χριστοφόρῳ πανδουρ(ιστῇ) [
40 Σερήνῳ τοῦ αὐ(τοῦ) Παπνουθ[ίου
Θεοδώρῳ Ἰουλίου [
Ἀλτίνᾳ γαμ(ετῇ) αὐ(τοῦ) [
ἄπα Ὥρῳ υἱῷ τοῦ αὐ(τοῦ) Θεοδώρ[ου
Ἰουλίῳ υἱῷ τοῦ αὐ(τοῦ) Θεοδώ[ρου
45 Σερήνῳ υἱῷ τοῦ αὐ(τοῦ) Θεοδώ[ρου
Μηνᾷ υἱῷ τοῦ αὐ(τοῦ) Θεοδώρου [
Θεοδότῃ θυγατρ(ὶ) τοῦ αὐ(τοῦ) Θεοδ[ώρου
Μινερίῳ υἱῷ Εὐφημίας [
ἀπέθανε ⟦Εὐφημίᾳ μητρ(ὶ) αὐ(τοῦ) ἀδελφ(ῇ) Ἰουλ[ίου   ⟧

96. WAGE ACCOUNT

50 Φὶβ υἱῷ ἄπα Νακίω μαγίρ(ῳ) [
τῷ αὐ(τῷ) ὑπὲρ παραμυθ(ίας) [
Ἰωάννῃ υἱῷ αὐ(τοῦ) [
Γεωργίῳ υἱῷ Ψεείου Ἰακώβ [

In margin at left, written at right angles:

54 † Φλαουίῳ Ἀπίωνι τῷ πανευφήμῳ καὶ ὑπερφυεστ(άτῳ) ἀπὸ ὑπάτων ὀρδιναρ(ίων).

Verso

55 † Φιλοξένῳ μειζοτέρ(ῳ)
τῷ αὐ(τῷ) ὑπὲρ παραμυθίας
Φοιβάμμωνι πατρ(ὶ) αὐ(τοῦ) ἀπὸ μειζ(οτέρων)
Ἰακὼβ υἱῷ τοῦ αὐ(τοῦ) Φοιβάμμωνος
Σερήνῳ ἀπὸ μειζο(τέρων)
60 Βίκτορι υἱῷ τοῦ αὐ(τοῦ)
Μαρίνῳ υἱῷ Λέοντος
Χρυσερῶτι Μαύρ(ου)
Ἄννιδι ἀδελφ(ῷ) τοῦ αὐ(τοῦ)
Ὑπατίᾳ θυγατρ(ὶ) Βίκτορι ἀπὸ μειζ(οτέρων)
65 Ἀρκαδίᾳ θυγατρ(ὶ) αὐ(τοῦ)
Γεωργίᾳ ἀδελφ(ῇ) αὐ(τῆς)
Ἀνδρέᾳ Μηνᾶ ρουας
Φοιβάμμωνι υἱῷ αὐτοῦ
Ἴσιδι θυγατρὶ τοῦ αὐ(τοῦ) Παπνουθίου
70 Φιλοξένῳ μειζ(οτέρῳ)
τῷ αὐτῷ ὑπὲρ παραμυθίας
Φοιβάμμωνι πατρ(ὶ) αὐ(τοῦ) ἀπὸ μειζ(οτέρων)
Ἰακὼβ υἱῷ τοῦ αὐ(τοῦ) Φοιβάμμωνι
Σερήνῳ ἀπὸ μειζ(οτέρων)
75 Βίκτορι υἱῷ τοῦ αὐ(τοῦ)
Μαρίνῳ υἱῷ Λέοντος

At left, written at right angles:

77 † Φλαουίῳ Ἀπίωνι τῷ πανευφήμ(ῳ) καὶ ὑπερφυεστ(άτῳ) ἀπὸ ὑπάτων ὀρδιναρ(ίων)
γεουχοῦντι καὶ ἐνταῦθα τῇ λαμπρᾷ Ὀξυρυγχιτῶν πόλει. λόγος λημμάτων
καὶ ἀναλωμ(άτων) γενομ(ένων) δι' ἐμοῦ. † λήμμ(ατα) καὶ ἀναλώμ(ατα) τῆς
λογι(ζομένης?) ιδ ἰνδ(ικτίονος).

Written just above the last three lines:

80 [[Φλ[αου]ί[ῳ Ἀπ]ι]]   λόγ(ος) λημμ(άτων) καὶ ἀναλωμ(άτων) τῆς
λογι(ζομένης?) ιδ ἰνδ(ικτίονος).

Written just above the last line, but upside down:

81 † λόγ(os) λημμ(άτων) καὶ ἀναλωμ(άτων) τῆς λογι(ζομένης ?)
82 ιδ ἰνδ(ικτίονος).

In lower left corner, written in very large letters:

83 σχιδάρ(ιον) σχιδάρ(ιον)
84 σχιδάρ(ιον) σχιδάρ(ιον)

1, 3. παιδαρρ/. 12. σερηνα corrected to σερηνο (read Σερήνῳ). 14. υιω (so passim). 18, 19. Read Χρυσερῶτι. 50. Read Νακίου. 64. Read Βίκτορος. 73. Read Φοιβάμμωνος. 83 f. Read σχεδάρ(ιον).

6-7. τῷ αὐ(τῷ) ὑπὲρ παραμυθ(ίας). Philoxenus appears to have required some special compensation not covered by the payment recorded in lines 4-5. Cf. line 51. παραμυθία here, as often in Byzantine texts, probably has the sense of *salary* or *wages*. Maspero (Rev. d. ét. grec., XXV [1912], 222), commenting upon the use of the word in P. Lond. 1452. 12, equates it with the Latin *solacium* and proposes *traitement* as the French equivalent.

8. ἀπὸ μειζοτέρ(ων). Cf. P. Oxy. 2056. 6. A phrase used to designate one who had served as μειζότερος. For the office of μειζότερος (or μείζων) cf. P. Oxy. 1835. 2, note, and Stud. Pal. XIX, pp. 41 ff.

20. Ἄννι (= Ἀννιδι). Cf. line 63.

24. ἄπα Σίωνος. Cf. P. Oxy. 192 (see Preisigke, BL.). It is impossible to explain why this and the two following entries have been crossed out. It is unlikely that the erasure has been caused by the death of the persons in question, as in line 49, where the death of Euphemia is noted in the margin as an explanation of the erasure of her name. The corresponding entries do not appear in the duplicate list of names on the verso. In the latter Ἀνδρέας follows Γεωργία (lines 66-67).

27. ρουας. (?). The word evidently served to distinguish this Menas from the pastry-cook of the same name who appears in line 38, but there is no clue to its meaning. Cf. line 67. The reading in both cases is very clear.

32. Cf. line 69. This is the only entry in Col. II which is duplicated on the verso.

34. Πετρωνίᾳ. The duplication of this entry would seem to have been intentional, for this line has been crowded in between lines 33 and 35, and represents almost certainly a subsequent revision.

39. υἱῷ τοῦ αὐ(τοῦ) should perhaps be supplied at the end of the line, although no traces of writing are visible in the rather considerable space which follows the preceding word.

42. Ἀλτίνᾳ. This and Μινερίῳ (line 48) are new names.

43. ἄπα Ὥρῳ. Cf. P. Oxy. 1912. 47, 92 and 2019. 13, 18.

50. ἄπα Νακίω (read Νακίου). Cf. P. Oxy. 1912. 23 and 2019. 65. See P. Oxy. XVI, index v, s. v.

69-76. The list of names on the verso here ceases to follow the order found in the corresponding list on the recto. The two entries appearing in lines 29-30 find no counterpart in the duplicate list. The following entry (Ἴσιδι κ. τ. λ., line 32) reappears in line 69, but at that point the two lists part company, lines 70-76 reproducing the entries which had already been copied (?) in lines 55-61. The purpose of this duplicate list is difficult to conjecture. The amounts of the payments have been omitted throughout, unless these appeared far to the right of the list of names, on the verso of the strip which has been lost from Col. II. It should be noted, however, that the longest lines in the duplicate list are separated from the edge of the papyrus by a space of at least 3.5 cm. On the recto the blank space separating the names from the payment totals varies from 1.5 to 7.5 cm. The totals were arranged in a straight column, the position of which was determined more or less arbitrarily when the first entry in the column was inscribed. In the case of Col. I on the recto the initial total was recorded at a distance of 5.5 cm. from the concluding letter of the name. The same procedure may have been followed on the verso, in which case the column of totals was doubtless written near the outer edge of the strip which has been lost. Since this column would have been written in a straight vertical line, it is not surprising that no traces of it remain. The previous existence of this column of totals is thus open to conjecture.

97. Letter

Garrett Dep. 7619.   9.5 × 23.5 cm.   Provenance unknown.   326/327 A.D.   Plate IX.

In the following letter the writer gives instructions to his "brother" (?) to issue receipts to certain farmers and vine-dressers who have delivered the required number of pigs in settlement of claims against them. He is instructed further to credit these deliveries on his accounts. The writer was doubtless the owner of a large estate, receiving small annual contributions of pigs from his tenants, who thus discharged certain obligations imposed upon them. The deliveries are stated to have been in varying quantities under the following classifications: ὑδρο(φυλακίας), νεοφύτου ἀμ(πελῶνος), ἱπ(ὲρ) μυλαίον, and πωμ(αρίου). In most cases the delivery of one pig is offered in satisfaction of each obligation, though in some instances two are required. Deliveries are credited for the years 325/326 and 326/327.

The addressee is also instructed to make settlement for the taxes (δημόσια) on the estate under his supervision (προστασίας).

The text is written on the verso, the papyrus having been torn off from a larger piece, on the recto of which there had been inscribed a rather extensive account. The remains of this account are too fragmentary to permit a restoration.

Ὡρίων [.]π οι[. . .]   [ἀδελ-
    φῷ   χαίρειν.
τῶν χοίρων ἀπενεχθέντ[ων
ὑπὸ τῶν γεωργῶν καὶ ἀμπ[ε-
5 λουργῶν τοῦ ἐποικίον, φρ[όν-
τισον λαβὼν μου τὰ γράμμ[α-
τα ἔκδος ἄποχα γράμμα-
τα τοῖς ἑξῆς ἵνα [ἐπὶ
τῶν λόγων σου λημματ[ί-

```
10    σης. εἰσὶ δὲ
      ἐπὶ μὲν τοῦ διελθόντος
      κ∫ ι∫ β∫// Μόσχ(ου ?) ς ˉ (ἀρουρῶν) ὑδρο(φυλακίας)    325/326
      χοίρ(ος) αˉ, νεοφύτου ἀμ(πελῶνος)
      χοῖ(ρος) αˉ, Εὔφρο(νος) ὑπ(ὲρ) μυ-
15    λαίου χοῖ(ρος) αˉ, γ (ἀρουρῶν) ὑδρο(φυλακίας)
      καὶ ἀμ(πελῶνος) χοῖ(ροι) β/, καὶ [ἐπὶ τοῦ
      ἐνεστῶτος κα∫ ια[∫ γ∫//                              326/327
      Μόσχ(ου ?) ς (ἀρουρῶν) ὑδρο(φυλακίας) χοῖ(ρος) α[ˉ,
      ἀμ(πελῶνος) χοῖ(ροι) β/, Ἑλέν(ου) ς′ (ἀρουρῶν ?) ὑδρ[ο(φυλακίας)
20    χοῖ(ρος) αˉ, ἀμ(πελῶνος) χοῖ(ρος) αˉ, μυλ[αίου
      ⟦Ἑλένου ͞ς ὑδρο(φυλακίας) χοῖ(ρος) ā⟧ . . . . . [
      χοῖ(ροι) β/, γˉ (ἀρουρῶν) ὑδρο(φυλακίας) χοῖ(ρος) αˉ,
      ζ (ἀρουρῶν) ὑδ[ρο(φυλακίας)] χοῖ(ροι) β, Παναν( )
      πωμ(αρίου) χοῖ(ρος) αˉ, Τιμοθέου
25    ὑπ(ὲρ) μυλαίου ιε∫ ἰνδ(ικτίονος) χοῖ(ρος) α[ˉ,        326/327
      νεοφύτου ἐκτ(ολογουμένου) . . . / ἀμ(πελῶνος)
      χοῖ(ρος) αˉ. πλήρωσων δὲ
      τὰ δημόσια τῆς σῆς προ-
      στασίας. ἐρρῶσ[θαί σε
30              εὔχομαι.
```

27. Read πλήρωσον.

1-2. ἀδελφῷ. A real brother or a formal mode of address? Quite possibly the former. The writer does not appear to be writing to a subordinate, such as an agent or bailiff (φροντιστής).

7. ἀποχα γράμματα. Receipts. See note to P. Thead. 28. 13 and cf. Preisigke, WB., s. v.

10. εἰσὶ δέ. For the plural verb cf. P. Oxy. 890. 13. The singular is more commonly found in this phrase.

12. κ∫ ι∫ β∫. Cf. P. Oslo 44. 13. The regnal years are those of Constantine, Crispus, and Constantius (P. Oslo II, p. 107).

17. For the date see note to line 12.

21. This line was carefully crossed out by the writer. There is probably a repetition of some of the items recorded in lines 19-20.

98. Letter

Garrett Dep. 7647.   6 × 24.5 cm.   Provenance unknown.   4th cent. A.D.

The writer chides his correspondent on his failure to deliver some hemp for which he has been waiting two months and requests that delivery be made to one whom he names as his agent (a second name has been added by a later hand). To lend urgency to his plea the writer reminds the addressee that the hemp belongs not to him (the writer), but to his master. As an afterthought Theodoulus suggests alternatively the payment of the money value of the hemp.

No address appears on the verso.

    Κυρίῳ μου πατρὶ
      Εὐλογίῳ Θεόδουλος
        χαίρειν.
    καὶ ἄλλοτε ὅτε ἀνῆλθα
5 πρὸς σὲ μετὰ τοῦ
    ἀδελφοῦ μου Νίκωνος
    χάριν Εὐανθείας
    καὶ χάριν τῶν
    στιππίων ὧν χρε-
10 ωστεῖς μοι οὕτως
    οὖν καθὼς ἠξίωσάς
    με τότε τοῦ συγχωρῆ-
    σαί μέ σοι πρὸς ὀλίγας
    ἡμέρας ἄχρις οὗ ἀπαν-
15 τήσῃς μετὰ τῶν στιππί-
    ων. ἐθαύμασά σε οὖν
    ἰδοὺ δύο μῆνες σήμε-
    ρον οὐδὲν δέδωκάς μοι,
    οἶδας γὰρ ὅτι οὐκ ἔστιν
20 ἐμὰ ἀλλὰ δεσποτικά ἐστιν.
    ἠξίωσα οὖν τὸν ἀδελφὸν
      Καλόκαιρον ʿκαὶ Πανίσκον᾿
    ἵνα αὐτῷ αὐτὰ παράσχῃς.
      ἐρρῶσθαί σε εὔχομαι
25   πα⟨μ⟩πόλλοις χρόνοις.
  ἢ τὴν τιμὴν αὐτῶν.

17. ἰδου.

4. ἀνῆλθα. For the form see Mayser, *Grammatik*, I, 368-369.

9. στιππίων. References to the cultivation and use of hemp are asssembled by Calderini, *Raccolta Lumbroso*, 77-81.

17. ἰδοὺ δύο μῆνες. For the nominative with ἰδού see Mayser, *op. cit.*, II², 187.

22. Καλόκαιρον was inserted between lines 21 and 23 by the original writer after the completion of the letter. καὶ Πανίσκον was added subsequently by a second hand, αὐτῷ in the following line not being corrected, however, to αὐτοῖς.

25. πα⟨μ⟩πόλλοις. A nasal is frequently dropped before a following labial. Cf. Mayser, *op. cit.*, I, 190.

99. Letter

Garrett Dep. 7646.   26 × 8.5 cm.   Philadelphia.   4th cent. A.D.

A letter from Ptolemaius, an irenarch, addressed to the comarchs of Philadelphia, importuning them to come to "the city" (Arsinoë) immediately. There may be a reference to an ἀρχέφοδος in line 6, but this as well as other details are obscure, partly owing to the faulty orthography of the writer.

Π(αρὰ) τοῦ εἰρηνάρχου Πτολεμέου
κωμάρχαις κώμης Φιλαδελφίας. αὐτῆς ὥρας ἀνέρχεσθαι ἐπὶ τὴν
πόλιν ἕνεκεν Πιαρίου τοῦ συμμάχου. ἰ δὲ μὴ πέμπουσι συμμάχους
ἐπεὶ ὑμᾶς καὶ μήτε ἐνοχλῖσθαι πάντως ἀνέρχεσθαι ἐπεὶ τὴν πόλιν
5 ἐπεὶ ὀρτῇ τῆς ἰρήνης. [μὴ] ἐνοχλῖσθαι περὶ ὑμῶν καὶ παραστησάτω
ὁ ἀρχέπους τὰ πάντ[α ..]αε[......] περὶ τοῦ χοιριδίου. ὀναφα εντα̣χυν[.]α.
         ἐρρ[ῶσ]θαί [σ]ε
7   εὔχομαι.

1. Read Πτολεμαίου. 2. Read ἀνέρχεσθε. 3. ἰ. Read εἰ. 4. Read ἐπί, ἐνοχλεῖσθε, ἀνέρχεσθε. 5. ἰρηνης. Read ἐπὶ ἑορτῇ (?), εἰρήνης, ἐνοχλεῖσθε. 6. Read ἀρχέφοδος (?).

100. Letter

Garrett Dep. 7691a.   11.5 × 11.5 cm.   Oxyrhynchus.   4th cent. A.D.

A letter, of which both the beginning and conclusion are missing, referring to a visit to Toca on the preceding day. The writer requests the sending of a tax list (ἀπαιτήσιμον) together with information relative to the measure which his correspondent desires to use.

. . . .
[....]σιωτ[.] . [.] νιος ὑπὸ Εὐ-
[θα]λείου τοῦ χωματεπίκτου αὐτῶν
καὶ πάλειν ἐν τῇ ἐχθὲς ἡμέρᾳ ἀπῆλ-
θον εἰς Τόκα καὶ εὗρον αὐτοὺς ἐλαβό⟨ν⟩τας
5 κριθὴν ἀπὸ Ἑρμία ἐλεοπώλῃ καὶ ἐδή-
τησα εἰς τὸ χαρτάριν ὃ ἔδωκας τῇ μη-
τρί σου καὶ οὐκ εὑρέθη τὸ ὄνομα αὐτοῦ.
σπούδασον οὖν τὸ ἀπετήσιμον γράψαι
καὶ ἀποστῖλέ μοι καὶ γράψαι ὅτι ἐν ποίῳ
10 μέτρῳ βούλῃ μετρῆσαι. ὁ γὰρ λοιπὸς
ἤδη ἔσχεν ἀπὸ τοῦ μέτρου τοῦ προσ-

βυτέρου καὶ εἰ βούλει ἀνενεχθῆναι
........] .... [......] ουν γράψιν
. . . .

On the verso:

14 [   ]ι   Διονύσιος.

2. The deletion of the first two letters is uncertain.   5. Read ἐλαιοπώλου.
5-6. Read ἐξήτησα (?).   9. Read ἀποστεῖλαι.   11-12. Read πρεσβυτέρου.

4. Τόκα. A village situated in the Oxyrhynchite nome. Cf. P. S. I. 219. 4, P. Oxy. 1659. 74, 79, and 2140. 10 (see note). ἐλαβό⟨ν⟩τας. For the augment see Mayser, *Grammatik*, I, 345.
6. χαρτάριν (= χαρτάριον). For the spelling cf. P. Oxy. 1297. 18.
7. οὐκ εὑρέθη. For the disappearance of the rough breathing see Mayser, *op. cit.*, I, 202-203 (especially p. 203, Anm. 2). Cf. **70**. 8.
9. ὅτι. For ὅτι *recitativum* in the papyri see Mayser, *op. cit.*, II³, 46-47.

101. Letter

AM 8958.   7 × 10 cm.   Provenance unknown.   4th cent. A.D.

Letters of recommendation are frequently found among the papyri. For similar texts the reader is referred to P. Oslo 51 and 55, where references are given to other letters of the same type. The text of the letter presented here is fragmentary, only the opening lines having been preserved.

Τῷ κυρί]ῳ μου ἀδελφῷ
Εὐδαί]μονι Σεουῆρος
   εὖ πράττειν.
ὁλοκλ]ηροῦντι σοι εὔχομαι
5   τῷ κυ]ρίῳ θεῷ ἀποδοθῆναί
σοι τα]ῦτα μου τὰ γράμματα.
... ὁ] ἀναδιδούς σοι τὰ γράμ-
ματά] μου οἰκῖος τοῦ πατρὸς
τοῦ Σ]τεφάνου τυγχάνει. γρα-
10 ....] [.] [...] ....ος
. . . .

3. πρατ'τειν.

1-2. In Christian letters the prescript usually takes this form, the name of the recipient preceding that of the sender. Although this form is also found in non-Christian letters as early as the second century B.C., its use in pagan correspondence was strictly limited to cases in which a superior was addressed by a person of inferior rank. Christian letter writers, on the other hand, adopted this form regularly without observing distinctions of rank. Ghedini (*Lettere Cristiane*, 13) suggests that Christian writers may have been mindful of the precept which Jesus gave His disciples when they had disputed among themselves, who should be the greatest: εἴ τις θέλει πρῶτος εἶναι, ἔσται πάντων ἔσχατος καὶ πάντων διάκονος (Mark ix. 35). The essential characteristics of Christian epistolography are summarized by Ghedini, *op. cit.*, 1-13 and Meecham, *Light from Ancient Letters*, 112-157.

3. εὖ πράττειν. Used instead of the more usual χαίρειν. Cf. P.S.I. 207, 299, and P. Oxy. 822. ἐπέστειλε is understood (cf. Mayser, *Grammatik*, II^3, 5-6). The occasional use of εὖ πράττειν in the concluding salutation is cited by Schubart (*Einfuhrung in die Papyruskunde*, 223), who characterizes it as a *literarische Feinheit*. The attribution of this formula to Plato is rejected by Ziemann (*De epistularum Graecarum formulis sollemnibus quaestiones selectae*, 290-291) and Ghedini (*op. cit.*, 87). It is likely that εὖ πράττειν stood alone in this line. The prescript was frequently separated from the body of the letter in this manner, the last line of the prescript being often indented. Such lines were usually somewhat shorter than the average. Cf. P. Lips. 111, P. Oxy. 1493, 1495, and P. Grenf. II. 73 (= Wilcken Chrest. 127).

4-6. Cf. P. Oxy. 1593. 2-3 and P. Lond. 405. 4 for close resemblances in thought and expression. ἀποδοθῆναι. This verb is used technically to denote the act of *delivering* a letter. Cf. Ghedini, *op. cit.*, 158.

7. [... ὁ] ἀναδιδούς ... τυγχάνει. Cf. P. Oxy. 1424. 3-4. The name of the bearer may have appeared in the lacuna, although space was available for not more than three or four letters. Cf. P. Oslo 51. 3, note. In P. Oxy. 1773 the writer requests her mother, upon receipt of the letter, to repay to the bearers a rather large loan recently made by them in her behalf.

102. Letter

AM 8957.   11 × 16 cm.   Provenance unknown.   4th cent. A.D.   Plate X.

The writer of the following letter sends a message of comfort to a friend who has just suffered the loss of his son. He expresses at the same time his regret that, owing to the difficulty of the journey, he was prevented from coming at once to him (evidently prior to the death of the son) and fulfilling humanitarian obligations which are now increased twofold by the son's death. That the writer was a Christian would seem clearly indicated by the phrase υἱὸς ὁ θεοῦ in line 15, as well as by the form of the prescript (see **101.** 1-2, note).

Letters of condolence are rare among the papyri. Cf. Winter, *Life and Letters in the Papyri*, 134-135, 190-191, and Deissmann, *Light from the Ancient East* (4th ed. in trans.), 176-178.

Κυρίῳ μου ἀδελφῷ Κι διενῳ
Ἀλέξανδρος χαίρειν.
ἐβουλόμην μὲν αὐτοθέντην
ὁρμήσασθαι πρός σαι καὶ τὰ

5 τῆς φιλανθρωπίας τοῦ εὐμύρου σοι υἱοῦ ἀποπληρῶσαι,
   ἃ ἐπὶ ἐνποδών μοι γεγένηται
   δι]ὰ μὴ δύνασθέ μαι ἀπαντῆσαι,
   ἐπιδήπερ δυσκόλως ἀνερχό-
10 μεθα εἰς τὴν πόλειν, δὶς δὲ τὸ
   ἀνθρώπινον φέρει. τοιγαροῦν
   ἀπόθου τὸ λυπηρὸν τοῦ ἀνθρω-
   πίνου πτέσματος καὶ ἀπόβλη-
   ψον ὅτι οὐδεὶς ἐν ἀνθρώποις ἀθά-
15 νατος εἰ μὴ υἱὸς ὁ θεοῦ καὶ
   μνημόνευσον τῆς ὑποσχέσε-
   ως τὰ ?] κακὰ σ[.....] λου καθὼς

. . . .

In margin at left:

18 ἐ[ρ]ρ̣[ῶσθαί σε εὔχο]μαι πολλοῖς χρόν[ο]ις κ[ύριέ μου ἀδελφέ].

On the verso:

Κι[..] [... ἀδε]λφῷ.

5–6. Read εὐμοίρου. ἀποπληρῶσε corrected to ἀποπληρῶσαι.   7. Read ἐπεί.
8. ναι corrected to μαι (= με).   10. δι.   13–14. Read πταίσματος,
ἀπόβλεψον υιδει corrected to οὐδείς, σ being added above the line.
15. [[τον]].

3. αὐτοθέντην. *Immediately, at once.* The word is found only here in this form.
Cf. αὐτομάτην (Diod. II. 25. 8).

5–6. εὐμύρου (= εὐμοίρου). On the application of this word to deceased persons
cf. Deissmann, op. cit., 176, note 4.

12–15. The same injunction occurs commonly in funerary inscriptions, though in
briefer form. Cf. SB. 3514: μὴ λυπ[ῇς], οὐδεὶς ἀ[θάνα]τος ἐν κό[σμῳ].

15. εἰ μὴ υἱὸς [[τόν]] ὁ θεοῦ. The revised form of the article was written just above
the erasure. τόν rather than τοῦ appears to have been the original reading.
The dotted letters may fairly be classed as doubtful, and yet the alternative reading, εἰ μηνὸς ὁ θεός, is devoid of meaning. That υἱός may have
been in the writer's mind is rather doubtfully suggested by the erasure
in the preceding line (see *app. crit.*).

103. LETTER

Garrett Dep. 7637.   30.5 × 10 cm.   Provenance unknown.   5th cent. A.D.

An urgent request to despatch to the writer certain sums of money supplied by various individuals as surety for a certain Ammon. There is

appended a similar request to send or bring 25½ pounds of woolen waste. The absence of an introductory salutation is noteworthy. The writing runs across the fibres. On the verso fragments of an account.

Τὰ εἴκοσι δύο νομίσματα τοῦ θαυμασιωτάτου Συμεωνίου τοῦ πραγματευτοῦ καὶ
τὰ δέκα τοῦ Ἰακὼβ καὶ τὰ ἑ[ξ τοῦ
Σαμπαθίου καὶ τὰ ἑξ τὰ ἀντεφώνησ[ε]ν με ἡ σὴ θαυμασιότης ὑπὲρ Ἄμμωνα
καταξίωσον ταῦτα
ἀποστῖλαι, καὶ γὰρ χρία⟨ν⟩ αὐτῶν ἔχω, διὰ γὰρ τούτου ἠναγκάσθην ἀποστῖλαι
Σιλουανὸν τὸν σύμμαχον
διὰ τὸ ἐμὲ χρίαν ἔχειν τούτων, τὰς δὲ εἴκοσι πέντε ἥμισυ λίτρας τῶν [γν]αφάλλων
5 καταξ[ί]ωσον ἢ ταῦτα ἀποστῖλαι ἢ γοῦν ταῦτα ἀνένεγκον μετὰ τῆς ἀπο[κρί]σεως.

2. τὰ ἀντεφώνησ[ε]ν με . . . ὑπὲρ Ἄμμωνα. For the phrase cf. P. S. I. 76. 3. The accusative following ὑπέρ is irregular. Perhaps Ἄμμωνο(s) should be read. A dot appears above the final letter, possibly marking an abbreviation. For τά = ἅ cf. Mayser, Grammatik, I, 310-311. με was doubtless written in error for μοι. The vocalism οι ⟩ ε is unknown.

104. LETTER

Garrett Dep. 7632.   10 × 9.5 cm.   Provenance unknown.   5th cent. A.D.

The opening portion of a letter addressed by Collouthus, a fruit-grower, to his master, the owner of a large estate. Of sole interest is the reference to village liturgists.

ΧΜΓ
Δεσπότῃ μου καὶ
πάτρωνι γαιούχου
Κολλοῦθος πωμαρίτης
5 ἐν κ(υρί)ῳ χαίρ(ειν).
καθὼς ἐδήλωσας
τοῖς λιτουργοῖς τῆς
κώμης οὐ προσεποίη-
[σας ?   ] . [

7. τοῖς.   2. Read γεούχῳ.

1. ΧΜΓ. For various explanations of the meaning of these letters see Ghedini, Lettere Cristiane, 283-284.

105. LETTER

AM 8964.   32 × 8 cm.   Oxyrhynchus.   6th cent. A.D.

A brief letter of introduction addressed to Phoebammon, an assistant of the *protocometae* of the village of Coba, instructing them to entertain for one evening a certain official making his way to Oxyrhynchus. They are further requested to furnish hay to their guest's six pack animals.

† Τῷ τιμιωτάτ(ῳ) Φοιβάμμωνι βοηθ(ῷ) πρωτοκωμ(ητῶν) Κόβα
    Φλαβιανὸς σχολ(αστικός).
† θελήσατε ὑποδέξασθαι τὴν μίαν ἑσπέραν Ἰωάννην τὸν καὶ Πετ [...] τὸν
    ἐλλογιμιώτατον
σχολαστικὸν σὺν θεῷ ἀνερχόμενον ἐπὶ τὴν Ὀξ[υ]ρύγχων. παράσχετ[ε] δὲ καὶ
    ὀλίγον χόρτον
τοῖς ἓξ ζῴοις αὐτοῦ τὴν μίαν ἑσπέραν. ℟ γένηται. ℟   ℟℟℟
5   ΧΜΓ

On the verso:

6 † ἐπίδ(ος) τῷ τιμιωτ(άτῳ) Φοιβάμμωνι βοη(θῷ) πρωτοκ(ωμητῶν) Κόβ[α]
    Ο Ο   π(αρὰ) Φλαβιανοῦ σχολ[(αστικοῦ)].

1. πρωτοκωμμ ʃ.   2. ὑποδεξ., ιωαννην.   6. πρωτοκκ/.

1. πρωτοκωμ(ητῶν). For the significance of the term see P. Oxy. 1835. 2, note.
2. ἐλλογιμιώτατον. An honorary title commonly applied to the *scholasticus*. It appears to have corresponded to the Latin *eloquentissimus*. Cf. Hornickel, *Ehren- und Rangpradikate in den Papyrusurkunden*, 7-8.
4. ℟℟℟. As in P. Oxy. 2063. 12 and P. Lond. 1701. 13.
6. The two symbols which appear before π(αρά) seem to have been added for decorative purposes.

106. LETTER

Garrett Dep. 7653.   29.5 × 10 cm.   Provenance unknown.   6th cent. A.D.

A letter urging the recipient to secure wine for the writer, who has given him two solidi for the purpose. The wine is to be purchased at the rate of not less than 45 pint measures (σηκώματα ξ(εστιαῖα)) for each solidus. The addressee is further instructed either to despatch a boat to the city in order that the writer may send back some (empty) jars, or to purchase [the wine in jars (?)]. The rest is obscure.

Καθὼς παρεκάλεσα τὴν σὴν θαυμασιότητα σπούδασον λαβεῖν μου τῶν δύο
    χρυσίνων
ὧν παρεσχόμην αὐτῇ τὸν οἶνον μὴ παρὰ μέντοι τεσσαράκοντα πέντε σηκώματα
    ξ(εστιαῖα)
8

ἑκάστου χρυσίνου μετὰ τῆς ἄλλης ἐπινοίας καὶ ἢ πέμψον μοι πλοῖον ἐρχόμενον
εἰς τὴν
πόλειν ἵνα κατάγω κοῦφα ἢ ἀγόρασον   [. μ]ετρητ[. . . . .] ἔχω τὸ αὐτὸ τοῦ
οἴνου τὸ τίμημα ὅ ποτε
5 ὁ θαυμασιώτατος Ὑ(πα)τίων εἶπεν ἡμ[ῖν   ca. 21   ]ου . . δυς ὅτι
παρέχει τὰ κοῦφα
καὶ σὺν θεῷ ταῦτα ἠνεγκεῖν μοι ἢ ἀπο[πέμψαι   ca. 19   ] . a . . .
Σερήνου τοῦ παιδαρίου σου.

On the verso:

7 † ἐπίδος τῷ δεσπότῃ μ[ου τ]ῷ θαυμ(ασιωτάτῳ) καὶ ἐναρ(έτῳ) ἀδελφῷ
Θεωδώρῳ βοηθ(ῷ)   π(αρὰ) Διογένους.

107. GNOSTIC FEVER AMULET

AM 8963.   13 × 15.5 cm.   Provenance unknown.   4th-5th cent. A.D.

Numerous specimens of amulets, both pagan and Christian, are presented by Preisendanz (P. Gr. Mag., II). The text published here is one of a rather large group pertaining more particularly to fevers. Of especial interest are three quotations from the Scriptures, in the reproduction of which the writer has become guilty of numerous errors and omissions. The few phrases taken from the Lord's Prayer have been set down very incoherently.

Among similar texts are C. P. R. 2, 12; P. Oxy. 924, 1151; P. Teb. 275; and B. G. U. 956, all of which have been re-edited by Preisendanz (*op. cit.*). The use of amulets by Christians and Gnostics is discussed by Budge, *Amulets and Superstitions*, xxvii f., 200 ff.

† Πρὸς . . . . . . ρε ο γωβα σ . μω . .
νουσηα ειεγε . . οσαρκ . . . αυσε
ρυγοπύρετον ὁρκίζω σε Μιχαὴλ ἀρχάγγελε γῆς καθημερινὸν ἢ νυκτ-
5 ερινὸν ἢ τεταρτέον τὸν παντοκράτο-
ρα Σαβαὼθ μηκέτι ἄψῃ τῇ ψυχῇ τοῦ
φοροῦντος μηδὲ παντὸς τοῦ σώματ-
ος αὐτοῦ ὁρκίζω σε καὶ νεκροὺς ἀπαλλάσ[σε-
ται ὀχλησις ιδοτ υγρσβωνωη . .
10 ὁ κατικὸν ἐν βοηθίᾳ τοῦ ὑψίστου ἐν σκέ-
πι τοῦ θ(εο)ῦ τοῦ οὐρανοῦ αὐλ[ι]στήσεται. ἐρ[εῖ]
τοῦ θ(εο)ῦ καὶ καταφυγή μου καὶ βοηθώς μου,
ἐλπιδῶ ἐφ' αὐτῶν. πατὴρ ὑμῶν ἐν τῆς
οὐρανῆς, ἁγιασθήτω τὼ θέλημα σου, τὼ-

15   ν ἄρτον ὑμῶν τῶν ἐπιούσιων. ἅγιος
     ἅγιος κ(ύριο)ς Σαβαώθ, πλήρος οὐρανὸς
     καὶ δίκης ἅγιος ὁ δόξης ανιααδα ι-
     α Μιγαὴλ τῶν κ(ρίω)ν Ἀβράμ, Ἰσάκ,
     Ἰακώβ, Ἐλωεί, Ἐλ⟨ω⟩έ, Σαλα[μάν . . . . .]
20   Σαβ]αὼθ Ωηλ [

3. Read ῥιγοπύρετον.   5. Read τεταρταῖον.   10. εσκε.
                                                  ·ν·

1. Perhaps Πρὸς ῥιγοπύρετον, although the original hardly supports this conjecture.
3–4. Μιχαὴλ ἀρχάγγελε. For the rôle of archangels in Gnostic amulets cf. Budge, op. cit., 203.
8. ἀπάλλαξ[ον] should perhaps be read at the end of the line, ται standing for δέ at the beginning of the following line. But what follows is wholly unintelligible.
10–13. Quoted from Psalms xc. 1-2: Ὁ κατοικῶν ἐν βοηθείᾳ τοῦ ὑψίστου ἐν σκέπῃ τοῦ θεοῦ τοῦ οὐρανοῦ αὐλισθήσεται. ἐρεῖ τῷ θεῷ Ἀντιλήμπτωρ μου εἶ καὶ καταφυγή μου, ὁ θεός μου, ἐλπιῶ ἐπ' αὐτόν (Rahlfs). Quotations from the same Psalm are also found in P. S. I. 719, Stud. Pal. XX. 294, and P. Oxy. 1928, 2065. The use of passages from the Psalms in magical papyri is discussed by Collart, *Aegyptus*, XIII, 209-211 and Préaux, *Chr. Eg.*, XX (1935), 365-367. Cf. also Kortenbeutel-Böhlig, *Aegyptus*, XV (1935), 418.
13–15. Cf. Matthew vi. 9-11. The Lord's Prayer is commonly quoted in Christian magical papyri, either in whole or in part, but nowhere, it seems, as incoherently as here.
15–16. The writer is evidently thinking of Isaiah vi. 3[b], but the quotation breaks off abruptly. The LXX has Ἅγιος ἅγιος ἅγιος κύριος σαβαωθ, πλήρης πᾶσα ἡ γῆ τῆς δόξης αὐτοῦ (Rahlfs).
17–18. ανιααδα ια. Perhaps a magical word. Ἀδωναί cannot be read.
19. Possibly Σαλα[μάν, Ταρχει]. Cf. P. Oxy. 2061. 2-3 and P. Oslo 5. 2.
20. ωηλ. Ἰωήλ cannot be read. For the names of the angels see P. Oslo, 1, pp. 77 ff. It is difficult to determine whether or not the text broke off at this point. The lower edge of the papyrus has been trimmed by modern hands. Yet the crowding of the last two lines would seem to indicate that the writer was aware that he had but little space at his disposal.

INDEXES

I. KINGS AND EMPERORS.

PTOLEMY VI (PHILOMETOR) AND CLEOPATRA (?)
  23rd year (159/158 B. C.) **16**, 5, 8.

AUGUSTUS
  Καῖσαρ, 42nd year (12/13 A. D.) **23**, 7.

TIBERIUS
  Τιβέριος Καῖσαρ Σεβαστός, 7th year (20/21 A. D.) **24**, 7-8, 26-27.

CALIGULA
  Γάιος Καῖσαρ Σεβαστὸς Γερμανικός, 4th year (39/40 A. D.) **65**, 16-17.

CLAUDIUS
  Τιβέριος Κλαύδιος Καῖσαρ Σεβαστὸς Γερμανικὸς Αὐτοκράτωρ, 9th year (48/49 A. D.) **40**, 1-2.
  ———, 10th year (49/50 A. D.) **41**, 1-2.

TITUS
  Αὐτοκράτωρ Τίτος Καῖσαρ Οὐεσπασιανὸς Σεβαστός, year uncertain (79-81 A. D.) **31**, 1.

DOMITIAN
  Δομιτιανός, 12th year (92/93 A. D.) **42**, 1.

TRAJAN
  Αὐτοκράτωρ Καῖσαρ Νέρουα Τραιανὸς Σεβαστὸς Γερμανικός [ ], 3rd year (99/100 A. D.) **32**, 12-13.

HADRIAN
  Αὐτοκράτωρ Καῖσαρ Τραιανὸς Ἀδριανὸς Σεβαστός, 10th year (125/126 A. D.) **33**, 20-22.

ANTONINUS PIUS
  Αὐτοκράτωρ Καῖσαρ Τίτος Αἴλιος Ἀδριανὸς Ἀντωνῖνος Σεβαστὸς Εὐσεβής, 4th year (140/141 A. D.) **43**, 1-2, 6-7, 11-12; 5th year (141/142 A. D.) **44**, 1-2; 7th year (143/144 A. D.) **34**, 1-3.
  Ἀντωνῖνος Καῖσαρ ὁ κύριος, 17th year (153/154 A. D.) **56**, 8.
  ———, year unknown (138-161 A. D.) **75**, 17.

MARCUS AURELIUS
  Αὐρήλιος Ἀντωνῖνος Καῖσαρ ὁ κύριος Ἀρμενιακὸς Μηδικὸς Παρθικὸς μέγιστος, 14th year (173/174 A. D.) **45**, 1-3.

COMMODUS
  Αὐτοκράτωρ Καῖσαρ Λούκιος Αἴλιος Αὐρήλιος Κόμμοδος Εὐσεβὴς Εὐτυχὴς Σεβαστὸς Ἀρμενιακὸς Μηδικὸς Παρθικὸς Σαρματικὸς Γερμανικὸς μέγιστος Βρεταννικός, 32nd year (191/192 A. D.) **27**, 4-6 (cf. lines 6-7, 11).

SEPTIMIUS SEVERUS

Αὐτοκράτωρ Καῖσαρ Λούκιος Σεπτίμιος Σεουῆρος Εὐσεβὴς Περτίναξ Σεβαστὸς Ἀραβικὸς Ἀδιαβηνικός, year uncertain (195-197 A. D.) **36**, 8-10.

SEPTIMIUS SEVERUS, CARACALLA AND GETA

Λούκιος Σεπτίμιος Σεουῆρος Εὐσεβὴς Περτίναξ καὶ Μάρκος Αὐρήλιος Ἀντωνῖνος Εὐσεβὴς Σεβαστοὶ καὶ Πούβλιος Σεπτίμιος Γέτας Καῖσαρ Σεβαστός, 14th year (205/206 A. D.) **48**, 1-4.

CARACALLA

Ἀντωνῖνος ὁ κύριος Σεβαστός, 25th year (216/217 A. D.) **49**, 7-8.

ELAGABALUS

Αὐτοκράτωρ Καῖσαρ Μάρκος Αὐρήλιος Ἀντωνῖνος Εὐσεβὴς Εὐτυχὴς Σεβαστός, 2nd year (218/219 A. D.) **28**, 23-26 (cf. lines 15-17, 19-21).

MAXIMINUS AND MAXIMUS

οἱ κύριοι ἡμῶν Αὐτοκράτωρ Γάιος Ἰούλιος Οὐῆρος Μαξιμῖνος Εὐσεβὴς Εὐτυχὴς Σεβαστὸς καὶ Γάιος Ἰούλιος Οὐῆρος Μάξιμος ὁ ἱερώτατος Καῖσαρ, 3rd year (236/237 A. D.) **21**, 6-10.

PHILIPPI

Ἰούλιοι Φίλιπποι οἱ κύριοι, year uncertain (246-249 A. D.) **22**, 15.

VALERIANUS AND GALLIENUS

οἱ κύριοι ἡμῶν Οὐαλεριανὸς καὶ Γαλλιηνὸς Σεβαστοί, 2nd year (254/255 A. D.) **37**, 11; 3rd year (255/256 A. D.) **37**, 25; **50**, 1-3.

VALERIANUS, GALLIENUS AND SALONINUS

Αὐτοκράτορες Καίσαρες Πούπλιος Λικίννιος Οὐαλεριανὸς καὶ Πούπλιος Λικίννιος Οὐαλεριανὸς Γαλλιηνὸς Γερμανικοὶ μέγιστοι Εὐσεβεῖς Εὐτυχεῖς καὶ Πούπλιος Λικίννιος Κορνήλιος Σαλωνῖνος Οὐαλεριανὸς ὁ ἐπιφανέστατος Καῖσαρ Σεβαστοί, 6th year (258/259 A. D.) **29**, 21-27.

GALLIENUS

ὁ κύριος ἡμῶν Γαλλιηνὸς Σεβαστός, 11th year (263/264 A. D.) **61**, 4.

CONSTANTINE, CRISPUS AND CONSTANTIUS

20th, 10th and 2nd years (325/326 A. D.) **97**, 12; 21st, 11th and 3rd years (326/327 A. D.) **97**, 17.

HERACLIUS

ὁ θειότατος καὶ εὐσεβέστατος ἡμῶν δεσπότης μέγιστος εὐεργέτης Φλαούιος Ἡράκλειος ὁ αἰώνιος Αὔγουστος καὶ Αὐτοκράτωρ, 2nd year (611/612 A. D.) **87**, 1-7.

II. CONSULS.

οἱ δεσπόται ἡμῶν Κωνσταντῖνος ὁ Σεβ(αστὸς) τὸ ζ καὶ Κωνστάντιος ὁ ἐπιφανέστατος Καῖσαρ τὸ α (326 A. D.) **79**, 1.

Φλαού[ιοι] Λεόντιος ἔπαρχος τοῦ ἱεροῦ πραιτωρίου καὶ Σαλούστιος κόμες (344 A. D.) **81**, 1-3.

τοῖς μετὰ τὴν ὑπατείαν τοῦ δεσπότου ἡμῶν Φλ(αουίου) Ζήνωνος τοῦ αἰωνίου Αὐγούστου τὸ γ (481 A. D.) **82**, 1-2.

III. INDICTIONS.

a 86, 4.
β 89, 2.
γ 90, 1; 91, 1.
δ 82, 2.
ϛ 88, 1; 94, 2.

η 93, 1, 4.
ι 92, 2-3.
ιδ 96, 79, 80, 82.
ιε 87, 7; 96, 2; 97, 25.

IV. MONTHS AND DAYS.

(a) MONTHS.

Ἀδριανός (= Χοιάκ) 27, 19.
Ἀθύρ 36, 10; 53, 2, 20; 54, 4, 9; 90, 1.
Γερμανίκειος (= Παχών) 53, 26.
Ἐπείφ 39, 10; 40, 2; 45, 4; 51, 5; 53, 10, 28; 93, 4.
Θώθ 22, 15; 29, 28; 42, 6; 92, 1.
Καισάρειος (= Μεσορή) 33, 23.
Μεσορή 34, 4; 37, 12; 45, 3; 47, 8; 53, 11, 29; 65, 17.
Μεχείρ 16, 6, 8; 28, 27; 53, 5, 23; 54, 29; 91, 1.
Παῦνι 32, 11; 39, 9; 42, 3; 47, 7; 53, 9, 27; 92, 4.
Παχών 43, 3, 8, 13; 47, 7; 48, 4; 53, 8; 54, 48; 61, 3.
Σεβαστός (= Θώθ) 53, 12.
Τῦβι 24, 27; 47, 6; 53, 4, 22; 54, 22; 87, 7.
Φαμενώθ 53, 6, 24; 54, 35.
Φαρμοῦθι 18, 43; 23, 6; 41, 3; 43, 3, 8, 13; 47, 6; 49, 8; 53, 7, 25; 54, 41; 67, 6; 82, 2; 86, 4.
Φαῶφι 31, 1; 53, 13; 54, 9.
Χοιάκ 44, 3; 47, 5; 50, 3; 53, 3, 21; 54, 15; 61, 2; 90, 5.

(b) DAYS.

εἰκάς 51, 5-6.

V. PERSONAL NAMES.

Ἀβράμ, patriarch 107, 18.
Ἄγαθος 68, 12.
Ἀγαθὸς Δαίμων, Ἀ. Δ. ὁ καὶ Ἑρμαῖος, ex-βουλευτικὸς ὑπηρέτης 30, 7.
Ἄδμητος, f. of Διονύσιος 42, 21, 30.
Ἀειῶνις, traclator 86, 2.
Ἀθηνόδωρος, s. of Καρι( ) 54, 7 et saepe.
Ἀθηνώτωρος: see Ἀθηνόδωρος.
Ἀθρῆς, s. of Ἀρθώνιος, δέκανος 40, 3.
Αἰλουρᾶς 59, 4.
Ἀϊῶν 47, 1.
Ἀκοῦς 78, 5.
Ἀκύλλας, f. of Παῦλος 64, 6.
Ἀκῶρις, s. of Σάτυρος 46, 6.

Ἀκῶρις, f. of Αὐρ. Ἰοβῖνος 82, 92.
Ἀλέξανδρος, f. of Τιμόθεος 64, 4.
———, f. of Δωρόθεος 64, 5.
——— 73, 15.
——— 102, 2.
Ἀλίνη 38, 7.
Ἄλτινα, w. of Θεόδωρος 96, 42.
Ἀμᾶϊς, φροντιστὴς Τάνεως 37, 3, 14.
Ἀμέριμνος, f. of Ὀνήσιμος 48, 7.
Ἄμμων 103, 2.
Ἀμμώνιος, herdsman 28, 14.
———, Αὐρ. Ἀ., s. of Πτολλᾶς 28, 27.
——— 70, 1.
———, riparius 94, 6.
Ἀμ[ ], f. of Κολλοῦθος 84, 13.

Ἀνδρέας, s. of Μηνᾶς, ρovas (?) 96, 27, 29, 67.
──────, f. of Μηνᾶς 96, 36 (?).
Ἀνίκητος 54, 10.
Ἄννις, s. of Μαῦρος 96, 20, 63.
Ἀνουβίων, Ἀνοῦπις ὁ καὶ Ἀ. 59, 5.
Ἀνοῦπ, vine-dresser 88, 3.
Ἀνοῦπις, Ἀ. ὁ καὶ Ἀνουβίων 59, 5.
Ἀντίπατρος, Αὐρ. Ἀ., ἀπαιτητής 49, 2.
Ἀντώνιος 57, 10.
Ἀπάρτων, f. of Εὐδαίμων 59, 7.
Ἀπετε[ ], f. of Εὔπορος 25, 2.
Ἀπία, m. of Ἡρακ(λῆς?) and Διόδωρος 43, 9, 14.
Ἆπις, f. of Θαμῖνις 52, 26.
Ἀπίων, Αὐρ. Ἀ., nomarch 48, 5.
──────, s. of Ἀπίων 58, 1.
──────, f. of Ἀπίων 58, 1.
──────, Φλ. Ἀπίων, ex-consul 96, 54, 77, 80.
Ἀπολλόδωρος 19, 7.
Ἀπόλλων, s. of Κόμων 46, 9.
──────, f. of Ἱέραξ 58, 9.
────── 78, 4.
──────, f. of Θεόφιλος 82, 6.
Ἀπόλλ(ων?), f. of Κέρδων 46, 15.
Ἀπολλωνιανός, Ἀ. ὁ καὶ Διον[ύσιος?], s. of Ἑρμίππος (?) 27, 9.
Ἀπολλώνιος, f. of Σωκράτης 17, 2.
──────, Αὐρ. Ἀ.(?) ὁ καὶ Ἱέραξ, strategus of the Heraclides division 29, 1.
──────, s. of Ἀπολλώνιος 52, 19.
──────, f. of Ἀπολλώνιος 52, 19.
──────, Ἀ. ἐπικαλ. Οὐάλενς 63, 9.
──────, Ἀ. ὁ μέγας 58, 14.
Ἀρᾶισις, d. of Πετεσοῦχος (?) 31, 2, 8, 10.
Ἀπφουᾶς, f. of Αὐρ. Φίβ 87, 16.
──────, s. of ἄπα Σίων 96, 24.
Ἀρείων, s. of Βησᾶς, elder 82, 5 et saepe.
Ἀρεμῖφις, f. of Θαμῖνις 52, 6.
Ἀρητίων, s. of Νάσων 35, 1.
Ἀρθώνιος, f. of Ἀθρῆς 40, 3.
Ἀρθῶνις, m. of Κέρδων 46, 15.
Ἀρθώτης, s. of Μαρρεῖς 23, 3.
Ἄριος, Ον[...]ιου( ) ὁ καὶ Ἀ. 47, 2.
Ἀρκαδία, d. of Βίκτωρ 96, 22, 65.
Ἀρμίας 54, 24. See Ἀρμίεις.
Ἀρμίεις, s. of Ὠρίων 54, 1, 5 et saepe. Also written Ἀρμίας (l. 24) and Ἀρμίες (l. 30).

Ἀρμίες 54, 30. See Ἀρμίεις.
Ἁρπ( ), f. of Θαμοῦνις 58, 3.
Ἁρπαῆσις, f. of Θοῶνις 42, 7, 26.
──────, f. of Παπоντῶς 46, 2.
──────, s. of Ἀρσιῆσις 46, 3.
Ἀρσᾶς, f. of Ἄσινος 80, 3.
Ἀρσεῖς, m. of Ἀκῶρις 46, 6.
Ἀρσιῆσις, f. of Ἁρπαῆσις 46, 3.
Ἄρτεμις 39, 1.
Ἀρχίβιος 68, 13.
Ἄσινος, s. of Ἀρσᾶς, wool-dealer 80, 3.
Ἀσκλᾶς, s. of Ὠρίων 46, 12.
Ἀσκλατάριον, Αὐρ. Ἀ. ἡ καὶ Κόπριλλα, d. of Ἑρμῖνος ὁ καὶ Ἀσκληπιάδης 30, 3; 38, 3.
Ἀσκληπιάδης, Ἑρμῖνος ὁ καὶ Ἀ., s. of Χαιρήμων and f. of Ἀσκλατάριον ἡ καὶ Κόπριλλα 30, 3-4.
Ἀσόεις, Αὐρ. Ἀ., s. of Παυσεῖρις 29, 3, 20; 37, 4, 16.
Ἀτάμμων, Αὐρ. Ἀ., s. of Παυσεῖρις 29, 6, 10; 37, 4, 16.
Αὔγαρος 73, 1.
Αὔγχις, m. of Ὧρος 34, 7-8, 24.
Αὐρηλία: see Ἀσκλατάριον, Σερηνίλλα, Ἰσάριον, Βησοῦς.
Αὐρήλιος passim.
Ἀφθόνιος 80, 1.
Ἀφύγχις 73, 1.
Ἀχαιός, s. of Φαθρῆς, pilot 26, 3.
Ἀχιλλεύς, Αὐρ. Ἑρμῖνος ὁ καὶ Ἀ., s. of Εὐδαίμων, eutheniarch 38, 2.
──────, Αὐρ. Ἀ. ὁ καὶ Ἑρμῖνος, cosmete 38, 5.

Βαλάνιος, f. of Μυσθᾶς 54, 8 et saepe.
Βάσσος, Β. ὁ καὶ Κόλαινος 52, 18.
Βελλῆς, f. of Πτολεμαῖος 59, 9.
Βησᾶς, f. of Κῦρος, Δανιήλιος, and Ἀρείων 82, 6.
──────, Αὐρ. Β. 82, 93.
Βησοῦς, Αὐρ. Β. 77, 11.
Βιθαρίων, Αὐρ. Β. ὁ καὶ Εὐδαίμων, ἀρχιερεύς 50, 6-7.
Βίκτωρ 93, 4.
──────, s. of Σερῆνος 96, 14, 15, 60, 75.
──────, f. of Ὑπατία, Ἀρκαδία, Γεωργία and ἄπα Σίων (?), ἀπὸ μειζοτέρων 96, 21, 64.

V. PERSONAL NAMES

Γεωργία, d. of Βίκτωρ 96, 23, 66.
Γεώργιος, Αὐρ. Γ., s. of Φοιβάμμων 87, 8, 23.
———, secretary 90, 4, 6; 91, 5.
———, s. of Παπνούθιος 96, 37.
———, s. of Ψέεις 96, 53.
Γλαυκίας, s. of Πτολεμαῖος 46, 4.

Δανιήλιος, s. of Βησᾶς, elder 82, 5 et saepe.
Δεῖος, Συριακός 18, 9.
Δη( ) 58, 3.
Δημητρία, Αὐρ. Σερηνίλλα ἐπικαλ. Δ., d. of Φιλιππιανὸς ὁ καὶ Κοπρέας 38, 1.
Δημήτριος, χρηματιστῶν (?) ὑπηρέτης 16, 22.
——— 18, 4.
———, f. of Πανίσκος 52, 25.
Διδυμάριον, d. of Ἐπ.[ ] 58, 6.
Διδύμη, m. of Πτολεμαῖος 76, 14-15, 21.
Δίδυμος, Δ. ὁ καὶ Ἑρμείας, f. of Σερῆνος 26, 5-6.
———, πράκτωρ ἀργ. 44, 3.
———, f. of Κλεόπατρος 46, 10.
Διογένης, s. of Διογένης 58, 2.
———, f. of Διογένης 58, 2.
———, s. of Ὀκ...[ ] 58, 7.
——— 74, 4.
——— 106, 8.
Διοδώρα, m. of Χαιρήμων 43, 4.
Διόδωρος, s. of Χαιρήμων 43, 13.
———, f. of Σύρος 46, 13.
Διονυσία, d. of Πετοσῖρις 42, 2.
———, m. of Σύρος 46, 13.
Διονύσιος, μάχιμος 18, 10.
———, Ἀπολλωνιανὸς ὁ καὶ Διον[ύσιος?], s. of Ἑρμίππος (?) 27, 9.
———, κατασπορεύς 40, 4.
———, f. of Ἡρακλείδης (?) 42, 5.
———, s. of Ἄδμητος 42, 21, 30.
———, s. of Ἐπιτυγχ(άνων?) 46, 11.
———, f. of Πεκύλλος 64, 7.
——— 65, 1.
——— 67, 1, 7.
———, s. of Διοσκουρίδης and f. of Αὐρ. Ὡρίων, Αὐρ. Εὐδαίμων, and Αὐρ. Εὐλόγιος 79, 2, 3.
———, Αὐρ. Δ., s. of Σόϊς 82, 91.
——— 100, 14.
Διονυτᾶς 65, 18 (= Διονύσιος, l. 1).
Δῖος, s. of Στέφανος 36, 14.

Διόσκορος, s. of Διόσκορος 46, 8.
———, f. of Διόσκορος 46, 8.
———, Αὐρ. Δ. 49, 5.
——— 70, 5, 14.
——— 89, 1.
Διοσκουρίδης, f. of Διονύσιος 79, 2.
Δομίττιος, Δ. Ροῦφος, procurator in charge of granaries at Alexandria 26, 15.
Δράκων 49, 3.
Δωρίων 18, 5.
Δωρόθεος, s. of Ἀλέξανδρος 64, 5.

Εἰσσάκ 73, 16.
Ἔκυσις, s. of Πανεσνεὺς 34, 10 et saepe.
Ἑλένη, m. of Πτολεμαΐς 76, 13, 20.
Ἕλενος 97, 19, 21.
Ἐπ.[ ], f. of Διδυμάριον 58, 6.
Ἐπιτυγχ(άνων?), f. of Διονύσιος 46, 11.
Ἑρμαῖος, Ἀγαθὸς Δαίμων ὁ καὶ Ἑ., ἐκβουλευτικὸς ὑπηρέτης 30, 7.
Ἑρμείας, Δίδυμος ὁ καὶ Ἑ., f. of Σερῆνος 26, 5-6.
Ἑρμείων, s. of Ἑρμείων 59, 6.
———, f. of Ἑρμείων 59, 6.
Ἑρμίας, dealer in olive oil 100, 5.
Ἕρμινος, Ἕ. ὁ καὶ Ἀσκληπιάδης, s. of Χαιρήμων and f. of Ἀσκλατάριον ἡ καὶ Κόπριλλα 30, 3-4.
———, Αὐρ. Ἕ. ὁ καὶ Ἀχιλλεύς, s. of Εὐδαίμων, eutheniarch 38, 2.
———, Αὐρ. Ἀχιλλεὺς ὁ καὶ Ἕ., cosmete 38, 5.
Ἕρμιππος, f. of Ἀπολλωνιανός (?) 27, 10.
Ἐσοῦρις, s. of Ὡρίων 54, 6 et saepe.
——— 59, 4.
Εὐάνθεια 98, 7.
Εὐδαίμων, Αὐρ. Ε., strategus of the Alexandrian χώρα 21, 1.
———, f. of Ἕρμινος ὁ καὶ Ἀχιλλεύς 38, 2.
———, Αὐρ. Βιθαρίων ὁ καὶ Εὐ., ἀρχιερεύς 50, 6-7.
———, s. of Ἀπάρτων 59, 7.
———, f. of Φιβῖχις 59, 8.
———, Αὐρ. Εὐ., s. of Διονύσιος 79, 2, 6, 8.
——— 101, 2.
Εὐθάλειος (?) 100, 1-2.
Εὐλόγιος, Αὐρ. Εὐ., s. of Διονύσιος 79, 2.

Εὐλόγιος 98, 2.
Εὔμηλος 70, 1.
Εὔξεινος: see Πακίλλιος.
Εὔπορος, s. of Ἀπετε[ ] 25, 2.
——— 72, 1.
Εὐφημία, d. of Ἰωάννης, nun 84, 4. 9.
———, d. of Θεόδωρος 96, 48, 49.
Εὔφρων 19, 1. 14.
——— 97, 14.
Ἐφέλιος (= Ὀφέλλιος?), overseer 80, 6.
Ε. [..], m. of Διονύσιος 46, 11.

Ἡλιόδωρος 71, 7.
Ἡρακλείδης, Αὐρ. Ἡ., ex-cosmete 37, 1, 10, 13.
———, f. of Κλαύδιος 42, 4.
———, s. of Ἡρακλείδης (?) 58, 8.
Ἡρακ(λείδης?), s. of Διονύσιος 42, 5.
Ἡρακ[λείδης?], f. of Ἡρακλείδης 58, 8.
Ἡρακλῆς 83, 4.
Ἡρακ(λῆς?), s. of Χαιρήμων 43, 8.
Ἡρᾶς, s., f., and g. of same name 31, 2.
———, m. of Ἀσκλᾶς 46, 12.
———, s. of Τρύφων 46, 14.
——— 54, 55.
Ἡροΐς, d. of Θονῶνις (?) and Ἀραῖσις 31, 4.
Ἥρων, s. of Φάσεις 44, 3.
———, f. of Πωλίων 45, 5.

Θα[.....], m. of Ἥρων 44, 4.
Θαῆσις (?), d. of Ὧρος and m. of Ἡρᾶς 32, 1-2.
——— 68, 11.
Θαμῖνις, s. of Ἀρεμίφις 52, 6.
———, s. of Ψανσνῶς 52, 15.
———, s. of Ἆπις 52, 26.
Θαμοῦνις, s. of Ἁρπ( ) 58, 3.
Θαϋβάσθις, m. of Παμμίας 59, 3.
Θεανώ 67, 1.
Θεογένης, χρηματιστῶν εἰσαγωγεύς 16, 5.
Θεοδότη, d. of Θεόδωρος 96, 47.
Θεόδουλος 98, 2.
Θεόδωρος 83, 4.
———, ὁ ἅγιος Θ. 87, 15.
———, s. of Ἰούλιος and f. of Ὧρος, Ἰούλιος, Σερῆνος, Μηνᾶς, Θεοδότη, and Εὐφημία 96, 41 et saepe.
———, βοηθός 106, 8.
Θεόφιλος 18, 2.

Θεόφιλος, s. of Ἀπόλλων, deacon 82, 6 et saepe.
Θεραῖτις, s. of Ψενγῆρις 52, 9.
Θήδε(σις?), s. of Ἰάκοβος 42, 19, 21, 32.
Θονῶνις, h. of Ἀραῖσις 31, 5, 8.
Θοῶνις, s. of Ἁρπαῆσις 42, 7, 26 (Θῶνις), 39.
Θώνιος, f. of Σαραπάμμων 64, 2.
Θῶνις, freedman of Ἀπολλωνιανός 27, 9.
——— (= Θοῶνις), s. of Ἁρπαῆσις 42, 26.
———, βουλευτής 50, 10.

Ἰάκοβος, f. of Θήδε(σις?) 42, 21, 32.
Ἰακώβ, s. of Φοιβάμμων 96, 10, 11, 58, 73.
———, f. of Ψέειος 96, 53.
——— 103, 1.
———, patriarch 107, 19.
Ἰάσων, Αὐρ. Ἰ., ἀπαιτητής 49, 1.
Ἱέραξ, Αὐρ. Ἀπολλώνιος (?) ὁ καὶ Ἱ., strategus of the Heraclides division 29, 1.
———, s. of Ἀπόλλων 58, 9.
Ἱέρων 39, 2.
Ἰησοῦς: see Index VII, a.
Ἰοβῖνος, Αὐρ. Ἰ., s. of Ἀκῶρις 82, 92.
Ἰούλιος: see Σουίλλιος.
———, Αὐρ. Ἰ., ἀπαιτητής 49, 1.
———, f. of Θεόδωρος 96, 41.
———, s. of Θεόδωρος 96, 44, 49.
Ἰσάκ, patriarch 107, 18. Cf. Εἰσσάκ.
Ἰσάριον, Αὐρ. Ἰ. 77, 7.
Ἰσίδωρος, Ἰ. ὁ καὶ Μάρων, s. of Μάρων 41, 3.
———, s. of Παμῖνις 59, 2.
———, s. of Σαραπάμμων 64, 3.
——— 68, 14.
Ἶσις, m. of Αὐρ. Γεώργιος 87, 9.
———, m. of Σερῆνος 87, 11.
———, d. of Παπνούθιος 96, 32, 69.
Ἰσόδωρος, Ἰ. ὁ [καὶ 6-8] 16, 1.
Ἰωάννης, f. of Εὐφημία 84, 9.
——— 85, 6, 14.
——— 93, 2.
———, overseer 96, 31.
———, s. of Φίβ 96, 52.
———, Ἰ. ὁ. καὶ Πετ.[...], scholasticus 105, 2.
Ἰωσήφ, senator 86, 1.

Καλόκαιρος 33, 9.
——— 98, 22.
Κάμοκος 56, 2.
Καρι( ), f. of Ἀθηνόδωρος 54, 7 et saepe.
Κασέπος 18, 15.
Κᾶτις 70, 15.
Κέρδων, s. of Ἀπόλλ(ων ?) 46, 15.
Κέρεκος (?), f. of Μακάριος 90, 2; 91, 3.
Κεφάλων 42, 19 et saepe.
Κι. διενος (?) 102, 1, 19.
Κλαύδιος, Τιβέριος Κ. Σαραπίων, strategus of the Oxyrhynchite nome 25, 1.
———, s. of Ἡρακλείδης 42, 4.
Κλεοπάτρα, m. of Γλαυκίας and Σαραπ(ίων ?) 46, 5.
Κλεόπατρος, s. of Δίδυμος 46, 10.
Κλεοχάρης 58, 10.
Κοΐντος: see Πακίλλιος.
Κόλαινος, Βάσσος ὁ καὶ Κ. 52, 18.
Κολλοῦθος, s. of Μάξιμος 36, 10-11.
———, Αὐρ. Κ. 81, 8.
———, Αὐρ. Κ., s. of Βησᾶς 82, 90.
———, s. of Ἀμ[ ] 84, 13.
———, Κ. ὁ καὶ Στέφανος 94, 1-2, 5, 10.
———, fruit-grower 104, 4.
Κόμων, f. of Ἀπόλλων 46, 9.
Κοπρέας, Φιλιππιανὸς ὁ καὶ Κ., f. of Σερηνίλλα, ex-senator 38, 1.
Κόπριλλα, Αὐρ. Ἀσκλατάριον ἡ καὶ Κ., d. of Ἑρμῖνος ὁ καὶ Ἀσκληπιάδης 30, 3; 38, 3.
Κοσμᾶς, vine-dresser 88, 2.
Κῦρος, s. of Βησᾶς, bishop 82, 4 et saepe.

Λαέρτης 55, 2.
Λευκάδιος 72, 1.
Λέων, f. of Μαρῖνος 96, 16, 17, 61, 76.
Λικίννος 55, 3.
Λόγγος, Αὐρ. Οὐαλέριος Λ., veteran 38, 2.
Λοίσανδρος: see Λύσανδρος.
Λυκόφρων 55, 1.
Λύσανδρος 55, 4.

Μακάριος, advocatus fori 82, 15.
———, s. of Κέρεκος (?) 90, 2; 91, 2.
Μάκρος 73, 15.
Μάξιμος, f. of Κολλοῦθος 36, 11.
Μαρία, w. of Παπνούθιος 96, 35.

Μαρῖνος, s. of Λέων 96, 16, 17, 61, 76.
Μαρρεῖς, f. of Ἁρθώτης 23, 3.
Μάρων, Ἰσίδωρος ὁ καὶ Μ., s. of Μάρων 41, 3.
———, Μ. ν(εώτερος), f. of Ἰσίδωρος ὁ καὶ Μάρων 41, 4.
Μαῦρος, f. of Χρυσερῶς and Ἄννις 96, 18, 19, 62.
Μενα: see Μένανδρος.
Μένα(νδρος ?) 55, 1 (note).
Μερκούλιος 68, 12.
Μηνᾶς, s. of Ἀνδρέας (?) and f. of Ἀνδρέας and Παπνούθιος 96, 27, 36, 67.
———, s. of Παπνούθιος, pastry-cook 96, 38.
———, s. of Θεόδωρος 96, 46.
Μινέριος, s. of Εὐφημία 96, 48.
Μιχαήλ, archangel 107, 3, 18.
Μυσθᾶς, s. of Βαλάνιος 54, 8 et saepe.
Μόσχος 97, 12, 18.
Μύσθης, f. of Νεῖλος 35, 1.
Μ...ε.[ ], f. of Σεντασνῶς 52, 7.

Νάκιος, ἄπα, f. of Φίβ 96, 50.
Νάσων, f. of Ἀρητίων 35, 1-2.
Νεῖλος, h. of Ἡροῒς 31, 4.
———, s. of Μύσθης and f. of Χαιρήμων 35, 1.
Νεκφερῶς, f. of Παποντῶς 17, 1.
Νεμεσίων 65, 1.
Νίγερ 52, 20.
Νικάσιππος 18, 13.
Νίκων 98, 6.

Ξενοφῶν (?), f. of Ὠρίων 36, 13-14.

Ὀκ...[ ], f. of Διογένης 58, 7.
Ὀλύμπιος, secretary 83, 2.
Ον[...]ιου( ), Ο. ὁ καὶ Ἄριος 47, 2.
Ὀνήσιμος, s. of Ἀμέριμνος 48, 7.
Οὐάλενς, praepositus 63, 2.
———, Ἀπολλώνιος ἐπικαλ. Οὐ. 63, 9.
Οὐαλέριος, Αὐρ. Οὐ. Λόγγος, veteran 38, 2.
Ὀφέλλιος 75, 17.

Παᾶς, g. of Ὧρος 32, 3-4.
Παγχ[ ], f. of Σενψενενοῦπις 52, 4.
Παγχ( ), f. of Θαϋβάσθις 59, 3.
Παθερμοῦθις, f. of Ἥρων 45, 5.

Παι( ), f. of Βελλῆς **59**, 9.
Πακίλλιος, Κοίντος Π. Εὔξεινος ἐπιστάτης φυλακιτῶν **23**, 1.
[Παμ]ῖνις, f. of Τύρων **59**, 1.
———, s. of Τύρων **59**, 1.
[Π]αμῖνις, f. of Ἰσίδωρος **59**, 2.
Παμμίας, s. of Θαϋβάσθις **59**, 3.
Παμνοῦς **19**, 1.
Πάμφιλος **68**, 13.
Πανεσνεῦς, f. of Ἔκῦσις **34**, 11.
Πανεχάτης, f. of Σενπανεχάτης **52**, 3.
———, s. of Πουρανοῦπις **52**, 11.
Πανίσκος, s. of Δημήτριος **52**, 25.
——— **98**, 22.
Παπνούθιος, s. of Μηνᾶς and f. of Σερῆνος, Ἶσις, Πετρωνία, Γεώργιος, Μηνᾶς, and Χριστόφορος (?) **96**, 29 et saepe.
Παποντῶς, s. of Νεκφερῶς **17**, 1.
———, f. of Πετεσοῦχος **46**, 1.
———, s. of Ἁρπαῆσις **46**, 2.
——— **74**, 1, 13.
Πατερηοῦς **63**, 8.
Πάτρων **37**, 4, 15.
Παϋαν( ) **97**, 23.
Παῦλος, s. of Ἀκύλλας **64**, 6.
——— **74**, 12.
———, h. of Τλοῦλλα **95**, 4.
Παυσεῖρις, f. of Ἀσόεις and Ἀτάμμων **29**, 3-4.
Πεκύλλος, s. of Διονύσιος **64**, 7.
Πέλοψ, ὑπηρέτης **16**, 8.
Πετ[ ], f. of Τανεχᾶτις (?) **52**, 14.
Πετεμῖνις **18**, 12.
Πετερμούθης **33**, 2.
Πετεσοῦχος, ἀρτοκόπος (?) **18**, 16.
——— (?), f. of Ἁρᾶσις **31**, 2.
———, s. of Παποντῶς **46**, 1.
Πετεφνοῦθις, f. of Φαθρῆς **26**, 3.
Πετοσῖρις, f. of Διονυσία **42**, 2.
Πέτρος, δι. ( ) (?) **89**, 4.
Πετρωνία, d. of Παπνούθιος **96**, 33, 34.
Πετσεῖρος, s. of Πετσεῖρις, herdsman **24**, 16.
———, f. of Πετσεῖρις **24**, 17.
Πετ.[...], Ἰωάννης ὁ καὶ Π., scholasticus **105**, 2.
Πιάριος **99**, 3.
Πλούταρχος, δεκάδαρχος **22**, 10.
Πομπηιανός **71**, 17.
Πουρανοῦπις, f. of Πανεχάτης **52**, 11.
Πρυν( ) : see Φρυν( ).

Πτολεμαῖος, royal scribe of the Themistes division and acting-strategus of the Heraclides division **26**, 21.
———, f. of Γλαυκίας and Σαραπ(ίων?) **46**, 4.
———, s. of Βελλῆς **59**, 9.
——— **74**, 2, 14.
———, s. of Διδύμη **76**, 13-14, 20.
———, εἰρηνάρχης **99**, 1.
Πτολεμαΐς **50**, 9.
Πτολεμαΐς, d. of Ἑλένη **76**, 12, 19.
Πτολλᾶς, f. of Αὐρ. Ἀμμώνιος **28**, 28.
Πωλίων, s. of Ἥρων **45**, 5.
Πω( ) **42**, 18.
Π..πω..., f. of Ἑρμείων **59**, 6.

Ῥοῦφος : see Δομίττιος.

Σαμπάθιος **103**, 2.
Σαραπάμμων, s. of Θώνιος **64**, 2.
———, f. of Ἰσίδωρος **64**, 3.
———, Φλ. Σ., proximus **78**, 1.
Σαραπιάς **70**, 14.
Σαραπίων, toparch **24**, 23.
———, Τιβέριος Κλαύδιος Σ., strategus of the Oxyrhynchite nome **25**, 1.
———, strategus of the Oxyrhynchite nome **27**, 2, 8.
——— **48**, 5.
Σαραπ(ίων?), s. of Ὧρος **46**, 7.
Σαραποῦς **27**, 11.
Σαρᾶς, ἱεροψάλτης **62**, 5.
Σατορνεῖλος **71**, 8.
Σάτυρος, f. of Ἀκῶρις **46**, 6.
Σεναρεμῖφις, s. of Ὧρος **52**, 12.
Σενπανεχάτης, s. of Πανεχάτης **52**, 3.
Σενπανεχπαστι[ ] **52**, 13.
Σενπετεμεῖνις, s. of Τανεχᾶτις **52**, 14.
Σεντασνῶς, s. of Μ...ε.[ ] **52**, 7.
Σενψενενοῦπις, s. of Παγχ[ ] **52**, 4.
Σεουῆρος **101**, 2.
Σερηνίλλα, Αὐρ. Σ. ἐπικαλ. Δημητρία, d. of Φιλιππιανὸς ὁ καὶ Κοπρέας **38**, 1.
Σερῆνος, s. of Δίδυμος, secretary **26**, 6.
———, Φλ. Σ., proximus **78**, 1.
——— **84**, 3.
———, s. of Σουροῦς **87**, 10.
———, f. of Βίκτωρ, ἀπὸ μειζοτέρων **96**, 12, 13, 59, 74.
———, s. of Παπνούθιος **96**, 30, 40.
———, s. of Θεόδωρος **96**, 45.

Σερῆνος, slave 106, 6.
Σιλουανός, σύμμαχος 103, 3.
Σινθοῶνις, m. of Παᾶς 32, 4-5.
———, m. of Σαραπ(ίων?) 46, 7.
Σίων, ἄπα, s. of Βίκτωρ (?) and f. of Ἀπφουᾶς 96, 24 ff.
Σοῖς, f. of Αὐρ. Διονύσιος 82, 91.
Σουίλλιος, Σ. Ἰούλιος, juridicus 27, 1, 14.
Σουίρ 92, 1.
Σουροῦς, f. of Σερῆνος 87, 10.
Σοφία, w. of Αὐρ. Τιθοῆς 81, 7.
Σπαρτιάτης, Αὐρ. Σ. ὁ καὶ Χαιρήμων, strategus of the Hermopolite nome 30, 1.
Στέφανος, f. of Δῖος 36, 14.
———, Κολλοῦθος ὁ καὶ Σ. 94, 1-2, 5, 10.
——— 101, 9.
Συμεώνιος, πραγματευτής 103, 1.
Σύρος, s. of Διόδωρος 46, 13.
Σωκράτης, s. of Ἀπολλώνιος 17, 2.
Σωσικλῆς, f. of Χαιρήμων 58, 4.

Τααρχωρσία 24, 4.
Ταεῦς, m. of Πωλίων 45, 5.
Τανεντῆρις, m. of Διόσκορος 46, 8.
Τανεχᾶτις, m. of Σενπετεμεῖνις 52, 14.
Ταποτάμων, m. of Ἀπόλλων 46, 9.
Τεβῶς, s. of Φατρεῖς 52, 13.
Τιβερεῖνος 57, 1.
Τιβέριος : see Κλαύδιος.
Τιθοῆς, Αὐρ. Τ., s. of Τιθοῆς, weaver 81, 4.
———, f. of Αὐρ. Τιθοῆς 81, 4.
Τίμαιος 18, 11.
Τιμόθεος, s. of Ἀλέξανδρος 64, 4.
——— 97, 24.
Τλούλλα, w. of Παῦλος 95, 3.
Τρύφων, f. of Ἡρᾶς 46, 14.
Τύρων, s. of Παμῖνις (?) 59, 1.
———, f. of Παμῖνις (?) 59, 1.

Ὑπατία, d. of Βίκτωρ 96, 21, 64.
Ὑπατίων 106, 5.

Φαθρῆς, f. of Ἀχαιός and s. of Πετεφνοῦθις 26, 3.
Φάσεις, f. of Ἥρων 44, 3.
Φᾶσις, s. of Χαιρήμων 33, 1.
Φατρεῖς, f. of Τεβῶς 52, 13.
Φείδιππος, f. of Χαιρήμων 58, 5.
Φίβ, Αὐρ. Φ., s. of Ἀπφουᾶς, doorkeeper 87, 14.
———, s. of ἄπα Νάκιος and f. of Ἰωάννης, cook 96, 50.
Φιβῖχις, s. of Εὐδαίμων 59, 8.
Φιλήμων 18, 7.
Φιλιππιανός, Φ. ὁ καὶ Κοπρέας, f. of Σερηνίλλα, ex-senator 38, 1.
Φιλοκράτης, ὑδροφόρος Φιλήμονος (?) 18, 6.
Φιλόξενα, sister of ἄπα Σίων 96, 26.
Φιλόξενος, strategus of the Oxyrhynchite nome 22, 1.
——— 78, 3.
———, s. of Φοιβάμμων, μειζότερος 96, 4, 5, 55, 70.
Φίλων 42, 19, 34.
Φλαβιανός, scholasticus 105, 1, 7.
Φλαούιος : see Σαραπάμμων, Σερῆνος, Ἀπίων.
Φοιβάμμων, ἐλαιουργός 86, 1.
———, f. of Αὐρ. Γεώργιος 87, 8, 23.
——— 89, 1.
——— 90, 4.
———, f. of Φιλόξενος and Ἰακώβ, ἀπὸ μειζοτέρων 96, 8 ff. et saepe.
———, s. of Ἀνδρέας 96, 28, 68.
———, βοηθὸς πρωτοκωμητῶν 105, 1, 6.
Φρυν( ) 54, 11. Also written Πρυν( ) 54, 50.

Χαιρέας, strategus of the Oxyrhynchite nome 24, 3.
Χαιρήμων, Αὐρ. Σπαρτιάτης ὁ καὶ Χ., strategus of the Hermopolite nome 30, 1.
———, f. of Ἑρμῖνος ὁ καὶ Ἀσκληπιάδης 30, 4.
———, f. of Φᾶσις 33, 1.
———, s. of Νεῖλος 35, 2.
———, s. of Χαιρήμων 43, 3.
———, f. of Χαιρήμων, Ἡρακ(λῆς ?), and Διόδωρος 43, 3, 8, 13.
———, g. of Χαιρήμων, Ἡρακ(λῆς ?) and Διόδωρος 43, 3, 9, 14.
———, s. of Σωσικλῆς 58, 4.
———, s. of Φείδιππος 58, 5.
——— 71, 1.
Χριστός : see Ἰησοῦς.

Χριστόφορος, s. of Παπνούθιος (?), πανδουριστής 96, 39.
Χρυσερῶς, s. of Μαῦρος 96, 18, 19, 62.

Ψανσνῶς, f. of Θαμῖνις 52, 15.
Ψέειος, s. of Ἰακώβ and f. of Γεώργιος 96. 53.
Ψενγῆρις, f. of Θεραῖτις 52, 9.
Ψενοσῖρις, f. of Ψηρῖφις 52, 10.
Ψενο[ ] 52, 5.
Ψηρῖφις, s. of Ψενοσῖρις 52, 10.

Ὠρήων 54, 17. See Ὠρίων, f. of Ἐσοῦρις.
Ὠριγένης 71, 6, 11.
Ὠρίων, s. of Ξενοφῶν (?) 36, 13.

Ὠρίων 39, 12.
———, f. of Ἀσκλᾶς 46, 12.
———, f. of Ἁρμίεις and Ἐσοῦρις 54, 5, 6 et saepe.
———, Αὐρ. ῶ., s. of Διονύσιος 79, 2, 8.
——— 97, 1.
Ὧρος, f. of Θαῆσις (?) 32, 2.
———, g. of Παᾶς 32, 4.
———, ἀπάτωρ 34, 7 et saepe.
———, f. of Σαραπ(ίων ?) 46, 7.
———, f. of Σεναρεμῖφις 52, 12.
———, ἄπα ῶ., s. of Θεόδωρος 96, 43.

[.]τπυν 68, 11.

VI. GEOGRAPHICAL.

(a) Countries, Peoples, Nomes, Districts, Toparchies.

Αἰγύπτιος 96, 1, 3.
Αἴγυπτος 20, 2; 77, 1.
Ἀρσινοΐτης 26, 2; 29, 2; 31, 2; 34, 5-6; 48, 5.
Ἑρμοπολίτης 30, 2, 4.
Ἡρακλείδης 16, 3; 26, 2, 23-24, 25; 29, 2.
Θεμίστης 26, 22; 34, 5.

Λίβυς 29, 8.
Ὀξυρυγχίτης 22, 1; 27, 2; 87, 13-14.
Περσής: see ἐπιγονή (Index XIII).
Προσωπείτης 26, 5.
Συριακός 18, 9. ἀπαιτηταὶ κριθῆς Σ. 49, 2-3.
τοπαρχία, λιβὸς τ. 50, 4. ἡ πρὸς λίβα τ. 24, 14-15. ἡ κάτω τ. 24, 18-19.

(b) Cities and Villages.

Ἄθρα, κώμης Ἄθρας ὅρων 26, 4.
Ἀθῦχις 42, 2 et saepe.
Ἀλαβανθίς 19, 2.
Ἀλεξάνδρεια 26, 18; 27, 15; 68, 2. ἡ λαμπροτάτη Ἀλεξανδρέων πόλις 37, 1-2, 13, 14. ἡ Ἀλεξανδρέων χώρα 21, 2.
Ἀλεξανδρεύς 16, 1.
Ἐντεῖις 42, 5 et saepe.
Ἑρμοῦ πόλις 30, 7; 38, 1 ff.
Θεαδέλφεια 23, 4; 34, 4; 40, 3.
Θηβαῖος 82, 16.
Θμοινεψῶβθις (?) 42, 6, 22, 37.
Ἰβιῶν Πετεαφθί 38, 6.
Καμίνου, κώμη [Κα]μίνου 29, 7.
Κερκεσοῦχα Ὄρρους (sic) 90, 1-2; 91, 2.
Κερκή 26, 18.

Κόβα 105, 1, 6.
Κροκοδίλων πόλις 16, 14.
Λο.[..].. 73, 8.
Λυκοπολίτης 82, 4.
Λύκων πόλις 82, 2, 18.
Μέμφις, λιμὴν Μέμφεως 51, 2.
Μοῖραι, χωρίον Μοιρῶν 93, 1.
Νέα πόλις 26, 15-16, 19-20.
Νῆσος Λευκάδιος, ἐποίκιον Ν. Λ. 88, 1.
Ὀξυρυγχιτῶν πόλις 22, 13; 25, 3; 27, 11, 13; 32, 2-3; 77, 3; 81, 5; 87, 16; 96, 78.
Ὀξύρυγχος 83, 6; 105, 3.
Πέλα 24, 14; 61, 11.
Προταρ( ) 42, 4, 5.
Πω( ) (?), 42, 18.
Σενέπτα 79, 7.

VI. GEOGRAPHICAL

Σέσφθα **24**, 18.
Σύρων, κώμη Σ. **63**, 5.
Τάνις **37**, 3 et saepe.
Τόκα **100**, 4.

Φιλαδέλφια **16**, 3, 11-12; **17**, 2-3, 4; **26**, 1; **29**, 4-5; **41**, 5; **47**, 4; **51**, 1; **69**, 2-3; **99**, 2.

(c) ἄμφοδα.

Ἄνω Παρεμβολή **46**, 8.
Δρόμος Γυμνασίου **46**, 4, 12; **77**, 11.
Δρόμος Θοήριδος **46**, 10, 15.
Θοῆρις : see Δρόμος Θοήριδος.
Ἰβιοταφεῖον **46**, 14.
Ἱππόδρομος **46**, 1 ff.

Κρητικόν **46**, 1, 2, 9.
Μακεδόνων **45**, 6.
Πλατεία **46**, 11.
Ποιμενική **46**, 13.
Συριακή **43**, 4, 10, 15.
Φρούριον λίψ **30**, 5.

(d) κλῆροι, τόποι, κτήματα.

Ἐρεμία, τόπος Ἐ. **93**, 2.
Ἑρμαίων, τόπος Ἐ. **94**, 1.
Μεγάλη Ταρουθῖνος, κτῆμα Μ. Τ. **87**, 12-13.

Ναυβη, Ν. κλῆρος **38**, 6.
Πτιαπ( ), κλῆρος Π. **37**, 5.
Φθιαπ( ), ἐν τόπῳ Φθι[απ( ) κλήρο]υ **37**, introd.

(e) Tribes and Demes.

Ἀδριάνειος **27**, 10.
Ἀλθαιεύς **26**, 7.

Ἡφαιστιεύς **16**, 2.

(f) Miscellaneous.

Πλωτ( ), διῶρυξ(?) **40**, 2.

VII. RELIGION.

(a) Christian.

Ἀβράμ, οἱ κύριοι Ἀβράμ, Ἰσάκ, Ἰακώβ **107**, 18-19.
ἅγιος **82**, 4, 7; **107**, 15, 16, 17. See also Θεόδωρος.
ἄπα, ἅ. Ὧρος **96**, 43; ἅ. Σίων **96**, 24 ff.; ἅ. Νάκιος **96**, 50.
ἀρχάγγελος **107**, 3-4.
δεσπότης **87**, 1.
διάκονος **82**, 7, 17.
ἐκκλησία **82**, 7. ἡ καθολικὴ Λυκοπολιτῶν ἁγίας τοῦ θεοῦ ἐ. **82**, 4-5.
ἐπίσκοπος **82**, 4 et saepe.
Θεόδωρος, ὁ ἅγιος Θ. **87**, 15.
θεός **82**, 4, 7; **87**, 2; **90**, 4, 6; **91**, 5; **105**, 3; **106**, 6; **107**, 11, 12. ὁ κύριος θ. **73**, 4; **101**, 5. υἱὸς ὁ θεοῦ (?) **102**, 15.
Ἰακώβ : see Ἀβράμ.

Ἰησοῦς, Ἰ. Χριστός **87**, 2.
Ἰσάκ : see Ἀβράμ.
καθολικός : see ἐκκλησία.
κύριος **87**, 1; **104**, 5. See also θεός, Σαρᾶπις, Σαβαώθ, Ἀβράμ, Ἰσάκ, and Ἰακώβ.
Μιχαήλ **107**, 3, 18.
μονάζουσα **84**, 9.
ὄνομα, ἐν ὀ. τοῦ κυρίου κ. τ. λ. **87**, 1.
οὐρανός **107**, 11, 14, 16.
παντοκράτωρ, π. Σαβαώθ **107**, 5-6.
πατήρ, π. ἡμῶν **107**, 13.
πρεσβύτερος **82**, 5, 10.
Σαβαώθ **107**, 6, 20. κύριος Σ. **107**, 16.
σωτήρ **87**, 2.
υἱός : see θεός.
χμγ **83**, 1; **104**, 1; **105**, 5.
Χριστός : see Ἰησοῦς.

(b) PAGAN.

Ἄρτεμις (?) **39**, 1 (note).
ἀρχιερεύς **50**, 7.
θεοί **70**, 8.

ἱερός, τοῦ ἱ. πραιτωρίου **81**, 2. ἱερώτατος, ὁ ἱ. Καῖσαρ **21**, 10.
ἱεροψάλτης **62**, 5.
Σαρᾶπις, ὁ κύριος Σ. **70**, 4.

VIII. MAGIC AND ASTROLOGY.

Αἰγόκερως **75**, 4.
Ἄρης **75**, 6-7, 8.
ἀστήρ **75**, 11, 12.
ἀστροθέσις **75**, 18.
Ἀφροδείτη **75**, 1.
Ἐλωεί **107**, 19.
Ἑρμῆς **75**, 3, 12.
Καρκίνος **75**, 2.
κλῆρος, κ. τῆς τύχης **75**, 2. κ. ὁ τοῦ δαίμονος **75**, 4. κ. ἔρωτος **75**, 6. κ. τῆς ἀνάγκης **75**, 8.
κλιμακτηρικός: see ὅρος.
Κριός **75**, 8.

Κρόνος **75**, 1.
μοῖρα **75**, 1 et saepe.
οἰκοδεσποτεία **75**, 13.
οἰκοδεσπότης **75**, 10-11, 15-16.
οἶκος **75**, 1 et saepe.
ὅριον **75**, 1 et saepe.
ὅρος, κλιμακτηρικὸς ὅ. **75**, 15.
Σαλαμάν **107**, 19.
Σελήνη **75**, 2-3.
σινωτικός, σ. ὅρος **75**, 14-15.
Ταῦρος **75**, 6.
Ωηλ (?) **107**, 20.
. κοαχαμιφωνχωωθψαχε **76**, 1 ff.

IX. OFFICIAL AND MILITARY TERMS.

(a) OFFICIAL.

ἀπαιτητής **50**, 4. ἀ. κριθῆς Συριακῆς **49**, 2-3.
ἀρχέφοδος (?) **99**, 6.
βασιλικὸς γραμματεύς **26**, 21, 24-25.
βοηθός **106**, 8. β. πρωτοκωμητῶν **105**, 1, 6.
βουλευτήριον **61**, 17.
βουλευτής **38**, 1; **50**, 10; **86**, 1.
βουλευτικός: see ὑπηρέτης.
γραμματεύς **90**, 4, 6; **91**, 5.
γυμνασίαρχος **71**, 6.
δεκανός **40**, 3.
δικαιοδότης **27**, 1.
δικαστήριον **82**, 13.
εἰρηνάρχης **99**, 1.
εἰσαγωγεύς, εἰ. χρηματιστῶν **16**, 5.
ἔπαρχος **20**, 1, 14; **77**, 1. ἐ. τοῦ ἱεροῦ πραιτωρίου **81**, 2.
ἐπιστάτης **16**, 12, 19. ἐ. φυλακιτῶν **23**, 2.
ἐπιτροπή, ἡ τοῦ ἰδίου λόγου ἐ. **22**, 4, 11, 14.
ἐπίτροπος, ἐ. Νέας πόλεως **26**, 15-16.
εὐθηνιάρχης **38**, 2.
ἡγεμών **20**, 17.
ἴδιος λόγος **22**, 4.
κόμες **81**, 3; **83**, 2.
κοσμητεία **71**, 20.
κοσμητεύω **37**, 1, 13.
κοσμητής **38**, 5.
κωμάρχης **99**, 2.
λειτουργός: see Index XIII.
μειζότερος **96**, 4 et saepe.
νομάρχης **48**, 5.
πραγματευτής **103**, 1.
πραιπόσιτος **63**, 2.
πραιτώριον, ἔπαρχος τοῦ ἱεροῦ π. **81**, 2.
πράκτωρ **16**, 10-11, 20; **70**, 11. π. ἀργυρικῶν **44**, 3.
πρεσβύτερος **63**, 11.
προαιρέτης **74**, 14.
προνοητής **80**, 6.
πρύτανις **71**, 2, 9.

IX. OFFICIAL AND MILITARY TERMS

πρώξιμος 78, 2.
πρωτοκωμήτης 105, 1, 6.
ριπάριος 94, 6.
σιτολόγος 26, 1.
σκρινιάριος 83, 2.
στρατηγία, διαδεχόμενος καὶ τὰ κατὰ τὴν στρατηγίαν 26, 22-23.
στρατηγός 20, 23-24. σ. Ἑρμοπολίτου 30, 1-2. σ. Ἀρσινοίτου Ἡρακλείδου μερίδος 29, 2. σ. τῆς Ἀλεξανδρέων χώρας 21, 1-2. σ. Ὀξυρυγχίτου 22, 1; 24, 3; 25, 1; 27, 2, 8.
σύμμαχος 99, 3; 103, 3.
συνήγορος, σ. τοῦ Θηβαίων φόρου 82, 15-16.

σχολαστικός 105, 1, 3, 7.
τελώνης 20, 3.
τοπάρχης 24, 23.
τρακτευτής 86, 3.
ὕπατος, ἀπὸ ὑ. ὀρδιναρίων 96, 54.
ὑπηρέτης 16, 8, 22; 22, 11. γενόμενος βουλευτικὸς ὑ. 30, 7.
ὑποδέκτης, ὁ ὑ. τῆς πόλεως 89, 3-4.
φυλακίτης, ἐπιστάτης φυλακιτῶν 23, 2.
χειριστής 54, 63.
χρηματιστής 16, 5, 17, 21.
χωματεπίκτης 100, 2.
χωματεπιστάτης 72, 14.

(b) Military.

δεκάδαρχος 22, 10; 71, 10.
ἱππικός 50, 5; 57, 3.
μάχιμος 18, 10; 38, 6.
ὅπλον, ὁ. ἱππικά 57, 3.

οὐετρανός 38, 3.
σπεῖρα, σ. (πρώτη) ἱππική 50, 5.
στρατιώτης 61, 11. ἀννῶνα στρατιωτῶν 50, 5.

X. PROFESSIONS, TRADES AND OCCUPATIONS.

ἀμπελουργός 97, 4-5.
ἀρτοκόπος 18, 17.
γέρδιος 81, 6.
γραμματεύς 26, 7. βασιλικὸς γ.: see Index IX, a.
ἐλαιοπώλης 100, 5.
ἐλαιουργός 86, 1.
ἐριέμπορος 80, 3.
θυρουρός 87, 14.
κυβερνήτης 26, 7-8.

μάγιρος 96, 50.
πανδουριστής 96, 39.
πλακουντᾶς 96, 38.
προνοητής: see Index IX, a.
πωμαρίτης 104, 4.
σκυτεύς 63, 10.
τέκτων 61, 12.
ὑδροφόρος 18, 7.
φροντιστής, φ. Τάνεως 37, 3, 15.

XI. WEIGHTS, MEASURES AND COINS.

(a) Weights and Measures.

ἄρουρα 16, 6; 17, 4; 37, 7, 19; 38, 6, 7 bis; 42, 4a, 14; 60, 15; 63, 6; 79, 7, 9; 97, 12 et saepe.
ἀρουρίδιον 70, 6.
ἀρτάβη 17, 8; 22, 7; 26 passim; 32, 9 bis; 33, 12, 14; 37, 21, 22; 42, 2 ff.; 51, 4; 54, 5 et passim; 60, 8, 12; 81, 13; 93, 2, 3; 96, 4 ff.

δρόμος: see μέτρον.
ἡμιαρούριον 23, 12.
καγκέλλον: see μέτρον.
κνίδιον (?) 88 passim.
λίτρα 103, 4.
μετρητής (?) 106, 4.
μέτρον 54, 56; 100, 10, 11. μ. δρόμῳ 33, 11-12. μ. δεκάτῳ ἐμπορικῷ 54, 57-

9

58. (sc. μ.) καγκέλλῳ ἀρτ. 96, 4 ff.
(sc. μ.) μοδίῳ σωλ(ηνικῷ?) 93, 3. μ.
μτλ (?) 54, 56. χαλκῷ μ. 54, 61-62.
μόδιος: see μέτρον.
ξέστης 86, 3, 5.

ξεστιαῖος (?), σηκώματα ξ(εστιαῖα?) 106, 2.
σήκωμα, σηκώματα ξ(εστιαῖα ?) 106, 2.
χοῖνιξ 42, 2 et passim; 60, 8.

(b) Coins.

ἀργύριον 22, 9; 31, 7; 39, 5; 41, 5; 44, 4; 57, 6, 13; 79, 6; 80, 2, 4. ἀ. Σεβαστοῦ νομίσματος 32, 7.
δηνάριον 27, 13, 14.
δίχαλκον (χ^β) 41, 6 bis; 44, 5; 52, 7 et saepe.
διώβολον (=) 41, 6 bis; 47, 5; 53, 23, 27, 28.
δραχμή 22, 8; 31, 7; 32 8 bis; 39, 5; 41, 5; 47, 4; 50, 8; 57, 7, 13-14; 71, 13; 81, 15. The abbreviation passim.
ζυγός, ἰδιωτικῷ ζ. 87, 19, 20. ἰδιωτικῷ ζ. Ὀξυρύγχων 83, 5-6 bis.
ἡμιώβολον (δ) 44, 5; 52, 6 et saepe.
κεράτιον 78, 8; 83, 5, 6, 7; 89, 2; 90, 2, 5; 91, 3 f.; 94, 3, 8.
μνᾶ 62, 7.

νόμισμα 83, 3, 5, 6; 103, 1. ἀρίθμιον (sc. ν.) 92, 3. Σεβαστοῦ ν. 32, 7.
νομισμάτιον 84, 7, 11; 87, 18, 20; 95, 6, 12.
ὀβολός (-) 43, 5, 10, 15; 44, 5; 45, 7; 53, 4 et saepe.
πεντώβολον (ϝ) 52, 8, 9; 53, 8 et saepe.
τάλαντον 16, 7 (note); 57, 6, 13; 71, 4, 17; 79, 6; 80, 4-5; 81, 14.
τετρώβολον (ϝ) 46 passim; 53, 3 et saepe.
τριώβολον (Γ) 41, 6 bis; 44, 5; 52, 5 et saepe; 53, 5, 6; 60, 9, 11 (?).
χαλκός 43, 5, 10, 15; 45, 7; 62, 6, 8; 65, 10.
χαλκοῦς 52, 11, 14, 15. See also δίχαλκον.
χρύσινος 106, 1, 3.

XII. TAXES.

ἀνδρισμός 92, 2.
ἀννῶνα 72, 12. ἀ. στρατιωτῶν 50, 5.
ἀρταβία 33, 5.
δεσμοφυλακία 44, 5.
δημόσια 39, 11-12; 94, 2; 97, 28.
διαγραφή 89, 2.
διακοσιοστή 26, 9, 11, 13.
διχοινικία 49, 6 (note). See χο( ).
ἑκατοστή 26, 9, 11, 13; 42, 5a.
ἐκτολογέω 97, 26.
ἐμβολή 93, 1.
ἐπιβολή 52, 17 (?).
ἡμιαρτάβιον 42, 3 ff. (note).
λαογραφία 43, 4, 9, 14; 45, 6; 47, 3.
λιμὴν Μέμφεως 51, 1-2.
μαγδωλοφυλακία 44, 5.

μερισμός 90, 1; 91, 1.
ναύβιον 60, 4.
ὀνηλάσιον 42, 5a.
πενθήμερος 40, 2; 72, 15.
ποταμοφυλακία 44, 5.
προσδιαγραφόμενα 43, 5, 10, 15; 45, 7.
σακκηγία 33, 16-17.
συντάξιμον 44, 4.
τέλος, τ. προβάτων 24, 21 (note). τ. μόσχου θυομένου 48, 6.
ὑϊκή 44, 5.
φυλακία 44, 5.
χειρωνάξιον 41, 4.
χο( ) (?) 49, 6.
χωματικόν 46 passim; 53, 17.

XIII. GENERAL INDEX.

ἀβάσκοντος 70, 12.
ἀγγέλλω 66, 1-2.
ἁγιάζω 107, 14.
ἅγιος: see Index VII, a.
ἀγοράζω 56, 3; 106, 4.
ἄγω 76, 12.
ἀγωγή 26, 8; 75, 5.
ἀδελφή 19, 3; 42, 5; 68, 10; 96, 22 et saepe.
ἀδελφός 29, 5, 9; 33, 2; 46, 5; 65, 2; 67, 1, 7-8; 69, 6; 70, 5; 73, 1, 14, 15; 74, 3; 82, 5, 15, 95; 96, 20, 63; 97, 1-2; 98, 6, 21; 101, 1; 102, 1, 18, 19; 106, 7.
ἀθάνατος 102, 14-15.
ἀθεράπευτος 29, 13.
αἰδέομαι 71, 7.
αἰδέσιμος 78, 2.
αἴξ 24 passim; 28, 3 et saepe.
αἱρέω 82, 14.
αἰτέω 71, 4.
αἰτιάζω 82, 9.
αἰτίασις 82, 9.
αἰώνιος: ὁ αἰ. Αὔγουστος 82, 1.
ἀκατάπλοος 70, 9.
ἀκολούθως 27, 14; 33, 6-7.
ἀκούω 71, 10; 82, 93, 94.
ἀλλά 29, 15; 70, 9; 71, 5; 73, 4, 11; 77, 13.
ἀλλήλων 79, 4; 82, 7.
ἄλλος 62, 8; 96, 2; 106, 3.
ἄλλοτε 98, 4.
ἀλυσίδιον 95, 22.
ἅμα 33, 16; 84, 4, 6, 11.
ἅμαξα 95, 11.
ἀμελέω 73, 5.
ἀμπελουργός: see Index X.
ἀμπελών 16, 6; 97, 13 et saepe.
ἀμφί 27, 2.
ἄμφοδον: see Index VI, c.
ἀμφότερος 27, 10.
ἀναβαίνω 16, 16; 70, 5, 9.
ἀναγκάζω 103, 3.
ἀναγκαῖος 20, 16.
ἀνάγκη 72, 4. See also κλῆρος (Index VIII).
ἀναγράφω 24, 23; 30, 4.
ἀναδίδωμι 33, 10; 101, 7.

ἀναδικέω 16, 13.
ἀνακομίζω 19, 3.
ἀναλαμβάνω 89, 4.
ἀνάλωμα 60, 3; 61, 2, 10; 86, 3; 96, 31, 79 ff.
ἀνατείνω 77, 15.
ἀναφέρω 100, 12; 103, 5.
ἀναχωρέω 71, 15.
ἀνδρισμός: see Index XII.
ἀνεμποδίστως 85, 3.
ἀνέρχομαι 98, 4; 99, 2, 4; 102, 9-10; 105, 3.
ἄνευ 22, 8.
ἀνήρ 31, 4, 5; 77, 3, 4; 95, 4.
ἀνθίστημι 71, 9.
ἀνθρώπινος 29, 18-19; 102, 11, 12-13.
ἄνθρωπος 67, 3; 102, 14.
ἀννῶνα: see Index XII.
ἀντί 60, 10.
ἀντικαταλλαγή 78, 7.
ἀντικνήμιον 29, 20.
ἀντιποιέομαι 85, 10.
ἀντίρρησις 82, 15.
ἀντιφωνέω 103, 2.
ἀνυπερθέτως 33, 19; 39, 11.
ἀνύω 67, 3-4.
ἀξιόω 23, 12; 29, 17; 98, 11, 21.
ἀξίωσις 77, 15.
ἄπα: see Index VII, a.
ἀπαιτέω 20, 5.
ἀπαιτήσιμον 100, 8.
ἀπαιτητής: see Index IX, a.
ἀπαλλάσσω 78, 4; 107, 8-9.
ἀπαντάω 82, 25; 98, 14-15; 102, 8.
ἀπάτωρ 34, 7, 23.
ἀπελεύθερος 27, 9.
ἀπέρχομαι 100, 3-4.
ἀπέχω 16, 15; 19, 7; 31, 6; 34, 14, 24-25; 35, 3; 37, 5, 18; 79, 4; 81, 10; 84, 6, 10-11.
ἀποβλέπω 102, 13-14.
ἀπογομέω 26, 11.
ἀπογράφομαι 24, 5; 28, 1, b-c, 8.
ἀπόδειξις 83, 8 (?); 94, 4, 9.
ἀποδίδωμι 32, 10-11; 33, 15; 39, 9; 71, 13 (?); 87, 21 (?); 101, 5.
ἀποθνήσκω 96, 49.
ἀποκληρονόμος 38, 4.

ἀπόκρισις 103, 5.
ἀποπέμπω 106, 6 (?).
ἀποπληρόω 102, 6.
ἀποστέλλω 82, 11; 100, 9; 103, 3, 5.
ἀπόστολος 26, 14.
ἀπότακτος, φόρος ἀ. 39, 4-5.
ἀποτίθημι 102, 12.
ἀποφέρω 16, 7; 97, 3.
ἀποχή 81, 16.
ἄποχος 97, 7.
ἀποχώρισις 20, 8.
ἅπτομαι 107, 6.
ἀργύριον: see Index XI, b.
ἀρετή 70, 11.
ἀρίθμησις 21, 5; 43, 3, 8, 13; 45, 4; 65, 14.
ἀρίθμιος: see νόμισμα.
ἀριστερός 31, 3, 6; 34, 10, 13. ἐξ ἀριστερῶν 31, 5.
ἀρκέω 71, 4.
ἄρνες 24, 12; 28, 3 et saepe.
ἄρουρα: see Index XI, a.
ἀρουρίδιον: see Index XI, a.
ἀρτάβη: see Index XI, a.
ἀρταβία: see Index XII.
ἀρτοκόπος: see Index X.
ἄρτος 54, 11, 49; 107, 15.
ἀρχάγγελος: see Index VII, a.
ἀρχαῖος 38, 1.
ἀρχέφοδος (?): see Index IX, a.
ἀρχιερεύς: see Index VII, b.
ἀσθενέω 29, 12.
ἀσπάζομαι 67, 5; 68, 10; 70, 12, 14, 15; 71, 21; 73, 14; 74, 2.
ἀστήρ: see Index VIII.
ἀστροθέσις: see Index VIII.
ἀσφάλεια 34, 17; 83, 7; 94, 4, 9.
αὐγουσταλιανόν 82, 9.
αὐλίζομαι 107, 11.
αὔριον 48, 6.
αὐτίκα 78, 4.
αὐτοθέντην 102, 3.
αὐτοῦ: see ἑαυτοῦ.
ἀφίστημι 85, 16, 17-18 (?).
ἀφίω, (= ἀφίημι) 73, 10.
ἄχρι 27, 17. ἄχρις 98, 14.
ἄχυρον 72, 6. πυρὸς ἐξ ἀχύρου 18, 27, 31, 40. κριθόπυρος ἐξ ἀχύρου 18, 41.

βαίνω 20, 14 (?).
βάλλω 61, 13; 68, 6-7; 73, 6.
βασιλεία 87, 3.

βασιλικός, β. γῇ 23, 10; 42, 4a, 15. β. γραμματεύς: see Index IX, a.
βεβαιόω 83, 8; 84, 7-8, 12.
βιαίως 95, 3.
βιβλίδιον 29, 16-17.
βιβλίον 77, 15.
βίος 38, 7; 79, 3.
βοήθεια 107, 10.
βοηθός 107, 12. See also Index IX, a.
βορινός 52, 21.
βοτανισμός 18, 14.
βουλευτήριον: see Index IX, a.
βουλευτής: see Index IX, a.
βουλευτικός: see Index IX, a.
βούλομαι 100, 10, 12; 102, 3.
βοῦς 66, 7.
βραβεῖον 75, 13.
βρεκτήριον 95, 7.
βρέονιον 96, 1, 3.

γαμετή 96, 35, 42.
γάρ 71, 8, 10; 98, 19; 100, 10; 103, 3.
γε 71, 11.
γεμώω 72, 6.
γένεσις 75, 17.
γένημα 16, 7; 36, 2-3.
γενηματογραφέω 22, 3-4.
γεουχέω 96, 78.
γεουχία 69, 1.
γεουχικός 80, 4.
γεοῦχος 104, 3.
γέρδιος: see Index X.
γεωργέω 23, 9-10; 33, 5-6; 37, 6, 19; 63, 7.
γεωργός 65, 3; 97, 3. δημόσιοι γ. 23, 5.
γῆ 39, 11; 77, 14; 107, 4. γ. βασιλική 23, 10.
γίγνομαι 16, 10; 29, 7-8, 14-15, 17-18; 30, 7; 31, 5; 38, 1; 66, 3; 69, 4; 75, 15; 96, 31, 79; 102, 7; 105, 4. γίνεται and γίνονται indicating sums passim.
γιγνώσκω 38, 5.
γνάφαλλον 103, 4.
γνῶσις 95, 1.
γονή 28, e, 10-11.
γόνυ 31, 6.
γοῦν 103, 5.
γράμμα 27, 18; 84, 13 (?); 97, 6-7, 7-8; 100, 6, 7-8.
γραμματεῖον 77, 13.
γραμματεύς: see Indexes IX, a and X.

XIII. GENERAL INDEX

γραμμάτιον **87**, 22.
γραφεῖον **31**, 1, 9.
γράφω **27**, 14; **38**, 3; **68**, 7; **71**, 3; **72**, 5; **81**, 16; **84**, 13 (?); **93**, 4; **100**, 8, 9, 13.
γύης, πέμπτος γ. **17**, 4.
γυμνασίαρχος: see Index IX, a.
γυνή **57**, 12; **81**, 7; **96**, 1.

δαίμων: see κλῆρος (Index VIII).
δάκτυλος **34**, 9, 12-13.
δαπανάω **21**, 4; **57**, 9.
δαπάνη **73**, 13.
δαπάνημα **85**, 17.
δεινότατος **16**, 18.
δεινῶς **20**, 4.
δέκα **39**, 8; **43**, 5, 10, 15; **45**, 7; **103**, 1.
δεκάδαρχος: see Index IX, b.
δεκαέξ **83**, 5, 7; **94**, 8.
δεκανός: see Index IX, a.
δεκαπέντε **84**, 12.
δεκατέσσαρες **90**, 5.
δέκατος **41**, 1, 5; **92**, 2. See also μέτρον.
δέομαι **74**, 8.
δεσμοφυλακία: see Index XII.
δεσπότης **104**, 2; **106**, 7. See also Indexes I, II, and VII, a.
δεσποτικός **98**, 20.
δεύτερος **37**, 8; **87**, 7.
δέχομαι **94**, 2, 7.
δηλόω **67**, 2-3; **104**, 6.
δῆμος **16**, 2. See also Index VI, e.
δημόσιος, δ. γεωργοί **23**, 4-5. See also Index XII.
δηνάριον: see Index XI, b.
δήποτε **85**, 9.
διαγραφή **71**, 3. See also Index XII.
διαγράφω **43**, 3, 8, 13; **44**, 3; **45**, 4; **47**, 1; **48**, 4; **50**, 3; **71**, 3.
διαδέχομαι **26**, 22.
διάδοχος **85**, 7, 15.
διαθήκη **38**, 3.
διακάτοχος **85**, 7, 15.
διάκονος: see Index VII, a.
διακοσιοστή: see Index XII.
διαλαλέω **82**, 12, 16.
διάλυσις **79**, 4, 5; **82**, 3, 87 et saepe.
διαλύω **82**, 93, 94.
διαπέμπω **27**, 3.
διασαφέω **19**, 5.
διασημότατος **77**, 1.

διαστολή **33**, 8.
διάταγμα **20**, 16-17 (?).
διατροφή **57**, 11.
διαφέρω **71**, 2.
διαφθείρω **28**, 6, f.
δίδωμι **18**, 7 (?); **38**, 10; **54**, 54; **70**, 6, 11; **71**, 19; **89**, 1; **98**, 18; **100**, 6.
διέρχομαι **20**, 4-5; **28**, 2, a; **79**, 3; **97**, 11.
διευτυχέω **29**, 19; **75**, 16.
δικάζω **82**, 16.
δικαιοδότης: see Index IX, a.
δικαιολογία **82**, 13.
δίκαιος **18**, 2; **36**, 7; **85**, 3.
δικαστήριον: see Index IX, a.
δίκη **82**, 14; **107**, 17.
διμνῶος **54**, 60 (note) (?).
διό **23**, 12.
δίς **102**, 10.
δισσός **81**, 16.
δίχαλκον: see Index XI, b.
διχοινικία: see Index XII.
διώβολον: see Index XI, b.
δοκέω **79**, 5.
δόξη **107**, 17.
δοῦλος **85**, 12.
δραχμή: see Index XI, b.
δρόμος: see Index XI, a.
δύναμαι **38**, 5; **102**, 8.
δυνατός **16**, 9.
δύο **73**, 12; **78**, 8; **79**, 8; **86**, 3; **90**, 3; **94**, 3; **98**, 17; **103**, 1; **106**, 1.
δυσκόλως **102**, 9.
δώδεκα **44**, 5.
δῶμα **29**, 11-12.

ἐάν **23**, 13; **65**, 5, 9; **70**, 5. (= ἄν) **68**, 7; **79**, 8, 9.
ἑαυτοῦ **38**, 5; **77**, 12; **79**, 5; **82**, 3. αὐτοῦ **85**, 17.
ἑβδομήκοντα **31**, 3 (?), 6; **79**, 6.
ἕβδομος **34**, 1.
ἔγγραπτος **34**, 16.
ἐγγυητής **87**, 9, 23.
ἐγκαλέω **23**, 14-15; **34**, 19 bis.
ἔγκειμαι **82**, 11.
ἔθος **27**, 2.
εἰ **16**, 15; **82**, 14; **100**, 12. εἰ μή **99**, 3; **102**, 15.
εἰκάς: see Index IV, b.
εἴκοσι **43**, 5, 10, 15; **45**, 7; **48**, 4; **80**, 5; **90**, 3; **103**, 1, 4.

εἰκός 77, 6.
εἰρηνάρχης: see Index IX, a.
εἰρήνη 20, 18; 99, 5.
εἰς 33, 14; 38, 6, 11; 51, 4; 57, 6, 13; 83, 3; 105, 2. 4.
εἰσαγωγεύς: see Index IX, a.
εἰσπράσσω 21, 3.
ἕκαστος 22, 7; 106, 3.
ἑκατόν 24, 9, 24; 33, 12-13; 50, 8.
ἑκατοστή: see Index XII.
ἐκδίδωμι 97, 7.
ἐκδικέω 79, 9; 85, 16.
ἐκεῖ 65, 13; 69, 4.
ἐκεῖνος 82, 13.
ἔκκειμαι 71, 19-20.
ἐκκλησία: see Index VII, a.
ἑκουσίως 26, 10.
ἐκπηδάω 76, 18.
ἐκτελέω 71, 20.
ἐκτίθημι 82, 13.
ἐκτολογέω: see Index XII.
ἐκτός 52, 21.
ἕκτος 92, 3; 94, 2 f.
ἐκφόριον 17, 6; 37, 6, 18; 70, 8.
ἔλαιον 86, 3.
ἐλαιοπώλης: see Index X.
ἐλαιουργός: see Index X.
ἐλάσσων 60, 10.
ἔλκεστον 95, 16.
ἐλλογιμώτατος 105, 2.
ἐλπίζω 107, 13.
ἐμβάλλω 26, 17.
ἐμβολή 26, 12-13. See also Index XII.
ἐμός 89, 4; 98, 20.
ἐμποδών 102, 7.
ἐμπορικός: see μέτρον.
ἔμπροσθεν 34, 21.
ἐνάγω 82, 14.
ἐνακόσιοι 57, 7.
ἐνάρετος 106, 7.
ἔνατος 40, 1.
ἐνδείκνυμι 74, 5, 10-11.
ἕνεκα 29, 5; 70, 8, 10. ἕνεκεν 63, 4; 71, 2.
ἐνίστημι 24, 6; 28, 4-5, c, 9; 32, 11-12; 34, 22-23; 37, 8, 20; 61, 3; 97, 17.
ἐννέα 24, 9-10, 24-25.
ἐνοίκιον 70, 10.
ἐνοχλέω 99, 4, 5.
ἔνοχος 27, 18.
ἐντάγιον 89, 3.

ἐνταῦθα 73, 12; 96, 78.
ἐντάχιον 66, 1, 5-6.
ἐντεῦθεν 20, 23; 87, 18.
ἔντευξις 82, 11.
ἐντρυγάω 39, 7.
ἐνώδιον 95, 22.
ἐξ 31, 6; 37, 22; 81, 15; 84, 7 (?); 103, 1, 2; 105, 4.
ἐξάγω 51, 3.
ἑξακόσιοι 37, 21.
ἐξαποστέλλω 19, 5.
ἐξαριθμέω 28, c.
ἐξέρχομαι 67, 4.
ἑξήκοντα 41, 5.
ἑξῆς 60, 10; 97, 8.
ἐξουσία 77, 4.
ἐξωνέομαι 20, 9.
ἐπάγω 16, 2.
ἐπακολουθέω 24, 12; 28, 10.
ἐπάν 69, 3.
ἐπάνω 66, 4.
ἔπαρχος: see Index IX, a.
ἐπεί 71, 5; 102, 7.
ἐπείγω 20, 7.
ἐπειδή 72, 2.
ἔπειμι 65, 8.
ἐπέλευσις 29, 9.
ἐπέξοδος 23, 16.
ἐπεντέλλω 65, 3.
ἐπέρχομαι 85, 5, 9 (?).
ἐπερωτάω 37, 9; 81, 17.
ἐπιβάλλω 23, 7-8; 35, 3-4.
ἐπιβολή: see Index XII.
ἐπιγένημα 16, 7 (note).
ἐπιγονή, Πέρσης τῆς ἐ. 32, 3.
ἐπιδημέω 72, 3.
ἐπειδήπερ 102, 9.
ἐπιδίδωμι 28, 29; 29, 16; 66, 7-8; 105, 6; 106, 7.
ἐπίδοσις 77, 18.
ἐπιζητέω 73, 9.
ἐπίθεμα 60, 5.
ἐπικαλέω 38, 1; 63, 9.
ἐπικρατέω 75, 11.
ἐπικτάομαι 85, 13.
ἐπιλύω 82, 14.
ἐπιμελέστερον 27, 3.
ἐπίνοια 106, 3.
ἐπιούσιος 107, 15.
ἐπίσημος 38, 4-5.
ἐπίσκοπος: see Index VII, a.

ἐπίσταλμα 26, 20-21.
ἐπιστάτης: see Index IX, a.
ἐπιστολή 16, 11, 19.
ἐπιτροπή: see Index IX, a.
ἐπίτροπος 50, 10; 72, 2-3. See also Index IX, a.
ἐπιφανέστατος, ὁ ἐ. Καῖσαρ 29, 27; 79, 1.
ἐποίκιον 97, 5. See also Index VI, b.
ἐποικ... [ ] 61, 7.
ἑπτά 78, 5.
ἐράω 77, 6.
ἐργάζομαι 40, 2.
ἐργαλίδιον 95, 12.
ἔργον 65, 4.
ἐριέμπορος: see Index X.
ἔριφος 24, 12-13.
ἔρχομαι 76, 19; 106, 3.
ἔρως: see κλῆρος (Index VIII).
ἑσπέρα 105, 2, 4.
ἔσχατος 75, 13.
ἕτερος 87, 11.
ἔτι 16, 17; 27, 15; 71, 18; 73, 6; 78, 7.
ἑτοῖμος 73, 10. ἑτοίμως 89, 3.
ἔτος 16, 7; 17, 6-7; 28, 2, a, 4-5, c, 9; 29, 20; 31, 2, 4, 6, 9; 32, 11-12; 34, 8, 11; 37, 8, 20; 39, 10; 41, 5; 42, 9; 43, 4, 9, 14 (?); 44, 4; 45, 6 (?); 47, 4; 53, 12, 17; 61, 3; 97, 12, 17, 25. See also Indexes I-III.
εὖ 101, 3.
εὐδοκέω 69, 7.
εὐεργέτης, μέγιστος εὐ. 87, 4-5.
εὐεργετικώτατος 77, 16.
εὐθηνιάρχης: see Index IX, a.
εὐθέως 16, 13.
εὐλαβέστατος 82, 5 et saepe.
εὐλαβής 82, 6.
εὔμοιρος 102, 5-6.
εὔνοια 74, 6, 9.
εὑρίσκω 67, 3; 75, 2 et saepe; 100, 4, 7.
εὐσεβέστατος 87, 4.
εὐτρεπίζω 79, 3-4.
εὐτυχέω 23, 17; 24, 22; 68, 16; 69, 7; 77, 17.
εὔχομαι 22, 14; 27, 4; 68, 15; 69, 6; 70, 3; 71, 22; 73, 3, 17; 97, 30; 98, 24; 99, 7; 101, 4; 102, 18.
ἐχθές 100, 3.
ἔχθεσις 88, 1.
ἐχθρός 75, 9.
ἔχω 29, 14; 32, 6; 33, 3, 7; 38, 6, 7; 49, 4; 52, 17; 65, 6; 72, 4; 73, 13; 75, 10, 12; 78, 11 (?); 79, 6; 87, 17; 89, 3; 92, 1; 100, 11; 103, 3, 4; 106, 4.
ἕως 61, 2; 65, 11, 13; 76, 17.

ζεῦγος 27, 13, 14.
ζητέω 38, 9; 63, 3; 100, 5-6 (?).
ζήτησις 20, 15.
ζυγός: see Index XI, b.
ζῷον 105, 4.

ἡγεμών: see Index IX, a.
ἡγέομαι 20, 16.
ἤδη 70, 11; 76, 21; 87, 18; 100, 11.
ἦθος 75, 5.
ἡμέρα 16, 13, 15; 19, 13; 34, 23; 39, 7; 65, 5; 73, 6; 78, 6; 82, 18; 98, 14; 100, 3. αἱ ἐπίσημοι ἡ. 38, 4-5.
ἡμερησίως 39, 6.
ἡμέτερος 77, 9.
ἡμιαρούριον: see Index XI, a.
ἡμιαρτάβιον: see Index XII.
ἥμισυς 37, 22; 79, 9, 10; 89, 2; 103, 4. Abbreviated passim.
ἡμιώβολον: see Index XI, b.
ἧπαρ 76, 16.
ἤτοι 95, 22.

θάτερον 82, 6.
θαυμάζω 98, 16.
θαυμασιότης 103, 2; 106, 1.
θαυμασιώτατος 103, 1; 106, 5, 7.
θειότατος 87, 3.
θέλημα 107, 14.
θέλω 68, 7; 74, 8; 105, 2.
θέμα 60, 7 (?).
θεός: see Index VII, a, b.
θεοσεβέστατος 82, 10, 95.
θεοφιλέστατος 82, 4, 12.
θέρμος 60, 14.
θέσις 54, 53; 75, 7; 83, 3.
θυγάτηρ 25, 4; 68, 11-12; 95, 2; 96, 21 et saepe.
θυρουρός: see Index X.
θύω: see τέλος (Index XII).

ἴδιος 74, 12. ἴ. λόγος: see Index IX, a.
ἰδιωτικός 83, 5, 6; 87, 19, 20.
ἰδού 98, 17.
ἱερός and ἱερώτατος: see Index VII, b.

ἱεροψάλτης: see Index VII, b.
ἱκανός 78, 6.
ἱμάτιον 27, 17; **57**, 4; **95**, 18.
ἵνα 20, 8; 70, 9; 72, 5; 73, 7; 97, 8; 98, 23; 106, 4.
ἱππικός: see Index IX, b.
ἰνδικτίων: see Index III.
ἴσος 42, 19, 21, 39; **74**, 9.

καγκέλλον: see Index XI, a.
κάδος 95, 8.
καθήκω 24, 21.
κάθημαι 16, 17.
καθημερινός 107, 4.
καθίστημι 23, 13-14.
καθολικός: see ἐκκλησία (Index VII, a).
καθόλου 32, 10.
καθότι 19, 1.
καθώς 98, 11; 102, 17; **104**, 6; **106**, 1.
καιρός, πρὸ καιροῦ 27, 3.
κακός 102, 17.
καλλίμορφος 56, 5.
καλῶς 70, 4.
καρδία 76, 17.
καταβαίνω 65, 11.
καταβάλλω 22, 9 (?).
καταγίγνομαι 16, 3; 29, 6.
κατάγω 26, 19; 73, 7-8 (?); **106**, 4.
κατάθεσις 39, 3.
καταλαμβάνω 16, 17; 65, 13; 82, 8, 12.
καταλείπω 28, 7; 38, 6; 95, 1.
καταξιόω 103, 2, 5.
καταπλέω 27, 15; 69, 5.
κατανέμω 23, 11.
καταπίπτω 29, 10-11.
κατασκευάζω 27, 12.
καταφυγή 107, 12.
καταχωρισμός 29, 17.
κατέχω 71, 18; 73, 12.
κατηδια (?) 57, 3.
κατηχέω 20, 3.
κατοικέω 107, 10.
κάτω 31, 5.
κεῖμαι 56, 2 (?).
κελεύω 27, 16; 68, 8-9.
κεράτιον: see Index XI, b.
κεφάλαιον 32, 9; 82, 11.
κιβώτιον 95, 15.
κίνδυνος 20, 24.
κλεπτοσπορία 63, 4.
κληρονομία 38, 4.

κληρονόμος 38, 4, 5; **85**, 6, 14; **94**, 1.
κλῆρος 17, 3 (note). See Indexes VI, d and VIII.
κλιμακτηρικός: see Index VIII.
κνίδιον: see Index XI, a.
κοινός 82, 3, 95.
κοινωνία 36, 7; 37, 7, 19. βίου κ. 38, 7.
κοίτη 38, 6.
κόλλησις (?) 62, 2.
κολόκυνθος 39, 4, 8.
κύμες: see Index IX, a.
κόπος 70, 10.
κοπρηγέω 65, 4-5.
κοσμητεία: see Index IX, a.
κοσμητεύω: see Index IX, a.
κοσμητής: see Index IX, a.
κότος 63, 11.
κουράτωρ 38, 2, 8 bis.
κοῦφον 106, 4, 5.
κρατέω 20, 7.
κράτιστος, ὁ κ. δικαιοδότης 27, 1.
κρεμούριον (?) 95, 17.
κριθή 17, 7-8; 18 passim; **49**, 6; **56**, 6; 72, 7; 100, 5. κ. Συριακή (or κυριακή ?) 49, 2-3, and note.
κριθόπυρος 18, 41.
κρίσις 20, 22.
κτῆμα: see Index VI, b.
κτήνη 56, 4; 72, 6.
κυβερνήτης: see Index X.
κυριακός 49, 2-3 (note).
κύριος 31, 3; 38, 2; 69, 6; 72, 2; 73, 1, 4; 98, 1; 101, 1; 102, 1, 19. See also Indexes I and VII, a.
κύριος (adj.) 36, 8; 37, 9; 81, 16.
κυρόω 77, 14.
κωλ( ) 60, 7.
κωμάρχης: see Index IX, a.
κώμη 16, 4; 23, 8; 28, 2, 10, 12; 29, 13; 38, 7; 47, 4; 48, 6; 52, 23; **104**, 8. See also Index VI, b.

λαμβάνω 16, 11, 16, 19; 65, 12 (note) (?); 95, 3; 97, 6; 100, 4; 106, 1.
λαμπάδιον 95, 21.
λαμπρός 77, 2; 82, 2; 96, 78. -ότατος 22, 12; 37, 2, 13-14; 38, 1-2; 77, 2.
λανθάνω 77, 5.
λαογραφία: see Index XII.
λαογραφέω 24, 17.
λαχανόσπερμον 60, 12.

λέγω 20, 2; 71, 10, 12; 106, 5; 107, 11.
λείαν: see λίαν.
λείπω 28, c.
λειτουργός 104, 7.
λῆμμα 36, 4; 61, 2, 5 (?); 96, 31, 78 ff.
λημματίζω 22, 13; 97, 9-10.
λίαν 67, 5.
λιβέλλος 82, 9.
λιμήν: see Index XII.
λιτουργός: see λειτουργός.
λίτρα: see Index XI, a.
λίψ: see τοπαρχία (Index VI, a) and Φρούριον (Index VI, c).
λόγευμα 36, 1.
λογίζομαι 96, 79 ff.
λόγος 22, 14; 42, 29; 54, 13, 20, 27; 56, 3; 62, 1; 70, 11; 80, 2, 7; 81, 11; 96, 31, 78, 80, 81; 97, 9. λ. ἀργυρικός 21, 3. λ. λημ. καὶ ἀναλ. 61, 2. ἴδιος λ.: see Index IX, a.
λοιπάζομαι 83, 6.
λοιπός 26, 12; 42, 27; 53, 15, 16, 30; 60, 7, 11; 68, 6; 100, 10.
λυπηρός 102, 12.
λωδίκιον 95, 14.

μά 70, 8.
μαγδωλοφυλακία: see Index XII.
μάγιρος: see Index X.
μακάριος 95, 2.
μάλιστα 77, 5.
μαρτυρέω 82, 91, 93, 94.
μαρτύρομαι 38, 5.
μάρτυς 78, 5.
μαφόριον 95, 19.
μάχιμος: see Index IX, b.
μέγας 38, 1; 68, 14; 72, 8-9; 82, 8, 13. -ιστος 87, 4. See also Index I.
μειζότερος: see Index IX, a.
μέλλω 72, 3; 85, 8.
μέν 82, 3; 97, 11; 102, 3.
μέντοι 106, 2.
μερίζω 22, 6.
μερίς: see Index VI, a.
μερισμός: see Index XII.
μέρος 35, 4; 36, 3; 79, 5, 6, 9; 82, 4; 94, 3.
μεταδίδωμι 19, 2.
μεταξύ 82, 17.
μέτοχος 44, 3; 85, 1.
μετρέω 26, 16; 32, 8; 100, 10.

μέτρησις 17, 5.
μετρητής: see Index XI, a.
μέτρον 75, 3. See also Index XI, a.
μέχρι 34, 22; 36, 2; 73, 11; 77, 10.
μηδέ 34, 18, 19, 20; 107, 7.
μηδείς 29, 18; 34, 17; 70, 9; 77, 5.
μηκέτι 107, 6.
μῆκος 16, 14.
μήν 32, 11; 33, 23; 39, 10; 40, 2; 44, 2; 75, 14; 92, 3; 98, 17. See also Index IV, a.
μήτε 99, 4.
μήτηρ 32, 1, 4; 34, 7, 24; 38, 3; 43, 4, 9, 14; 44, 4; 45, 5; 46, 4 et passim; 57, 12; 70, 5; 87, 9, 11; 96, 49; 100, 6-7.
μικρός 34, 9-10, 13; 82, 8.
μίσθωσις 17, 5-6; 36, 6-7; 37, 9.
μισθωτής 37, 4, 16.
μνᾶ: see Index XI, b.
μνήμη 82, 6.
μνημονεύω 102, 16.
μόγις 71, 13.
μόδιος: see Index XI, a.
μοῖρα: see Index VIII.
μονάζουσα: see Index VII, a.
μόνος 71, 9; 81, 14; 89, 2 (?); 90, 3, 5; 91, 4.
μόσχος: see τέλος (Index XII).
μυλαῖον 97, 14-15, 20, 25.

ναύβιον: see Index XII.
νεκρός 107, 8.
νέμω 24, 13; 28, 11.
νεόφυτος 97, 13, 26.
νεώτερος 41, 4.
νομάρχης: see Index IX, a.
νομεύς 24, 16; 28, 13.
νόμισμα: see Index XI, b.
νομισμάτιον: see Index XI, b.
νομός 24, 15; 27, 16; 28, 13. See also Index VI, a.
νυκτερινός 107, 4-5.
νῦν 74, 7.
νύξ 23, 5; 75, 18.

ξέστης: see Index XI, a.
ξεστιαῖος: see Index XI, a.

ὀβολός: see Index XI, b.
ὀγδοήκοντα 57, 8.

ὄγδοος 91, 4; 93, 1; 94, 3.
ὁδός 73, 10.
οἶδα 84, 13 (?); 98, 19.
οἰκεῖος 85, 17; 101, 8.
οἰκέω 38, 8 (?); 77, 2.
οἰκία 77, 10; 80, 4; 84, 5, 10.
οἰκοδεσποτεία: see Index VIII.
οἰκοδεσπότης: see Index VIII.
οἰκονομέω 21, 5.
οἶκος 33, 6; 70, 13; 73, 16. ἐξ οἴκου 31, 7; 32, 7, 8. See also Index VIII.
οἶνος 74, 12; 88, 1, 4; 106, 2, 4.
οἷος 71, 12; 85, 9.
ὀκτώ 57, 8.
ὀλίγος 98, 13; 105, 3.
ὁλοκληρέω 73, 3-4; 101, 4.
ὁλόκληρος 84, 5, 10.
ὅλος 24, 15; 28, 12; 60, 11; 71, 4, 19; 73, 16.
ὀμνύω 27, 6, 11; 28, 14, 30.
ὁμογνήσιος 82, 5.
ὁμοίως 41, 6; 47, 8; 52, 24; 54, 59.
ὁμολογέω 17, 3; 26, 16; 31, 2, 6-7; 32, 6; 34, 6; 36, 12 ff.; 37, 9; 77, 17; 81, 10, 17-18; 82, 7, 18; 84, 3; 87, 17, 20.
ὁμολογία 82, 3, 16.
ὀνηλάσιον: see Index XII.
ὄνομα 49, 5; 63, 1, 3, 7; 70, 13; 73, 17; 79, 7; 89, 1; 100, 7. See also Index VII, a.
ὄνος 51, 3.
ὅπλον: see Index IX, b.
ὅπως 19, 5.
ὁράω 73, 4, 11.
ὀρδινάριος: see ὕπατος.
ὅριον: see Index VIII.
ὀριχαλκοῦς 95, 16.
ὁρκίζω 107, 3, 8.
ὅρκος 27, 18; 28, 30.
ὁρμάω 87, 12; 102, 4.
ὅρμος 26, 17-18; 72, 4, 8.
ὄρνις 62, 4.
ὅρος: see Index VIII.
ὁρτή 99, 5.
ὅσος 34, 15, 26; 79, 8, 9.
ὅσπερ 85, 4.
ὅστις 65, 13.
ὅταν 38, 5.
ὅτε 98, 4.

ὅτι 68, 8; 77, 14; 98, 19; 100, 9; 102, 11; 106, 5.
οὐδείς 32, 9; 98, 18; 102, 14.
οὐετρανός: see Index IX, b.
οὐλή 29, 20; 31, 3, 6; 34, 9, 12.
οὖν 16, 9; 20, 10; 22, 5; 74, 7; 98, 11, 16, 21; 100, 8.
οὔπω 16, 2.
οὐρανός: see Index VII, a.
οὐσία 53, 16; 56, 4. οὐ. Πτολεμαΐς 50, 9.
οὔτε 16, 16.
οὗτος 57, 9; 70, 8; 75, 3 et saepe; 77, 10, 12; 78, 2; 79, 3; 82, 3 (?), 16, 87; 83, 7; 101, 6; 103, 2 ff.; 106, 6.
οὕτως 71, 19; 74, 5; 95, 5; 96, 2; 98, 10.
ὀφείλω 20, 6; 22, 2; 31, 8; 34, 15, 26; 35, 4; 71, 18.
ὄχλησις 107, 9.
ὀψώνιον 96, 1, 3.

παιδάριον 86, 2; 96, 1, 3; 106, 6.
παιδίον 57, 11; 71, 21.
παιδοποιέω 77, 8.
παῖς 79, 3; 92, 4 (?).
πάλιν 67, 6; 71, 6; 100, 3.
πάλλιον 27, 13.
πανδουριστής: see Index X.
πανεύφημος 96, 54, 77.
πανήγυρις 61, 15.
πανοικεί 68, 15; 69, 6.
πάμπολυς 72, 5; 98, 25.
παντοκράτωρ: see Index VII, a.
πάνυ 71, 11.
παραγγελία 16, 9.
παραγγέλλω 16, 8; 20, 9-10, 24-25 (?).
παραγίγνομαι 73, 11.
παράδοσις 27, 12, 18.
παρακαλέω 106, 1.
παραμένω 27, 17.
παραμυθία 96, 6 et saepe.
παρατίθημι 74, 4.
παραχρῆμα 20, 11-12; 31, 7; 85, 16.
παραχωρέω 79, 7-8.
πάρειμι 19, 1; 71, 5, 8, 12.
παρέρχομαι 75, 14.
παρέχω 70, 10; 80, 2, 7; 86, 2; 98, 23; 105, 3; 106, 2, 5.
παρικλ( ) (?) 27, 13 (note).
παρίστημι 99, 5.

πᾶς 16, 18; 20, 19, 21; 34, 14, 25-26; 36, 6, 7; 68, 8; 69, 7; 70, 3, 8, 13; 73, 3; 74, 6; 75, 9 ff.; 77, 7; 78, 11 (?); 84, 2; 99, 6; 107, 7. πάντως 99, 4.
πατήρ 31, 4; 79, 2, 3, 7; 82, 6; 96, 8, 9, 57, 72; 98, 1; 101, 8. See also Index VII, a.
πατητικός 95, 11.
πάτρων 104, 3.
παύω 20, 10.
παχύνω 63, 10-11.
πείθω 68, 8.
πειράω 69, 3.
πεκούλιον 85, 13.
πέμπτος 17, 4; 44, 1.
πέμπω 19, 2, 10; 27, 2; 66, 5; 73, 6 (?); 99, 3; 106, 3.
πενθήμερος: see Index XII.
πέντε 34, 9, 12; 38, 7; 79, 6; 103, 4; 106, 2.
πεντήκοντα 37, 21-22.
πεντώβολον: see Index XI, b.
πέπων 39, 8.
πιπράσκω 56, 6; 84, 4, 9; 85, 4, 11-12, 18.
πίσσα 19, 7.
πίστις 26, 5.
πλακουντᾶς: see Index X.
πλαστή 52, 21.
πλεονεξία 20, 11.
πλῆξις 29, 14.
πλήν 66, 2-3.
πλήρης 37, 8, 22; 107, 16.
πληρόω 84, 8; 94, 2, 7; 97, 27.
πλοιάριον 19, 2, 11.
πλοῖον 26, 8; 27, 15; 73, 7, 8; 106, 3.
πνεῦμα 76, 16.
ποδίζω 65, 12.
ποιέω 27, 11; 36, 1; 38, 3; 61, 12; 66, 2; 68, 10; 70, 4-5, 9; 79, 5; 82, 3; 83, 8; 94, 4, 9.
ποιμήν 23, 8.
ποῖος 100, 9.
πόλις 16, 15, 16; 32, 5; 38, 10; 78, 2; 81, 9; 89, 4; 99, 3, 4; 102, 10; 106, 4. See also Index VI, b.
πολιτεύομαι 22, 5-6 (?).
πολύς 29, 14; 70, 1; 71, 6; 73, 2, 17-18; 78, 6; 102, 18. ἐπὶ πλεῖον 20, 6-7. πλεῖστος 67, 2.

πόρρωθεν 69, 2.
πορφιροῦς 95, 14.
ποταμός 73, 7.
ποταμοφυλακία: see Index XII.
ποτέ 34, 15, 26; 106, 4.
ποτίζω 60, 12.
ποτισμός (?) 54, 13, 20, 27.
πρᾶγμα 82, 68.
πραγματευτής: see Index IX, a.
πραιπόσιτος: see Index IX, a.
πραιτώριον: see Index IX, a.
πράκτωρ: see Index IX, a.
πρᾶσις 84, 12 (?), 14 (?).
πράσσω 22, 9; 101, 3.
πρεσβύτερος 100, 11-12. See also Indexes VII, a and IX, a.
πρίν 69, 4.
προαιρέτης: see Index IX, a.
πρόβατον 24 passim; 28, 3 et saepe. τέλος προβάτων: see Index XII.
προγράφω 82, 9, 17; 84, 2.
προδηλόω 79, 3.
προθεσμία 82, 25.
προθυμότατα 68, 9-10.
πρόκειμαι 36, 3; 84, 4-5, 9, 10. ὡς πρόκειται 28, 30; 36, 12 ff.; 37, 10, 24; 83, 8; 84, 8, 12 (?); 94, 4, 10 (?).
προνοητής: see Index IX, a.
προσάγω 32, 10.
προσάπαξ 90, 3, 6; 91, 4.
προσδιαγραφόμενα: see Index XII.
πρόσειμι 82, 13.
προσεπακολουθέω 28, d-e.
προσέρχομαι 38, 4.
προσημαίνω 82, 8.
προσκύνημα 70, 3.
πρόσοδος 60, 3.
προσποιέω 104, 8-9.
προστασία 97, 28-29.
προσφέρω 16, 21; 71, 7-8.
πρόσωπον 79, 10; 82, 68.
πρότερον 82, 8.
πρόχθες 29, 10.
πρύτανις: see Index IX, a.
πρώξιμος: see Index IX, a.
πρωτοκωμητής: see Index IX, a.
πταῖσμα 102, 13.
πτυχίον 95, 22.
πύλη 51, 1.

πυρός **18** *passim*; **22**, 2; **26**, 14; **32**, 9 *bis*; **33**, 11, 14; **37**, 21, 22; **42**, 2, 8, 29; **54**, 5 *et passim*; **60**, 8.
πυρόω **76**, 15.
πωμάριον **97**, 24.
πωμαρίτης: see Index X.
πῶς **16**, 9.

ῥιγοπύρετον **107**, 3.
ῥιπάριος: see Index IX, a.
ρουας (?) **96**, 27, 67.
ῥώννυμι **22**, 14; **27**, 4; **65**, 15; **67**, 5, 6; **68**, 15; **69**, 5; **71**, 22; **72**, 13; **73**, 17; **97**, 29; **98**, 24; **99**, 6; **102**, 18.

σακκηγία: see Index XII.
σάκκινος **19**, 4.
σαλάχινος (?) **95**, 20.
Σεβαστός, Σ. νόμισμα **32**, 7. See also Index IV, a.
σήκωμα: see Index XI, a.
σημαίνω **75**, 3 *et saepe*.
σημεῖον **73**, 14.
σημειόω, σεσημείωμαι **27**, 7; **37**, 10; **40**, 4; **80**, 5.
σήμερον **98**, 17-18.
σιαγών **31**, 3.
σιδήρειος **95**, 12.
σιδήριον **66**, 6.
σικυήρατον **39**, 4.
σικύριον **39**, 7.
σινωτικός: see Index VIII.
σιτικός **63**, 6 (?).
σιτολόγος: see Index IX, a.
σῖτος **60**, 9 (?); **81**, 13; **93**, 2, 3; **96**, 4 ff.
σιτω... **54**, 60.
σκέπη **107**, 10-11.
σκεῦος **57**, 1 (?), 4; **95**, 1.
σκηνή **19**, 4.
σκιωτός **82**, 38.
σκρινιάριος: see Index IX, a.
σκυτεύς: see Index X.
σός **83**, 3, 7; **97**, 28; **103**, 2; **106**, 1.
σοφίζομαι **20**, 4.
σπεῖρα: see Index IX, b.
σπονδεῖον **62**, 3.
σπουδάζω **100**, 8; **106**, 1.
στίππιον **98**, 9, 15-16.
στοιχέω **89**, 4; **92**, 4; **93**, 4.
στρατηγός: see Index IX, a.
στρατιώτης: see Index IX, b.

στρῶμα **95**, 20.
συγγραφή, σ. συνοικεσίου **31**, 8.
συγκλεισμός **36**, 2.
συγχωρέω **31**, 10; **98**, 12-13.
συλλαμβάνω **70**, 5-6.
συμβαίνω **29**, 19.
σύμβιος **38**, 5; **70**, 13, 15; **71**, 21; **83**, 5 (?).
συμβίωσις **31**, 10; **77**, 3.
σύμμαχος: see Index IX, a.
συναίρω, σ. τὴν συμβίωσιν **31**, 10.
σύνειμι **22**, 10-11.
συνήγορος: see Index IX, a.
συνίστημι **30**, 5.
συνοικέσιον **31**, 8.
συντάξιμον: see Index XII.
σύνταξις **41**, 4. μαχίμων σ. **38**, 6.
συντάσσω **73**, 13-14; **77**, 12.
συντίθημι **82**, 16.
συντίμησις **27**, 12.
συντυγχάνω **69**, 4.
σύστασις **75**, 7.
σχεδάριον (?) **96**, 83, 84.
σχολαστικός: see Index IX, a.
σωληνικός: see μόδιος (Index XI).
σῶμα **107**, 7-8.
σωτήρ: see Index VII, a.

τάλαντον: see Index XI, b.
τάσσω **24**, 20.
ταυρικόν **65**, 9.
ταχύ **66**, 2; **76**, 21. ταχέως **73**, 5. τὸ τάχιον **20**, 8.
τέκνον **67**, 6; **70**, 12, 15; **85**, 6, 14.
τέκτων: see Index X.
τέλειος, πρόβατα τ. **28**, 3 *et saepe*.
τελειόω **31**, 9.
τελέω **51**, 1.
τέλος **66**, 8-9. See also Index XII.
τεσσαράκοντα **34**, 8-9; **106**, 2.
τέσσαρες **17**, 5; **22**, 8; **47**, 5; **83**, 3, 5; **95**, 18.
τεσσαρεσκαιδέκατος **45**, 6.
τεταρταῖος **107**, 5.
τέταρτος **38**, 11; **43**, 4, 9, 14; **82**, 2; **90**, 3; **91**, 3.
τετρώβολον: see Index XI, b.
τέχνη **81**, 6.
τήγανον **95**, 10.
τίκτω **76**, 13, 14, 21.
τιμάω **71**, 11.

τιμή **19**, 5, 7; **57**, 3; **62**, 2 *et saepe*; **74**, 7, 10; **84**, 8 (?). 11; **98**, 26.
τίμημα **106**, 4.
τιμώτατος **70**, 1; **71**, 1; **105**, 1, 6.
τίς **67**, 3.
τὶς **16**, 15; **20**, 8-9; **22**, 8; **85**, 11 (?).
τκουσου (?) **95**, 9.
τοιγαροῦν **77**, 9; **102**, 11.
τοιοῦτος **20**, 11.
τοπάρχης: see Index IX, a.
τοπαρχία: see Index VI, a.
τόπος **52**, 22; **75**, 8. See also Index VI, d.
τοσοῦτος **16**, 14; **71**, 2, 11.
τότε **74**, 5; **85**, 19; **98**, 12.
τρακτευτής: see Index IX, a.
τράπεζα **53**, 1, 18.
τρεῖς **24**, 10, 25; **31**, 3; **38**, 7; **41**, 6; **79**, 2, 5; **82**, 5; **87**, 19; **89**, 2; **91**, 3.
τριάκοντα **33**, 13; **34**, 11-12; **93**, 3.
τριακόσιοι **39**, 5-6; **57**, 14.
τρίκλινον **19**, 4.
τρισχίλιοι **57**, 7, 14.
τρίτος **32**, 12; **51**, 5; **79**, 8; **90**, 1; **91**, 1; **94**, 3.
τριώβολον: see Index XI, b.
τρόπος **75**, 5; **85**, 9.
τυγχάνω **101**, 9.
τύχη **27**, 7, 11; **28**, 17; **75**, 3. See also κλῆρος (Index VIII).

ὑγιαίνω **70**, 3.
ὑδροφόρος: see Index X.
ὑδροφυλακία (?) **97**, 12 *et saepe*.
ὕδωρ **66**, 3-4.
ὑϊκή: see Index XII.
υἱός **24**, 16; **35**, 2; **38**, 4; **59**, 3; **78**, 5; **87**, 8, 10, 15, 23; **96** *passim*; **102**, 6. See also Index VII, a.
ὑμέτερος **94**, 4, 9.
ὑπαγορεύω **38**, 3.
ὑπάρχω **25**, 8. τὰ ὑπάρχοντα γενηματογραφούμενα **22**, 3-4.
ὑπατεία: see Index II.
ὕπατος: see Index IX, a.
ὑπεναντίον **82**, 72.
ὑπέρθεσις **22**, 8.
ὑπερφυέστατος **96**, 54, 77.
ὑπηρέτης: see Index IX, a.
ὑπογραφή **77**, 16.
ὑποδέκτης: see Index IX, a.

ὑποδέχομαι **105**, 2.
ὑπόστασις **53**, 17; **75**, 15.
ὑπόσχεσις **102**, 16-17.
ὑποτάσσω **82**, 7-8.
ὑφίστημι **71**, 13.
ὕψιστος **107**, 10.

φαίνομαι **23**, 13.
φακός **56**, 7.
φανερός **82**, 11; **95**, 1.
φερνή **31**, 8.
φέρω **23**, 6; **89**, 3; **102**, 11; **106**, 6.
φιλανθρωπία **102**, 5.
φιλονεικεία (-νηκ-) **79**, 4.
φίλος **70**, 1; **71**, 8-9.
φίλτατος **68**, 15; **74**, 13.
φοῖνιξ **51**, 4; **61**, 16.
φορέω **107**, 7.
φόρος **39**, 4-5, 9. See also συνήγορος.
φροντίζω **22**, 5; **27**, 3; **97**, 5-6.
φροντιστής: see Index X.
φυλακία: see Index XII.
φωκάριον **57**, 9.

χαίρω **71**, 1; **74**, 1. χαίρειν in salutations **19**, 1; **27**, 2; **32**, 5; **33**, 3; **35**, 3; **37**, 5, 17; **65**, 2; **67**, 2; **70**, 2; **73**, 2; **80**, 6; **81**, 10; **82**, 8; **83**, 3; **97**, 2; **98**, 3; **102**, 2; **104**, 5.
χαλκός **66**, 8. See also Index XI, b.
χαλκός (adj.): see μέτρον.
χαλκοῦς **95**, 7 (?). See also Index XI, b.
χάριν **98**, 7, 8.
χάρις **65**, 9; **71**, 16.
χαρτάριον **100**, 6.
χείλιοι: see χίλιοι.
χείρ **34**, 10, 13. διὰ χειρός **31**, 7; **32**, 6.
χειρισμός **26**, 20.
χειριστής: see Index IX, a.
χειρωνάξιον: see Index XII.
χίλιοι **71**, 14; **81**, 15 (?).
χοῖνιξ: see Index XI, a.
χοιρίδιον **99**, 6.
χοῖρος **97** *passim*.
χόρτος **23**, 11-12; **105**, 3.
χο( ): see Index XII.
χράομαι **85**, 11.
χρεία **65**, 5-6; **103**, 3, 4.
χρεωστέω **81**, 12; **98**, 9-10.
χρήζω **20**, 20.

χρηματίζω **49**, 3-4.
χρηματιστής: see Index IX, a.
χρῆσις **33**, 4.
χρηστήριον **84**, 5-6, 10.
χρόνος **34**, 22; **73**, 18; **85**, 8; **98**, 25; **102**, 18.
χρύσινος: see Index XI, b.
χρυσίον **62**, 1.
χρυσός **84**, 7, 11; **87**, 18, 19; **89**, 2; **94**, 3; **95**, 6.
χωματεπίκτης: see Index IX, a.
χωματεπιστάτης: see Index IX, a.
χωματικόν: see Index XII.
χώρα, ἡ Ἀλεξανδρέων χ. **21**, 2.
χωρίον: see Μοῖραι (Index VI, b).
χωρίς **20**, 21.

χω( ) (?) **27**, 13.

ψεύδω **28**, 18, 22.
ψῆφος **75**, 11.
ψυχή **76**, 17; **107**, 6.

ὠνέομαι **77**, 10.
ὥρα **75**, 18; **99**, 2.
ὡς **49**, 3; **61**, 14; **71**, 15; **74**, 7; **83**, 6. ὡς ἐτῶν **31**, 6; **34**, 8, 11. ὡς πρόκειται: see πρόκειμαι.
ὧς **93**, 4 (?).
ὡσαύτως **36**, 5.
ὥσπερ **74**, 3.
ὥστε **26**, 18; **54**, 12. ὥ. εἰς **33**, 4-5; **54**, 49. ὥ. c. dat. **54**, 46, 51.

PLATE I.

No. 20. Edict of Prefect (II A.D.).

No. 40. Embankment Certificate (49 A.D.).

Plate II.

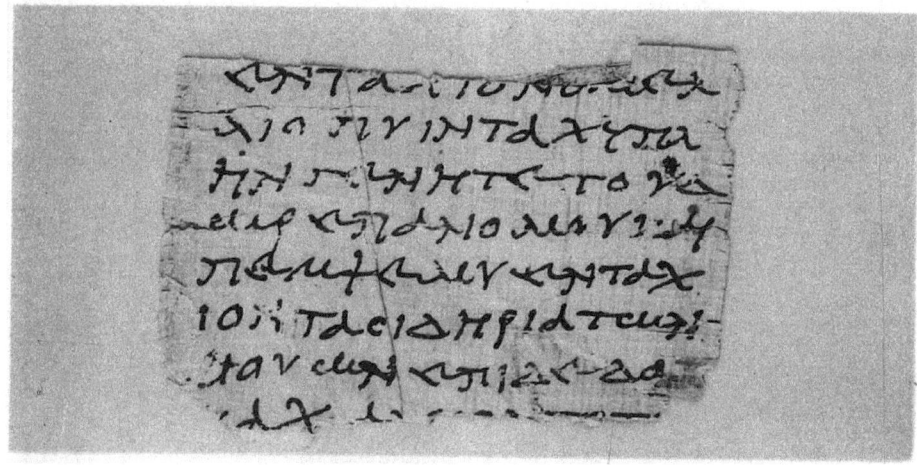

No. 26. Pilot's Receipt (about 154 A.D.).

No. 66. Letter (I A.D.).

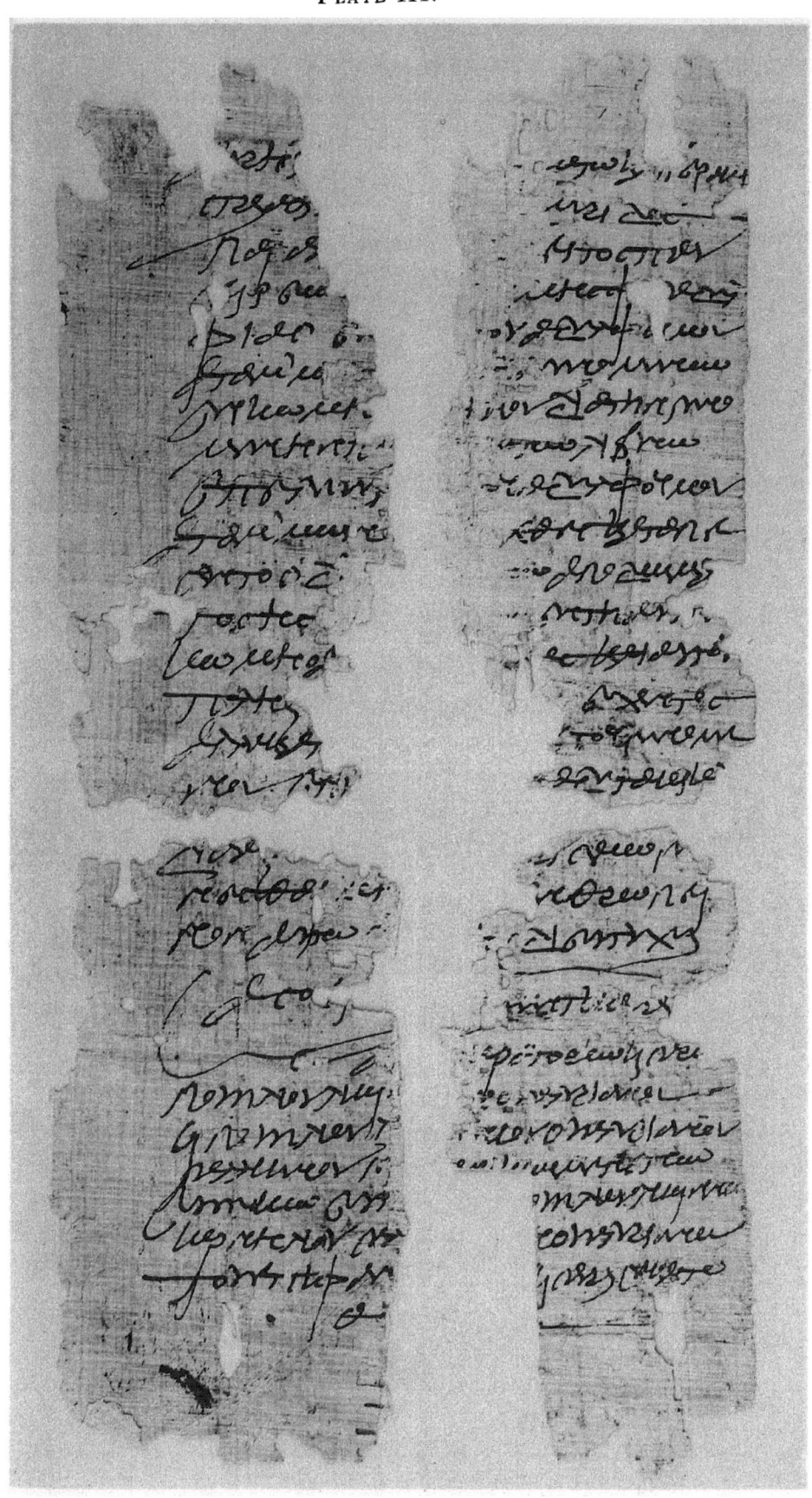

No. 29. Petition to Strategus (258 A.D.).

PLATE IV.

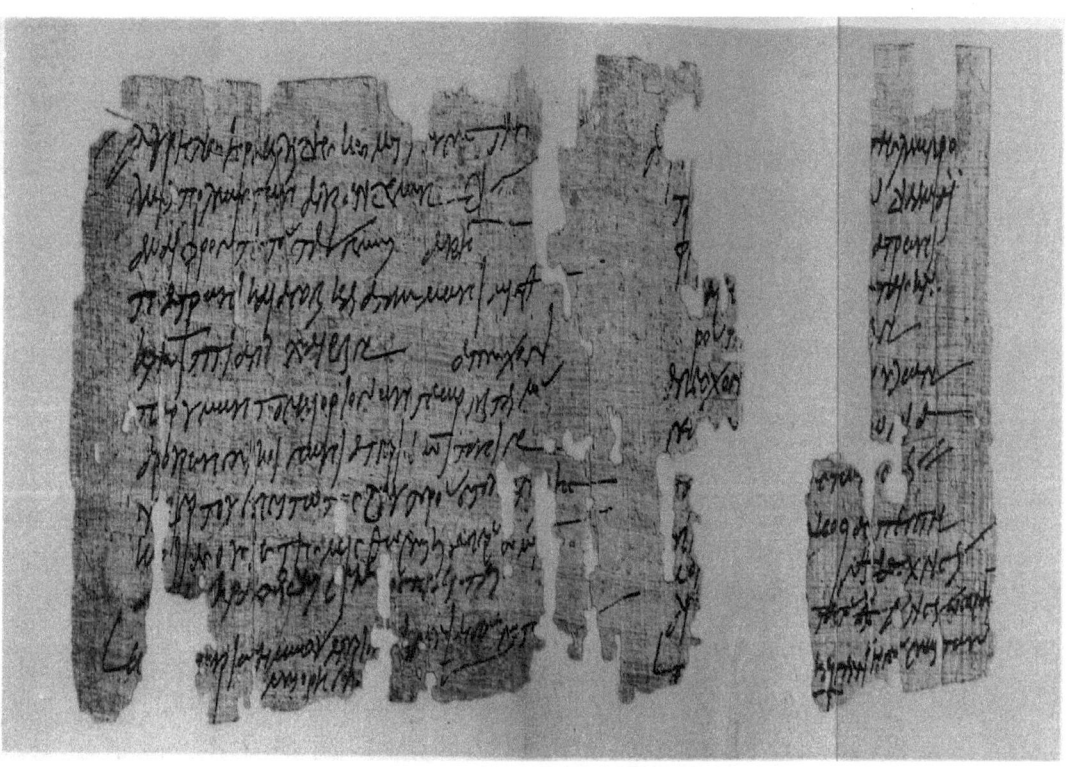

No. 37. Receipts for Payment of ἐκφόριον (255 and 256 A.D.).

No. 38. Roman Will (about 264 A.D.).

PLATE V.

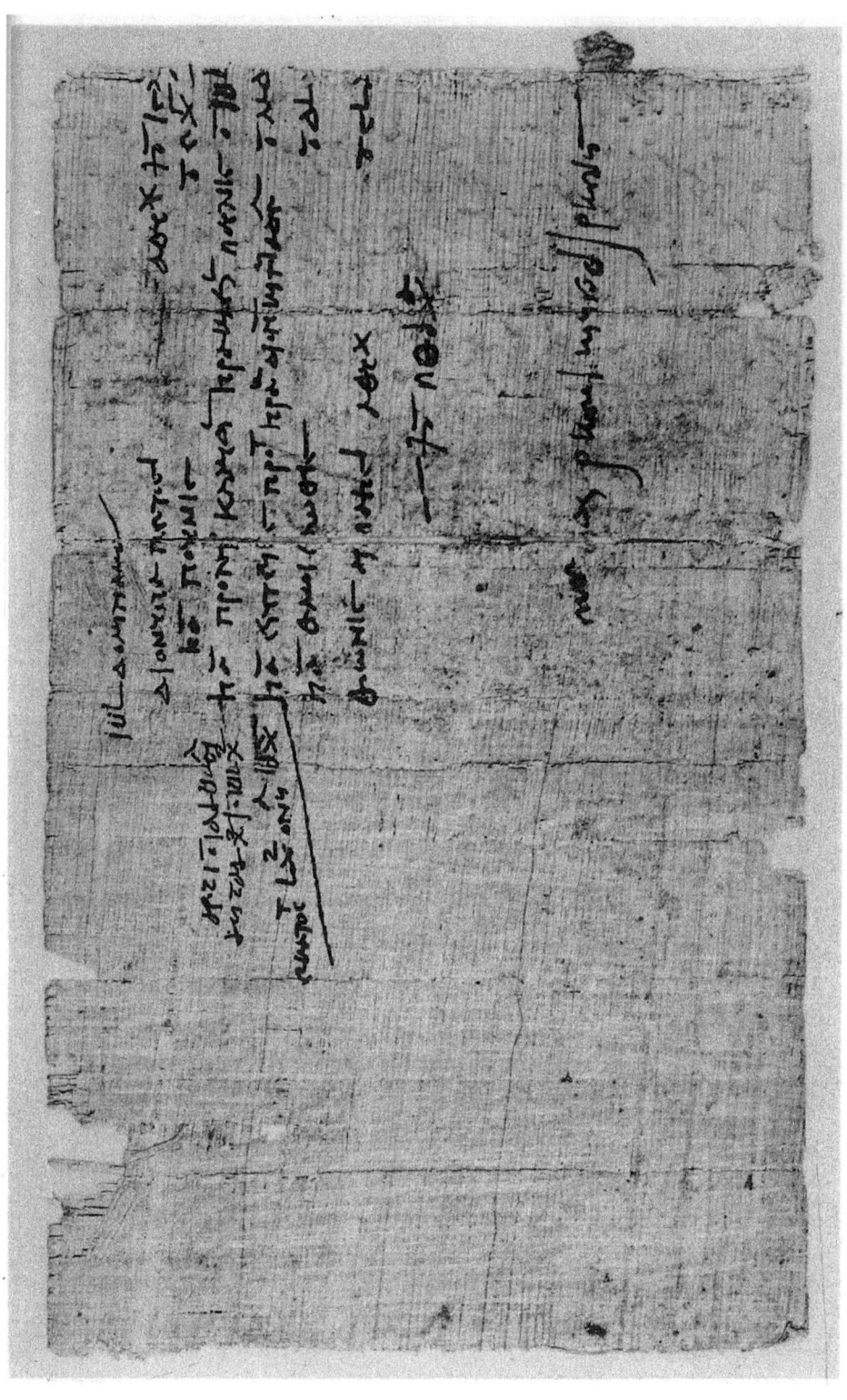

No. 42, recto. Grain Account (93 A.D.).

PLATE VI.

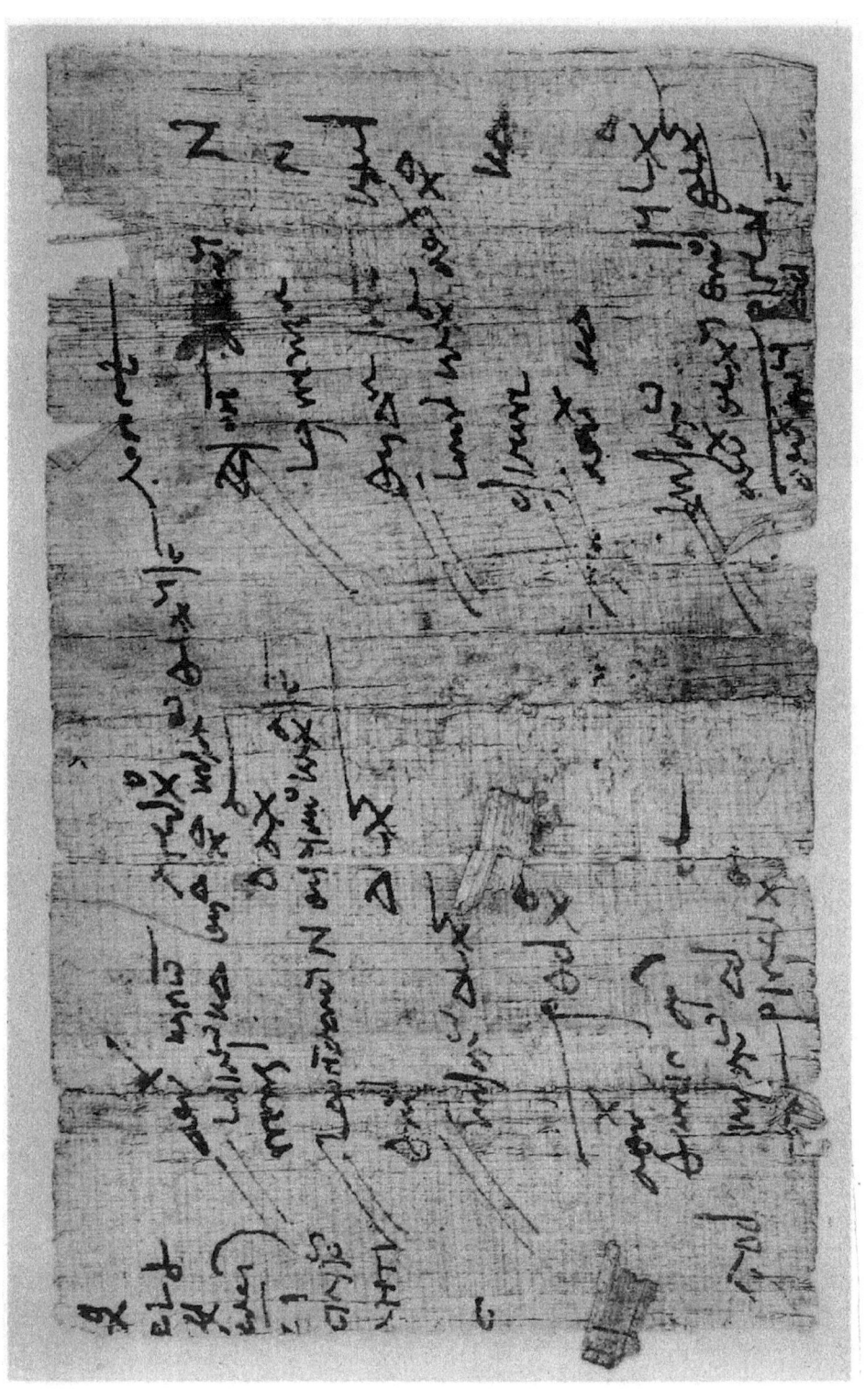

No. 42, verso. Grain Account (93 A.D.).

PLATE VII.

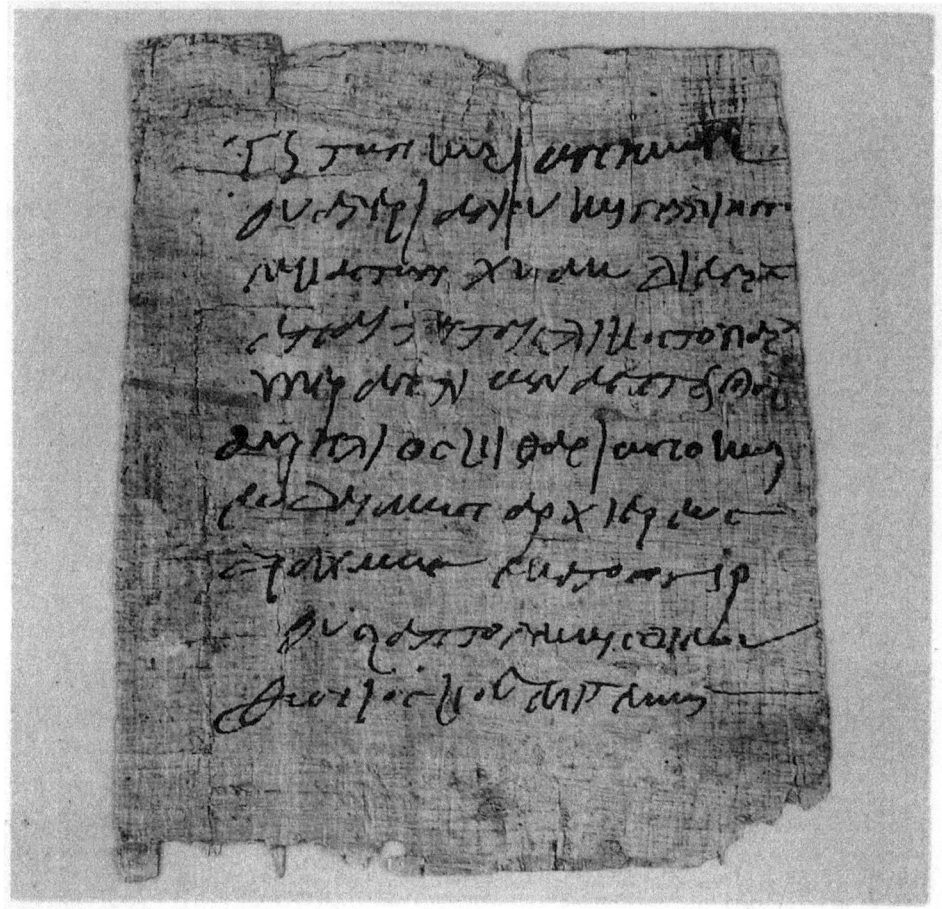

No. 50. Receipt for ἀννῶνα στρατιωτῶν (255 A.D.).

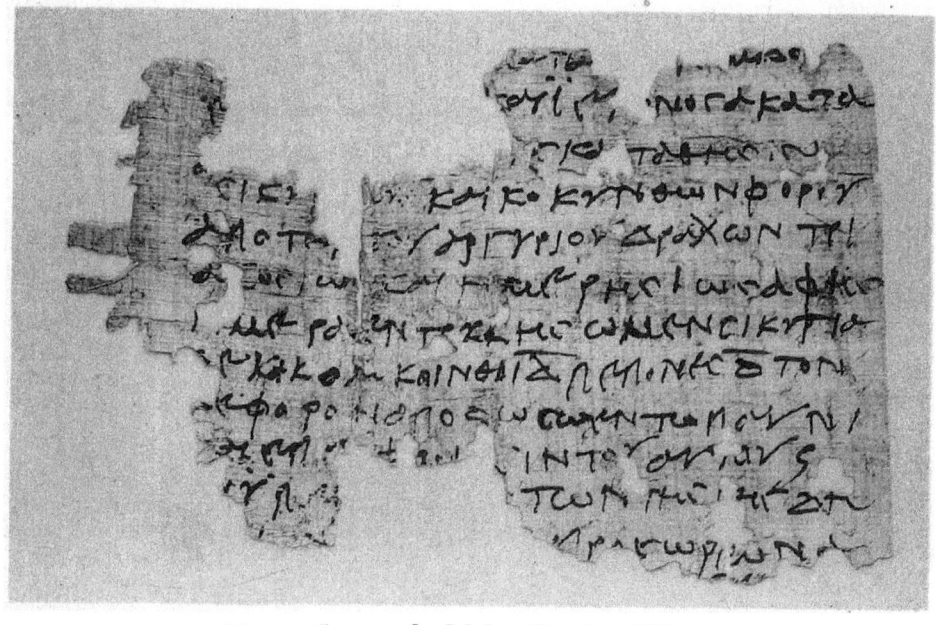

No. 39. Lease of a Melon Garden (III A.D.).

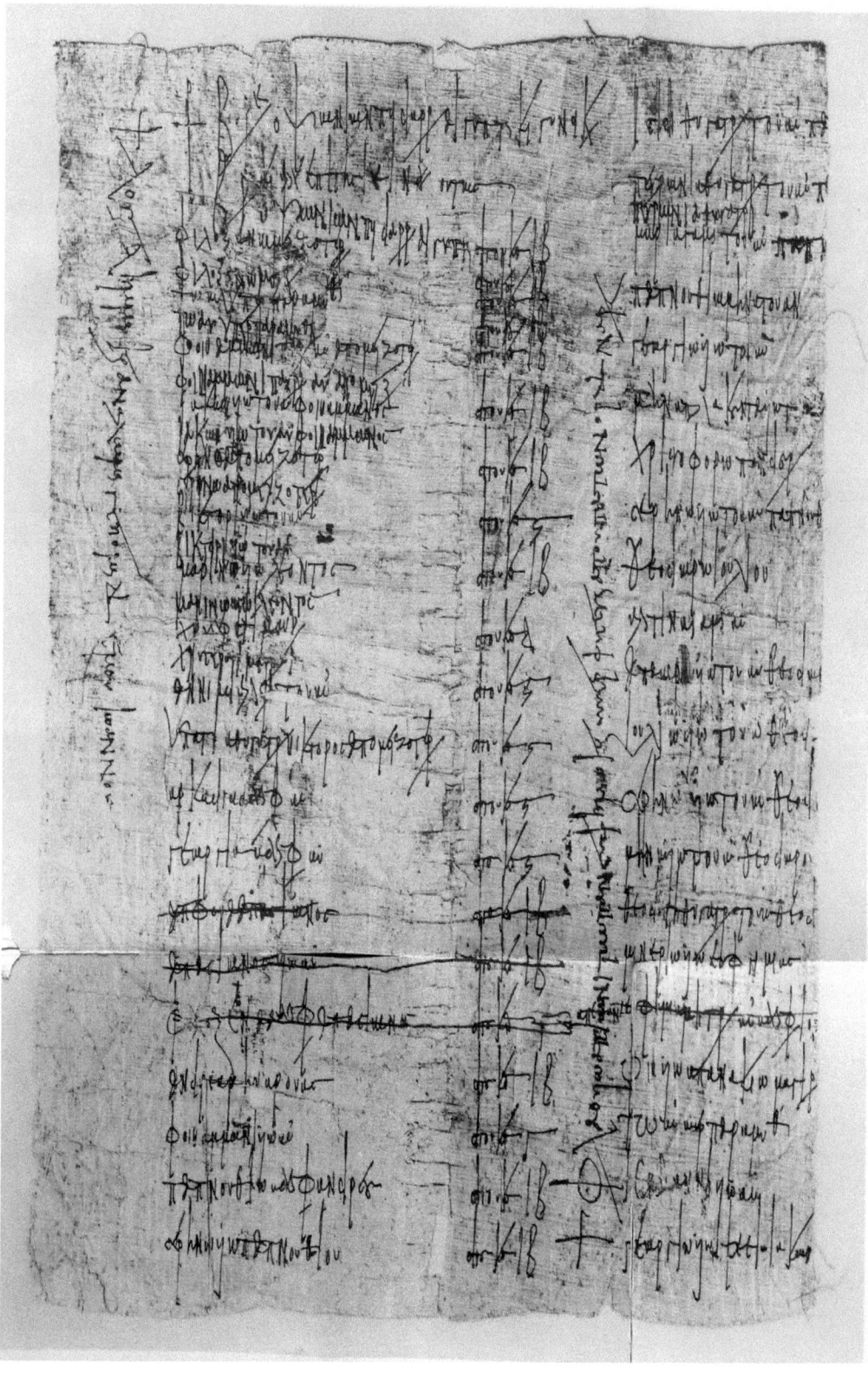

No. 96, recto. Wage Account (551/552 or 566/567 A.D.).

Plate IX.

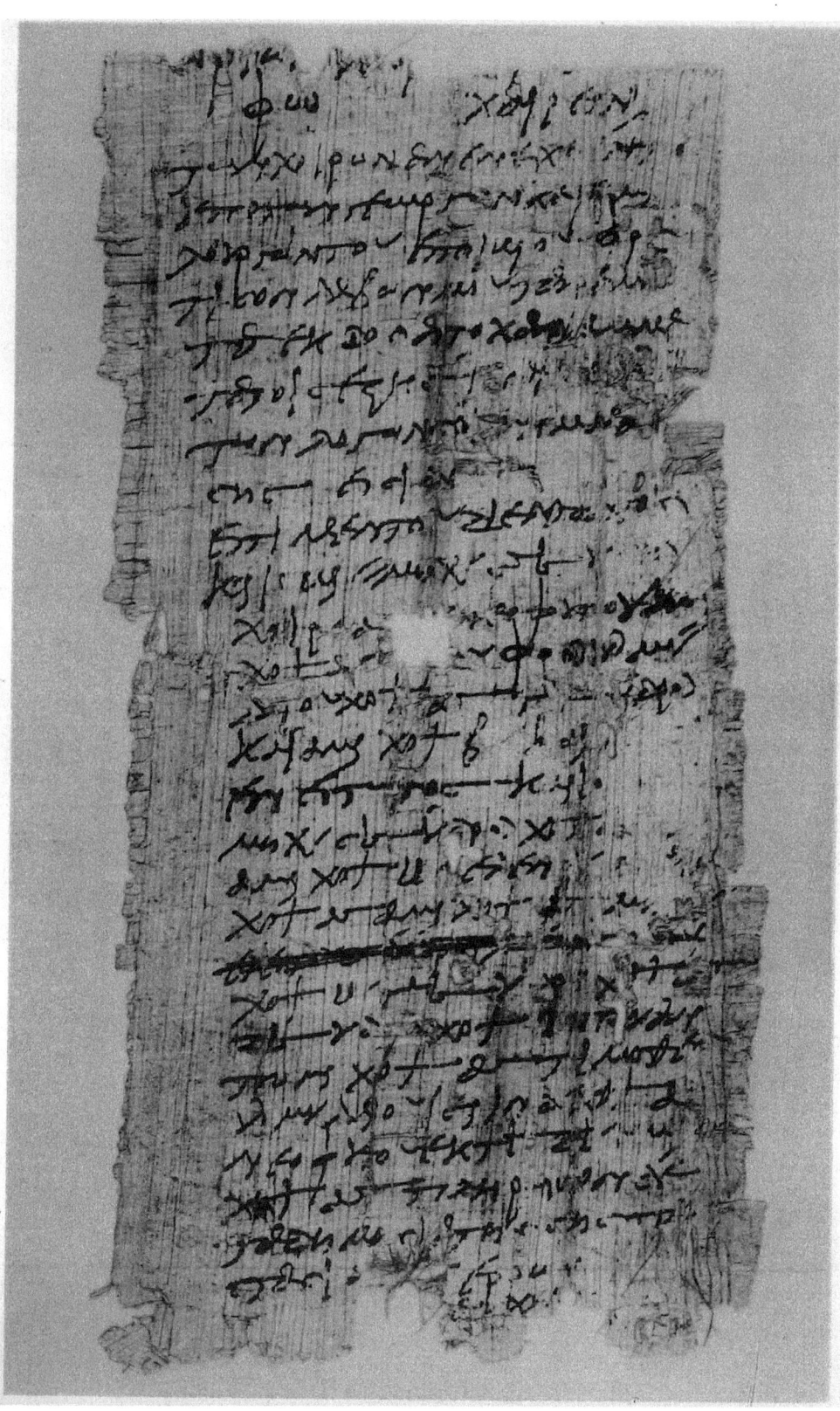

No. 97. Letter (326/327 A.D.).

PLATE X.

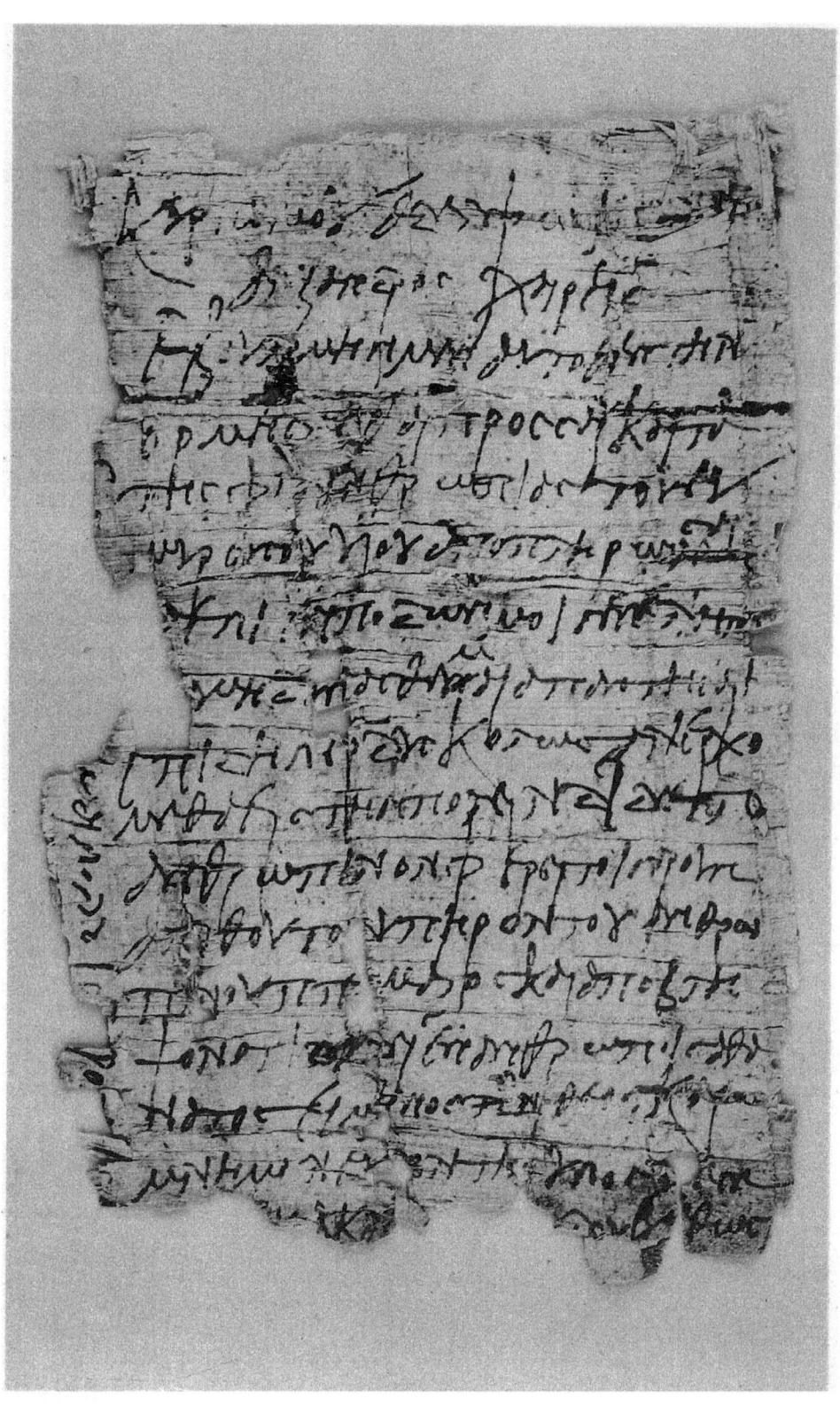

No. 102. Letter (IV A.D.).

Printed by Libri Plureos GmbH in Hamburg, Germany